RTI Applications, Volume 1

The Guilford Practical Intervention in the Schools Series

Kenneth W. Merrell, Founding Editor
T. Chris Riley-Tillman, Series Editor

This series presents the most reader-friendly resources available in key areas of evidence-based practice in school settings. Practitioners will find trustworthy guides on effective behavioral, mental health, and academic interventions, and assessment and measurement approaches. Covering all aspects of planning, implementing, and evaluating high-quality services for students, books in the series are carefully crafted for everyday utility. Features include ready-to-use reproducibles, lay-flat binding to facilitate photocopying, appealing visual elements, and an oversized format.

RTI Applications, Volume 1

Academic and Behavioral Interventions

Matthew K. Burns
T. Chris Riley-Tillman
Amanda M. VanDerHeyden

THE GUILFORD PRESS
New York   London

© 2012 The Guilford Press
A Division of Guilford Publications, Inc.
72 Spring Street, New York, NY 10012
www.guilford.com

Printed in the United States of America

This book is printed on acid-free paper.

Last digit is print number: 9   8   7   6   5   4   3   2   1

The authors have checked with sources believed to be reliable in their efforts to provide information that is complete and generally in accord with the standards of practice that are accepted at the time of publication. However, in view of the possibility of human error or changes in behavioral, mental health, or medical sciences, neither the authors, nor the editor and publisher, nor any other party who has been involved in the preparation or publication of this work warrants that the information contained herein is in every respect accurate or complete, and they are not responsible for any errors or omissions or the results obtained from the use of such information. Readers are encouraged to confirm the information contained in this book with other sources.

Library of Congress Cataloging-in-Publication Data

Burns, Matthew K.
  RTI applications / Matthew K. Burns, T. Chris Riley-Tillman, Amanda M. VanDerHeyden.
    p. cm. — (The Guilford practical intervention in the schools series)
  Includes bibliographical references and index.
  Contents: v. 1. Academic and behavioral interventions
  ISBN 978-1-4625-0354-4 (pbk.)
  1. Response to intervention (Learning disabled children)—Handbooks, manuals, etc.
I. Riley-Tillman, T. Chris.   II. VanDerHeyden, Amanda Mathany.   III. Title.
  LC4705.B87 2012
  371.9—dc23
                                                                  2011044444

In memory of Ken Merrell,
whose vision for The Guilford Practical Intervention in the Schools Series
framed this book, and whose leadership in school psychology
helped shape the profession

About the Authors

Matthew K. Burns, PhD, is Professor of Educational Psychology, Coordinator of the School Psychology Program, and Co-Director of the Minnesota Center for Reading Research at the University of Minnesota. Dr. Burns has published over 125 articles and book chapters in national publications and has coauthored and coedited several books. He is the Editor of *School Psychology Review* and past Editor of *Assessment for Effective Intervention*. Dr. Burns has conducted research on response to intervention (RTI), assessment of instructional levels, academic interventions, and facilitating problem-solving teams.

T. Chris Riley-Tillman, PhD, is Associate Professor in the Department of Educational, School and Counseling Psychology at the University of Missouri. His research focuses on improving education through the effective application of a problem-solving model. Specifically, he is interested in social behavioral assessment, intervention, single-case design, and consultation. Dr. Riley-Tillman has written numerous articles, books, and book chapters related to these research interests.

Amanda M. VanDerHeyden, PhD, is a private consultant, researcher, and national trainer who has worked in a number of school districts and is President of Education Research and Consulting, Inc., in Fairhope, Alabama. She is Associate Editor of *School Psychology Review* and serves on the editorial boards of several other journals, including *School Psychology Quarterly* and *Topics in Early Childhood Special Education*, and has published more than 60 articles, books, and book chapters related to RTI. In 2006, Dr. VanDerHeyden was named to a National Center for Learning Disabilities advisory panel to provide guidance related to RTI, and received the Lightner Witmer Award from the American Psychological Association for her scholarship on early intervention, RTI, and models of data-based decision making.

Acknowledgments

We begin by thanking our many mentors who have helped shape our beliefs and practices over the years. We would also like to thank Natalie Graham, Editor at The Guilford Press, for her editorial guidance. Chris would like to thank Shannon Brooks for her editorial eye with a number of the chapters in the book. Finally, we would like to thank our spouses, Mary Beth, Erin, and Chad, and our families for their continuous support.

Contents

CHAPTER 1

Introduction

OVERVIEW

Each of the three authors of this book works extensively in PreK–12 schools to help facilitate response-to-intervention (RTI) implementation, and the question we get the most is "What interventions should we use?" This clear desire to help children learn is admirable but often results in well-meaning practitioners using interventions for which there is questionable or little evidence to support their effects (e.g., learning styles and modality instruction). Using interventions that are not supported by scientific evidence leads to unsuccessful intervention efforts, frustration, and a sense of helplessness. The good news is that there is a more reliable way to identify the right intervention for a student and then get that intervention under way so that learning and behavior can improve. The key is knowing which questions to ask and how to use data to answer them.

During Matthew Burns's first year as a practicing school psychologist, a teacher asked for an intervention for a second-grade child with selective mutism; the little boy quite literally did not say a single word during his entire first-grade year. So he met individually with the

> **The key is knowing which questions to ask and how to use data to answer them.**

child. Predictably, the first 10 minutes of the interaction involved the young school psychologist asking questions to try and engage the child in a conversation, as if no one had thought of that intervention during the past 12 months. After a series of questions that were answered with blank stares, the school psychologist pointed down at the student's Teenage Mutant Ninja Turtles folder, named all of the turtles, and shared that he liked Rafael the best because he was the smart one. The little boy verbally replied that he liked Michelangelo the best because he was funny. After a short conversation, the little boy returned to class with his selective mutism "cured."

The teacher's response to the little boy speaking in class was joyous and the lucky school psychologist was viewed as a miracle worker, but the school psychologist was exactly that—lucky. He selected perhaps the worst possible intervention because he did not know what else to do and got lucky. Some might see the immediate change in the student's behavior and decide that a similar approach should be used for every child who was selectively mute, but the results would likely be very different. The point here is that just because something worked one time for one student does not mean that it is an evidence-based intervention (EBI) strategy. Similarly, just because an intervention is popular or widely used does not mean that it is effective.

Why do interventions fail? There are a number of reasons: (1) They are installed into environments where they are destined to fail, (2) they are incorrectly selected, (3) they are not correctly implemented, and (4) they are not effectively managed with ongoing progress monitoring and troubleshooting from those who are knowledgeable about implementation. The common ingredient necessary to ensure effective intervention implementation is correct use of data to inform decision making in:

- Evaluating the need for intervention.
- Selecting the right intervention for the student.
- Effectively deploying the intervention.
- Managing the intervention so that it can be successful.

Influential policy reports (Donovan & Cross, 2002; National Reading Panel, 2000) and legislation (Individuals with Disabilities Education Improvement Act, 2004; No Child Left Behind Act, 2002) echo a commonsense sentiment: we should know which students are struggling to learn, we should change instruction to those students so that they can learn better, we should select instructional strategies based on evidence showing they work, and we should evaluate our efforts locally to see whether we are indeed positively impacting learning. Central to the recommendations of policy and law is the use of evidence-based strategies. In education, there has been a legacy of adopting instructional strategies based on opinion, anecdotal reports, and theory. This legacy has been damaging, resulting in wasted resources and diminished learning outcomes for students exposed to strategies that often did not work.

WHAT ARE EVIDENCE-BASED INTERVENTIONS?

EBIs are interventions that have been shown to work in rigorous research studies. Evidence-based practice began in medicine (Sackett, Rosenberg, Gray, Haynes, & Richardson, 1996) and was viewed as the best way to improve the health outcomes for patients. Syntheses of research findings permit clinicians to rapidly integrate research evidence into their clinical decision making (e.g., what test to order, what follow-up test to order, what conditions to rule out, what intervention to initiate immediately). Moreover, evidence-based medicine gave clinicians a framework for data-based decision making where clinicians could (1) order tests to rule in or rule out a condition only if the test improved diagnostic accuracy that could be attained based on clinical suspicion or chance alone, and (2) select an intervention that had the least potential for harm and the greatest potential for improvement. This movement led to the founding of the Cochrane Database of Systematic Reviews (*www.cochrane.org*), which summarizes the findings of meta-analysis data so clinicians can readily identify treatments that will be of highest likely value.

The purpose of evidence-based practice in any field is to make the best evidence available to clinicians to guide their assessment practices and treatment recommendations. Recognition of empiricism as the best basis for diagnosis and treatment asserts that assessments and interventions should lead to appreciably positive changes in outcomes or clients should not be exposed to those assessments and treatments (Hayes, Nelson, & Jarrett, 1987; Messick, 1995). Psychology and education has embraced evidence-based practice as a basis for serving children (American Psychological Association Presidential Task Force on Evidence-Based Practice, 2006; American Psychological Association Task Force on Evidence-Based Practice for Children and Adolescents, 2008).

The What Works Clearinghouse (WWC) is a salient product of evidence-based practice in education. The WWC was built in 2002 to summarize evidence for educational interventions, but it raised thorny questions including what are the best sources of evidence and how much evidence is "enough." A special issue of *Exceptional Children* that was published in 2005 was dedicated to articulating standards for high-quality research; Cook, Tankersley, and Landrum (2009) edited a follow-up issue of *Exceptional Children*. Contributors to the 2009 special issue applied the quality indicators identified in the 2005 special issue and in WWC to evaluate common intervention strategies for reading, mathematics, writing, and behavior and concluded whether these practices were evidence-based or not. In an interesting commentary on the studies, Cook et al. highlight some of the challenges that limit the ability to reach broad conclusions about what does work, including poor operationalization of the quality indicators identified in the 2005 issue (and belying how difficult it is to specify quality indicators), inadequate documentation of interrater reliability, poor documentation of the integrity with which the independent variable was manipulated, failure to use multiple measures including at least one that was not closely tied to the independent variable, and failure to report effect sizes.

Despite the challenges in quantifying the quality of evidence (Feuer, Towne, & Shavelson, 2002), efforts to synthesize research findings to directly inform our practices may serve a dual purpose of helping improve the efficacy of our practices *and* increasing the quality of the research base over time. In this book, we argue that EBIs are a starting point for selecting interventions, and that selecting an intervention that has been shown to work for others is a necessary but insufficient step to ensuring intervention effects. EBIs should be the pool from which interventions are selected, but the specific intervention selected should be guided by individual student learning or behavior needs. RTI gives us a framework for matching the intervention to the student. We discuss RTI in more detail in Chapter 2, but discuss the role of EBIs within RTI below.

> **EBIs should be the pool from which interventions are selected, but the specific intervention selected should be guided by individual student learning or behavior needs.**

Evidence-Based Interventions and Response to Intervention

RTI has been described as application of the scientific method to educational problems. Educators want to know: Does this new math program work? Are most students thriving in general education? Which students are at risk academically and behaviorally? Did the reading intervention work for that first-grade student? RTI is a framework for using data to answer those questions. As those questions are answered, logical actions are implemented and system outcomes are enhanced over time. Where large groups of students are found to be at risk, for example, instructional teams can formulate hypotheses about what may be causing the group to perform in the risk range. Any causal explanation offered by the team becomes a hypothesis that can be tested, verified, and acted upon to improve learning.

RTI begins with quality core instruction and universal screening (Tier 1). Where large numbers of students (e.g., entire classes) perform below the risk criterion used at screening, the adequacy of core instruction must be evaluated and addressed prior to singling out individual students for individual intervention (VanDerHeyden & Witt, 2005). Thus, EBIs within Tier 1 should address the needs of an entire classroom as opposed to individual students. When most of the students score above the risk criterion on screening measures, then intervention efforts focus on small groups (Tier 2) of students or individual (Tier 3) student needs.

Because RTI is an integrated system of data collection, data interpretation, and actions that must occur in correct sequence, there are multiple opportunities for error to occur and implementation to go awry. One common source of error is failing to make use of student assessment data to identify the "right" intervention for the student, group of students, or whole class. Packaged programs may simplify intervention deployment by providing all needed materials to implement and providing scripted lessons. However, intervention packages require significant commitments for the teachers and school administrators in resources required for correct implementation. Often the decision to use a particular program is not based on evidence of effects obtained from sources other than the publisher. Efficacy data can be misleading because effect sizes report the "typical effect" of an intervention across the participants. Using this model, it is understood that a "strong" effect demonstrated across 10,000 children was not universally "strong" for all 10,000 children. In all likelihood, the intervention was in fact ineffective for some children, but there were other cases where there was a strong impact that balanced out the cases with a weak or absent effect. In the end, validation at the group level only means that an intervention is more likely to be effective, not that it will be effective with all children.

> A "strong" effect demonstrated across 10,000 children was not universally "strong" for all 10,000 children.

Problem Analysis and Response to Intervention

Educators examine data within an RTI framework to identify where learning or behavior is not successful, formulate hypotheses about what might be causing the lack of success and identify solutions to improve success, implement the solutions, and evaluate their success over time. Problem analysis in Tier 1 involves identifying whether a problem exists and if the problem is specific to an individual student or a group of students. Screening data are used to determine whether the core instruction and curriculum should be closely examined. Individual students for whom generally effective core curriculum and instruction do not lead to desired outcomes require a slightly more in-depth analysis and a subsequent Tier 2 intervention. Problem analysis within Tier 2 of an RTI system involves identifying the category of the deficit by isolating the root of the problem (e.g., reading decoding rather than reading fluency, recall of single-digit math facts within a two-digit by two-digit problem). Once the underlying deficit is identified, then those data are used to group the students accordingly and to deliver a correctly targeted intervention.

On average approximately 5% of the student population require intensive interventions despite good curriculum (Tier 1) and small-group interventions (Tier 2; Burns, Appleton, & Stehouwer, 2005). These are the students who most frustrate and concern practitioners. What do we do when a student is not learning at an acceptable rate despite our best efforts? Because there is such a high level of need and concern, there should be a correspondingly high level of analysis. Problem analysis within Tier 3 involves examining relevant and malleable environmental variables in order to identity which one is most closely related to the problem, which is then deemed to be the "causal" variable. After identifying the causal variable, it is manipulated to address the problem.

Problem Analysis and Individual Interventions

Problem analysis is the key to effective interventions, regardless of whether the intervention is applied to an individual or a group of students. An intervention is "a planned modification of the environment made for the purpose of altering behavior in a prespecified way" (Tilly & Flugum, 1995, p. 485). Interventions can occur for an entire school, smaller groups of students, or for an individual student.

Because interventions are planned modifications to the environment, the method with which they are planned is equally important as the target. Intervention efforts from previous decades relied heavily on intuitive appeal, but subsequent research did not support them. For example, interventions were frequently developed by matching instructional modality with the students' preferred learning style (i.e., visual, auditory, or kinesthetic learner; Kavale & Forness, 2000). However, meta-analytic research found such small effects ($d \leq .20$) for these interventions that their continued use is an example of philosophical and clinical beliefs overshadowing research data (Kavale & Forness, 2000).

Interventions that are built to resolve the root cause of the student's poor academic or behavior performance have been found to produce stronger effects (Daly, Witt, Martens, & Dool, 1997; Daly, Martens, Hamler, Dool, & Eckert, 1999; Graham, Harris, & MacArthur, 2004). Thus, we now have an assessment technology that can directly test the effectiveness of potential interventions before they are fully implemented. Practitioners implement interventions to test their effectiveness over the short term and the intervention that is the most effective is assumed to be linked to the causal variable and is implemented over an extended period (Daly et al., 1997; Jones & Wickstrom, 2002). There are two aspects of functional academic assessment or brief experimental analysis that make it effective. First,

	Acquisition Phase	Fluency Phase	Generalization Phase	Application Phase
General Focus	Increasing the accuracy and conceptual understanding	Increasing the speed of accurate responding	Applying the information across settings and stimuli	Using concepts to solve applied problems
Specific Principles	Explicit instruction in skill High modeling Immediate corrective feedback	Independent practice Immediate feedback on the speed of responding, but delayed feedback on the accuracy Contingent reinforcement for speed of response	Overlearning Training diversely Taking advantage of naturally occurring contingencies across settings	Problem identification (focusing on the necessary information) Encouraging multiple routes to same end
Examples	Modeling letter sounds while providing a visual cue of the letter Modeling with math manipulatives Supported cloze procedure for reading (Rasinski, 2003). Incremental rehearsal of words (Burns, 2007) and math facts (Burns, 2005)	Repeated reading (Samuels, 1979) Interspersal technique for math problems (Skinner et al., 1999) Word box for letter sounds (Joseph, 2002)	Instructional games with different stimuli Math word problems Reading passages containing previously taught letters and words	Schema-based math instruction (Jitendra, 2007) Learning centers Thematic units

FIGURE 1.1. Instructional hierarchy phases and corresponding instructional activities.

it utilizes sensitive measures, such as curriculum-based measurement (CBM; Deno, 1985) that can detect even relatively small differences in intervention effectiveness. Second, the interventions follow an intervention heuristic and are not just haphazardly selected. The heuristic most commonly used for functional academic assessment (Ardoin & Daly, 2007) is the instructional hierarchy in which interventions are identified by matching student skill with one of four phases of student learning (Haring & Eaton, 1978) that are outlined in Figure 1.1 and are described in Chapter 2.

THE INSTRUCTIONAL HIERARCHY AND RESPONSE-TO-INTERVENTION DECISIONS

Matching the student's skill to the "right" intervention produces greater learning gains. Similarly, a mismatch between student skill or capacity and the selected intervention forecasts a poor response to the intervention. Where interventions are selected in the absence of student assessment data, a poor intervention response cannot be taken as evidence that the student did not have a strong response to the intervention, but rather that the student was not necessarily matched with an adequate intervention. For example, teachers frequently ask their students to complete a sheet of math problems within a certain time length (e.g., 2 minutes) and the students are encouraged to beat yesterday's score with the idea that brief intervals of timed practice will build student capacity. This is likely an appropriate task *if* students have learned when and how to complete those problems accurately. If the student does not understand how to complete the math problems, then independent timed practice will actually do more harm than good in terms of building student capacity.

There are many research-based interventions from which to choose (Burns & Wagner, 2008; Kavale & Forness, 2000; Swanson, 1999; Swanson & Sachse-Lee, 2000). However, finding an effective intervention is not the primary challenge that faces most practitioners. As stated above, matching the right intervention to the child and implementing the intervention with intergrity are the two greatest challenges for school personnel. This book offers concrete step-by-step guidance to select the intervention that will improve learning and behavior performance.

> **Where interventions are selected in the absence of student assessment data, a poor intervention response cannot be taken as evidence that the student did not have a strong response to the intervention, but rather that the student was not necessarily matched with an adequate intervention.**

THE BOOK

In this book, we will show teachers, interventionists, and school psychologists how to match the intervention to the child for the greatest effect. The first section of the book describes RTI and provides a framework (in Chapter 2) for the chapters that address specific interventions. Then Chapters 3 and 4 deal with classwide and schoolwide (Tier 1) interventions, Chapters 5 and 6 focus on small-group interventions (Tier 2), and Chapters 7 through 12 address individual interventions (Tier 3) for the acquisition phase (Chapters 7 and 8), fluency phase (Chapters 9 and 10), and generalization phase (Chapters 11 and 12). Finally, Chapter 13 addresses the importance of intervention integrity for both systems and individual students.

Each chapter starting with Chapter 4 begins with an intervention description, the intervention objective (e.g., acquisition for reading fluency, fluency of math facts), and the population for which it is appropriate. The research supporting each intervention is summarized and step-by-step procedures are included so practitioners can use the book as a handy guide for implementing interventions.

This book is the first in a two-volume set. We address interventions in this book because without the "I," the "R" in RTI will not happen. The next book will go into more detail about the use of assessment data to make various decisions. These two books will hopefully provide information for practitioners to get a solid start on their RTI efforts, and we hope that this first book will address the most common questions. However, this book should be of use to just about any school-based practitioners who implement academic or behavioral interventions, regardless of whether those efforts occur within an RTI framework or not.

CHAPTER 2

Matching the "Right" Intervention to the Student

OVERVIEW

As noted earlier, interventions can fail for a number of reasons. In fact, intervention effectiveness studies tell us that when interventions fail, one common cause is that the wrong intervention was selected for the student. Selecting the wrong intervention commonly occurs when those making intervention selections do not have adequate data on student learning and capability. Intervention selection decisions are often made based on:

- Which interventions are readily available to the teacher.
- Which interventions are familiar to the teacher who will administer the intervention.
- Which interventions require the least amount of time or expertise.

These commonly selected bases for intervention selection are practical, but all too often have little to do with delivering effective behavior change for the student. For example, a school had attempted to resolve a kindergarten student's aggressive behavior by meeting with the child's parents, shortening the child's school day, and having the school psychologist observe the child in the classroom and make recommendations for intervention. The school psychologist had suggested that the teachers place the student in time out when he exhibited aggressive behavior. This intervention was not successful, and following a particularly severe episode, the district contacted an outside consultant for help. Following a functional analysis in the classroom, the data reflected that aggressive behavior reliably followed teacher commands and child noncompliance. When the child was offered brief breaks from an academic task only when he complied with teacher requests and not when he exhibited aggression, compliance increased and aggressive behavior decreased to zero. In other words, escape from a nonpreferred academic task was the reinforcer for aggression for this child. That is, time out was actually making things worse by reinforcing aggression rather than attenuating it. This example is a classic case of intervention selection being faulty and actually causing more harm than good.

There is a more effective way to select interventions.

In Chapter 1, RTI was defined as a framework for using academic and behavior data to allocate resources to assist the greatest number of students in the most efficient way. Data can be used to tell us when there is a problem with core instruction, or if core instruction is intact, which groups of students or individual students are in need of additional support. Data can tell us which strategies are likely to work if correctly applied. Knowing which interventions will work before we invest the resources to deploy those interventions allows implementers to focus on getting the intervention deployed successfully and troubleshooting that intervention until the desired effects are obtained (rather than wasting resources debating whether the intervention was appropriate or not). Implementers can think of this as a sort of "road test" for the intervention. We knew the intervention worked when it was applied well, so the goal in deployment is getting the intervention implemented well. This approach protects implementers against the attempt–attack–abandon (D. Deshler, personal communication, August 23, 2008) legacy that is so prevalent in education and is associated with the application of increasingly restrictive treatments implemented with worsening student outcomes.

THE INSTRUCTIONAL HIERARCHY AS A PROBLEM-ANALYSIS FRAMEWORK

The concept of measuring student proficiency to identify instructional strategies that will best work for that student is not a new idea (Betts, 1946; Gickling & Armstrong, 1978; Gickling & Thompson, 1985) and has been a key feature of recent reform efforts (National Council of Teachers of Mathematics, 2000; National Mathematics Advisory Panel, 2008; National Reading Panel, 2000). If the goal of instruction is to improve the student's "fit" with environmental expectations, then interventions can be designed to (1) improve student skill and/or (2) modify the task or environment to better support student skill development (Rosenfield, 2002). For many years, policy documents and experts have suggested that the hallmark of effective instruction is the use of assessment data to guide instruction and evaluate instructional efforts.

The instructional hierarchy (Haring & Eaton, 1978), as shown in Table 2.1, is a framework for matching interventions to a child's skill proficiency to produce the strongest gains for the student. Regardless of the skill being learned (e.g., reading, math computation, social skills), we know that learning progresses through a predictable sequence including:

1. Acquisition.
2. Fluency.
3. Generalization.
4. Adaptation.

TABLE 2.1. Assessment and Intervention Framework Based on Instructional Hierarchy Phases of Learning

Stage of learning	Student proficiency	How do you know?	Goal of intervention	Intervention example
Acquisition	Frustration	Responses are hesitant and incorrect.	Establish 100% correct.	• Cover, copy, and compare • Modeling • Guided practice • Prompt hierarchies and systematic fading • Immediate corrective feedback • Incremental rehearsal
Fluency building	Instructional	Responses are accurate but slow.	Build fluency.	• Flashcards • Timed performance with incentives • Response cards • Delayed feedback • Task interspersal • Goal setting • Fading of reinforcement
Generalization and adaptation	Mastery	Responses are fluent.	Establish robust application.	• Guided practice applying skill to solve more complex problems • Variation of task materials • Cues or prompts to generalize

Periodic assessment of students' skill proficiency gives teachers a clear basis for determining whether a student's skill is at the acquisition, fluency, generalization, or adaptation stage of learning. Knowing the stage of learning, in turn, gives teachers an unambiguous basis for:

1. Knowing when to increase task difficulty or accelerate learning content.
2. Knowing what type of instruction, practice, and feedback to provide to students.
3. Knowing how to maximize instructional time for the greatest effect.

Although it would be ideal if all intervention cases in schools were focused on academic difficulties, teachers unfortunately face a range of issues surrounding children who are misbehaving. The significance of the challenges educational professionals face has been noted in a number of government publications (e.g., National Research Council and Institute of Medicine, 2009; Public Agenda, 2004; Rose & Gallup, 2005; U.S. Department of Health and Human Services, 1999). It is clear that the traditional "wait to fail" approach used historically for both academic and social behavior problems has been an abject failure due to a tendency to avoid early use of EBIs with small social behavior problems before they become more serious (Albers, Glover, & Kratochwill, 2007; Gresham, 2008).

Alternative problem-solving models have been long advocated as an approach to provide more immediate assistance to teachers working with children who exhibit behavior problems. Going back to Bergan's (1977) original behavioral consultation model, there has been a series of problem-solving models suggested and validated for the purpose of selecting interventions for both academic and social behavior difficulties. Unfortunately RTI, which is the current national presentation of a schoolwide problem-solving model, has generally focused on academic intervention.

> **The traditional "wait to fail" approach used historically for both academic and social behavior problems has been an abject failure.**

In this book we have chosen to consider academic and social behavior intervention concurrently, as that is the actual challenge that teachers will face in a classroom on a daily basis. Academic and social behavior deficits can occur in combination, and a deficit in one can lead to problems in the other. Thus, the challenge at hand is to consider whether the functional framework presented in this chapter applies equally well to both academic and social behavior issues. Whereas traditionally the instructional hierarchy has been applied to academic issues, with some minor explanation, we believe it also is an effective system for quickly developing a hypothesis as to the function of social behavior difficulties as well. After all, a behavior is a behavior whether it is computing addition problems, solving word problems, or following teacher directions. Methods of changing behavior work whether you are teaching a student to compute sums or follow directions. We argue that it is ineffective to focus on one area (e.g., academics) to the exclusion of another (e.g., disruptive behavior) because problems in one area can undermine any chance of successful intervention in the other. Rather, we suggest that implementers set priorities that involve evaluating the adequacy of the instructional environment for the student, teaching the student expected behavioral skills to be successful in the classroom, giving the child work that he or she can be successful completing, and conduct more intensive (Tier 3) interventions when disruptive behavior persists in an environment that has been optimized (Witt, VanDerHeyden, & Gilbertson, 2004). It is fundamentally unfair and unproductive to ask children to quietly behave when the academic instruction is too challenging for them or too easy, and it is fundamentally unfair and ineffective to develop complicated behavioral interventions that are designed to suppress behaviors that are actually adaptive from the child's point of view because the instructional environment has been ignored by the assessment team.

Student Proficiency Is Linked to Intervention Using the Stages of Learning

Academic Skills Acquisition

When a new skill is being acquired or established, student responses will be slow and errors will be frequent (Haring & Eaton, 1978). The goal of instruction at this stage of learning is to establish the skill and help the student understand exactly the conditions under which a response is correct and the conditions under which a response is incorrect. To establish correct responding, substantial adult assistance and guidance may be required involving strategies like modeling correct responding, providing cues and more intensive prompts to facilitate correct responding, and providing immediate corrective feedback. During instruction, any external cues or prompts should be faded once correct responding is established. This stage of learning is complete when student responses are accurate and independent. The process is displayed in Figure 2.1.

At the acquisition stage of learning, it is unproductive (and potentially harmful) to permit the student to practice the skill without supervision because errors are too prevalent. Independent practice becomes an opportunity for the child to practice the skill incorrectly and can lead to errors that are intractable. Improving accuracy is associated with improved reading comprehension and time on task or active student engagement (Burns, Dean, & Foley, 2004; Gickling & Armstrong, 1978; Treptow, Burns, & McComas, 2007). How accurate must students be? A meta-analysis suggested that students should be able to complete 90–93% of the task (e.g., items within a math assignment or words within a reading task)

> **At the acquisition stage of learning, it is unproductive to permit the student to practice the skill without supervision because errors are too prevalent.**

correctly before they are allowed independent practice (Burns, 2004). Form 2.1 at the end of the chapter, provides a protocol to assess students' skills and make an instructional decision within the framework described below.

Behavioral Skills Acquisition

As with academic skills, it should not be assumed that children have appropriate social behaviors in their repertoire when they enter school or a new classroom experience. As with academic skills, there will be many cases where what was taught in the home environment or previous educational environment will not overlap with a particular current classroom. As such, it should be expected that unless a child demonstrates that he or she has a particu-

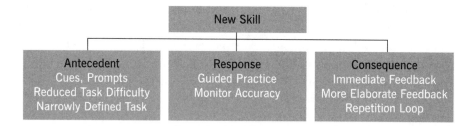

FIGURE 2.1. Instructional activities before, during, and after instruction for new skills. Instructional interactions can be broken down into antecedent–response–consequence sequences (sometimes referred to as learning trials). When a skill is new, antecedent variables need to be adjusted to occasion correct responding. The goal is to assist the student to discriminate the stimuli that should occasion a certain response and to make the correct response and provide the student corrective feedback that is immediate and more elaborate.

lar social behavior in his or her repertoire, the behavior must be directly instructed. From an assessment standpoint, evidence of a child being in the acquisition stage is either a total lack of behavior demonstration, or halting and inaccurate presentation of the target behavior. As with academic skills, there should be an expectation that initial student responses will be slow and errors will be frequent (Haring & Eaton, 1978).

The primary goal of behavior instruction in the acquisition phase is to establish the skill and help the student understand exactly the conditions under which a response is correct and the conditions under which a response is incorrect. Interventions in this initial stage of learning will be based on direct instruction with feedback when the behavior is exhibited incorrectly, or in the absence of the conditions indicating that the behavior is appropriate. For example, when children first enter kindergarten there is a long list of behaviors that must be directly instructed. The children must learn to stand in line, to put their coat in a cubby, to raise their hand when they would like to be called on, and to sit quietly and attentively when being read to. Clearly this list could go on for pages, but the defining feature is that these critical behaviors are ones that a child may simply have never developed before entering formal schooling. It is important to note that social behavior acquisition does not end in kindergarten or first grade. As a child enters any new classroom, a teacher's particular expectation of how a child requests to go to the bathroom or responds to a question may be somewhat different than in previous classrooms. In addition, as children develop they will begin to engage in new situations that can result in the need for both new and more advanced social behaviors.

Fluency Skills

Once a child can accurately respond, the skill is ready for fluency-building instruction, which follows the pattern shown in Figure 2.2. The goal of the fluency stage of learning is to facilitate rapid or automatic responding that remains accurate (Binder, 1996). At this stage of learning, the goal is to provide many opportunities to respond with delayed corrective feedback. When building fluency, it becomes counterproductive to interrupt the child's

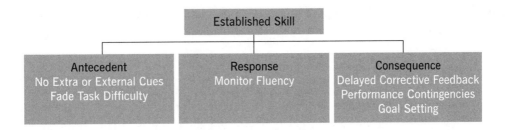

FIGURE 2.2. Instructional activities before, during, and after instruction for established skills. When a skill is established, meaning the student can perform the skill accurately and independently, the goal of instruction is to build fluency. At this stage, teachers should provide multiple opportunities to respond (antecedent manipulation), monitor fluency of responding, and provide delayed corrective feedback and rewards for more fluent performance (consequences).

response to give feedback, because it reduces opportunities to respond. Given that errors occur with much lower frequency at this stage of learning, delayed feedback can be tolerated. Setting goals and providing small rewards or privileges for more fluent performance is important, as is varying slightly the task presentation (e.g., order of words, types of problems) to facilitate robust skill development.

Haughton (1980) suggested that the outcome of effective instruction should be skills that are remembered, that endure over longer intervals of time, and can be applied in different contexts to solve novel problems. These goals are captured by the acronym REAPS (retention, endurance, application performance standards). REAPS are functional goals of instruction that suggest that a skill has been mastered to a level that it can be of use in the student's future learning. Fluency is usually, and perhaps most effectively, measured with CBM using a rate-based metric such as words read correctly per minute (WCPM) or digits correct per minute (DCPM). There are guidelines for WCPM to be considered within the fluency phase (first- and second-grade students—between 40 and 60 WCPM, third- through sixth-grade students—between 70 and 100 WCPM; Deno & Mirkin, 1977), but those criteria are not based on studies or well researched. Alternatively, all grades of students should be able to read at least 93% of the words correctly before they are considered to be within the fluency phase of learning, which is a criterion with a much stronger research base (Gickling & Armstrong, 1978; Gickling & Thompson, 1985; Burns, 2007; Treptow et al., 2007). Research on math fluency suggests that a student should be able to complete 14 to 31 DCPM among second- and third-grade students and 24 to 49 DCPM for fourth and fifth graders to be considered within a fluency phase (Burns, VanDerHeyden, & Jiban, 2006), again assuming sufficient accuracy of at least 90% correct (Burns, 2004).

Some practitioners use a norm-referenced framework for setting fluency goals. WCPM, for example, can be compared to the 25th percentile for a national normative group such as Hasbrouck and Tindal (2005) or AIMSweb (Pearson, 2008). The goal of intervention at the fluency-building stage is to attain performance associated with a certain percentile (e.g., 25th percentile). The problem with a norm-referenced approach is that the level of performance can vary substantially between high-achieving and low-achieving settings and does not necessarily indicate that a child is ready to progress to the next stage of the learning hierarchy. We suggest the use of functional outcome criteria such as REAPS or benchmark scores that indicate a child will perform in the proficient range on the year-end accountability assessment.

Fluency Behavior

As with academic skills, fluency building of social behavior is the logical goal after a child can accuracy display the desired target behavior. As such, the goal is to promote consistent presentation of the target behavior. When behavioral skills are dysfluent, children's responses will be halting, hesitant, and often unproductive. Behavior interventions often focus on acquisition of replacement behaviors and fail to build fluency. When interventions do not ensure that a new response is fluent for the student, then the response will not persist long beyond training. For example, a student may have been taught how to make a request of a peer during center time in kindergarten. The child may be able to effectively make a request during a practice session outside of the classroom or may be able to identify when it is appropriate to make a request and under what conditions making the request is likely to be successful. However, if the child's response is not fluent, the child will not fluidly use the new skill to obtain a desired item and will rapidly return to the use of other strategies (like simply taking the item), especially if the peer does not respond as expected.

In order to promote fluent behavior it is critical to adopt the orientation that behavior happens for a reason. Children respond to the contingencies that surround them and, as such, the development of proficient behavior is accomplished though the manipulation of the antecedents and consequences of a target behavior. In this stage it is typical to prompt children to increase the likelihood that a behavior is presented. In addition, consequences must be developed that reinforce the target behavior when presented. While these and other related issues are presented in depth later in the book, at this stage it is important to understand that developing behavioral fluency depends on the educational professional taking responsibility for creating conditions that support the target behavior. If the orientation of the educational setting or individual teacher is one that places the responsibility for appropriate social behavior squarely on the individual child, then it is unlikely that the environment will be one that increases the likelihood of fluent appropriate child behavior. More specifically, while some children might behave, in instances in which behavior intervention is necessary altering the environment to promote appropriate behavior by the target child is the only logical option.

Generalization and Adaptation Skills

Once the student responds fluently when presented with the task under conditions that are identical to training conditions, the student is ready for generalization training, which is reflected in Figure 2.3. The goal of learning at the generalization stage is to facilitate skill performance under slightly different task demands (slightly different conditions, settings, problem presentations). Productive instructional strategies that facilitate generalization include providing the student the opportunity to practice responding in different settings, different contexts, and with slightly variable tasks. Many of the strategies that were helpful at the acquisition stage of learning will be helpful at this stage too, including using cues and providing corrective feedback to guide, and then reinforce correct generalization. Extended practice intervals (similar to what might be used at the fluency-building stage of learning) can be used to help students recognize the need for generalization and correctly generalize the trained skill. For example, once a student can fluently solve sums to 20 and subtraction with answers to 20, the student is ready for exposure to word problems that require those computations, multidigit addition and subtraction, and fact family solutions (e.g., $5 + X = 8$). Adaptation occurs when the student changes the response to more efficiently solve problems encountered in the future (e.g., when confronted with $5 + 6$, the student may compute $5 + 5$ and add 1 to the answer to arrive at the correct answer, which is more efficient than counting if the sum is not memorized). For some students, generalization and adaptation may occur without specific instruction. For others, instruction may

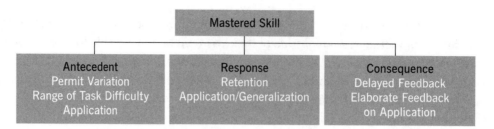

FIGURE 2.3. Instructional activities before, during, and after instruction for mastered skills. When a skill is fluent, generalization training may be needed to ensure it can be used robustly to solve slightly altered problems in contexts that differ from training. At this stage, increasing the range of stimuli to which the student is asked to respond (antecedent), tracking the response to ensure retention of fluent performance and assisting the student to adapt the response (response), and using corrective feedback and intermittent reinforcement to facilitate maintenance (consequences) are the goals of instruction.

be needed. Interventionists will know if generalization instruction is needed by assessing generalization directly as part of the intervention progress monitoring plan.

Intervention research tends not to focus on generalization and adaptation because most academic deficits seen by the interventionist are caused by inaccurate performance or dysfluent performance on the target skill or relevant prerequisites. That does not mean that these two phases of the learning hierarchy are not important. Applying newly learned information to a novel setting to solve a problem is the very goal of education and can be an efficient way in establish skills. However, most children who require intervention experience difficulty at the acquisition and fluency-building stages of learning.

Generalization and Adaptation Behavior

When a child can fluently exhibit a behavior skill in the classroom, the goal of intervention shifts to support the use of that skill in different environments or the adaptation of that skill to solve new problems or challenges that the student might encounter. Technically, the goal of behavior intervention at the generalization stage is to increase the likelihood that a trained behavior is presented across time, setting, and/or target in the absence of the conditions that promoted its acquisition (Stokes & Baer, 1977). A student who has had many years of practice understanding when interruptions are appropriate will not only be more successful in the classroom and with adults but will be more popular among his or her peers. The social skill of timing and making social initiations with others is a skill that builds over a number of years as the student encounters settings with different requirements (classroom instruction vs. dinner table vs. recess). To use this skill in a functional way, the child must fluently interrupt when it is tolerated and use the behavior that will work in a particular setting (e.g., raising a hand during classroom instruction to ask a relevant question about a task is appropriate and will work for the student, whereas raising a hand on the playground is not likely to be effective). While some children seem to naturally generalize fluent behaviors, others have some difficulty in this process. Considering that we typically expect children to transport appropriate behaviors as they move from classroom to classroom, or year to year, we must consider what to do when a child is having difficulty with the process of generalization of desired social behaviors. As with the fluency-building stage, intervention in the generalization programming stage is focused primarily on adapting the target environment (where you desire the child to exhibit the target behavior) to increase the likelihood of presentation. A simple reminder prompt may be all that is needed, assuming that the behavior is reinforced after exhibited. In addition, focus on promoting generalization can be placed in the original acquisition phase. At the time of initial skill acquisition multiple prompts and environments can be utilized so that the child learns that a specific behavior will be effective in a variety of locations. These issues are explored in depth later in this book.

Determining the Stage of Learning

The first step is to measure the child's skill proficiency on the expected task and a series of subsequently easier tasks. This process, referred to as survey-level assessment, requires only about 10 minutes per student and allows the interventionist to identify the stage of learning for the target skill. The interventionist needs to know whether the student can perform the target skill accurately, with speed, and if not, which prerequisite skills are lacking (see Figure 2.4 for a sequence of assessments and decisions needed for intervention planning).

Figure 2.5 provides an example. If the grade-level expected skill is multidigit multiplication, the interventionist first determines whether the student can perform the skill with greater than 90% accuracy. If the student is accurate, then fluency is checked. If the student correctly completes less than 31 DCPM for second and third graders or 49 DCPM for fourth and fifth graders, then an intervention designed to build fluency for multidigit multiplication should be selected. If the student is not accurate, then prerequisite skills should be checked. If the student can accurately regroup, then fluency with regrouping should be checked. Accuracy and fluency of multiplication facts should be verified. Accuracy is treated first, and interventions may be combined to provide intervention for two prerequisite skills simultaneously or may occur in sequence.

Once we have identified whether the student is accurate and fluent on the criterion or prerequisite skills, we can use functional academic assessment to verify the intervention effect with the student before we expend any resources implementing in the classroom. Functional academic assessment is similar to functional analysis of behavior (Iwata, Dorsey, Slifer, Bauman, & Richman, 1982; Mace, Yankanich, & West, 1988; McComas, Hoch, & Mace, 2000; McComas & Mace, 2000). Antecedent and consequent variables are manipulated to evaluate the effect of those manipulations on target behavior to reach a conclusion about the function of behavior. Generally, functional analysis of behavior focuses on identifying the function of problematic behaviors. Elevated occurrence under a given set of conditions (e.g., elevated aggression when task demands are present and escape from the task is permitted contingent on aggression) indicates a behavioral function. The behavioral function leads logically to an intervention designed to weaken the functional relationship and train adaptive replacement behaviors (e.g., reducing task demands, permitting brief breaks from task demands for an alternative behavior). Between 1986 (Lentz & Shapiro, 1986)

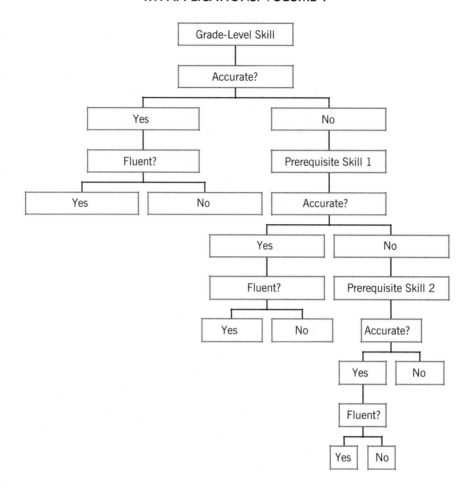

FIGURE 2.4. Flowchart for assessment.

and 1997 (Daly et al., 1997) a number of papers appeared suggesting that the same proce-dures could be used to identify the causes of poor academic performance (e.g., errors) and plan function-based interventions to improve learning. In 1986, Lentz and Shapiro wrote a seminal paper that laid out the application of functional assessment to academic or learning problems. Pioneered by behavioral researchers, especially Daly and colleagues (1997, 1999; Daly, Martens, Kilmer, & Massie, 1996), functional academic assessment exposes the child to a series of conditions designed to maximize performance including, for example, reducing task difficulty, providing incentives for improved performance, and providing extra practice on the skill. Elevated skill performance under a given condition provides a direct test of potential interventions and therefore empirical validation that the intervention is likely to work for that child if correctly implemented. Functional academic assessment has also been referred to as brief experimental analyses of academic responding.

Figure 2.6 shows data from a functional academic assessment. On the grade-level expected skill, the student scored 14 DCPM with no errors. This score is at the bottom of the instructional range and the goal is 31 DCPM (mastery criterion). Because the student

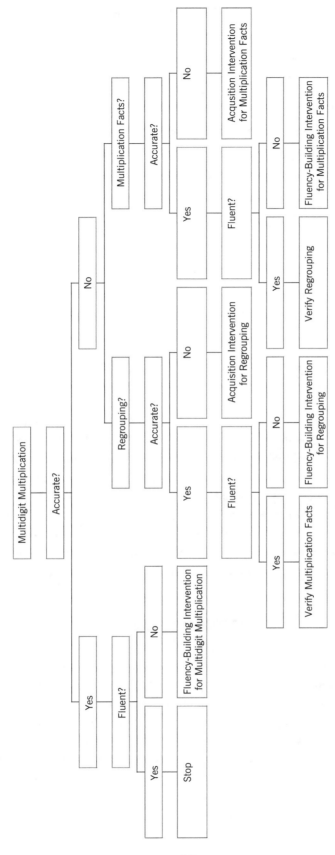

FIGURE 2.5. Sample prerequisite skill breakdown.

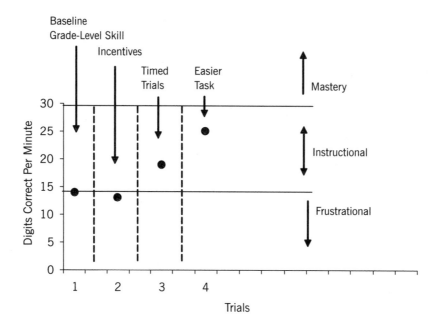

FIGURE 2.6. Sample academic functional assessment.

can respond accurately, he or she appears to be functioning in the fluency-building stage of learning. Brief functional assessment allows us to check the effects of some common fluency-building strategies. Offering incentives did not improve performance. A single session of timed trials produced an improvement to 19 DCPM. Reducing the task difficulty produced an even stronger improvement, raising the score to 25 DCPM, which was in the middle of the instructional range. Based on these data, reducing task difficulty slightly and providing practice opportunities on the easier task until the student reaches the mastery criterion (31 DCPM) and then increasing task difficulty in small increments would be a function-based intervention that should work for this student.

CONCLUSION

Selecting the appropriate intervention is the first and perhaps most important aspect of an effective intervention effort. There are many ways to analyze a problem, but using the instructional hierarchy seems to provide the most direct link between assessment and intervention. In other words, the appropriate intervention should be self-evident after determining in which phase the student is functioning. The chapters that follow discuss the interventions that match the phase, but even the best intervention will not work if it does not address the correct problem.

Assessment Protocols for Reading and Math

Assess Instructional Level for Reading

Student: _____   Date: _____

Have the student read for three 1-minute probes using material taken from the curriculum. Begin the assessment with grade-level material. Open the book to a page or provide the student a copy of a probe to read. If using a book, then randomly select three pages from the book: one at the beginning, one in the middle, and one at the end. Try to avoid passages with too many pictures or dialogue. Use the following directions:

> "When I tell you to, beginning reading out loud and keep going until I tell you to stop. Do your very best reading and if you come to a word you do not know, then I will give it to you. Ready? Begin. After 1 minute, ask the student to stop."

Record the data below. If the child reads less than 93% of the words correctly on three passages, then move down a grade level and repeat the assessment. Continue this process until an instructional level (93—97%) is reached.

On Grade Level

Percentage correct	Words read correctly per minute	Instructional level of 93–97%?	
First read		Yes	No
Second read		Yes	No
Third read		Yes	No
Median		Yes	No

1 Level Below Grade Level

Percentage correct	Words read correctly per minute	Instructional level of 93–97%?	
First read		Yes	No
Second read		Yes	No
Third read		Yes	No
Median		Yes	No

(cont.)

2 Levels Below Grade Level

Percentage correct	Words read correctly per minute	Instructional level of 93–97%?	
First read		Yes	No
Second read		Yes	No
Third read		Yes	No
Median		Yes	No

3 Levels Below Grade Level

Percentage correct	Words read correctly per minute	Instructional level of 93–97%?	
First read		Yes	No
Second read		Yes	No
Third read		Yes	No
Median		Yes	No

Error Analysis

_____ Child's performance is slow but accurate on grade-level task.

_____ Child can decode unknown words. If no, isolate letter sounds, blends, beginning and ending sounds? Is there a pattern?

_____ Child can read high-frequency words that are nondecodable.

_____ Does child commonly substitute or skip words? Does passage preview and/or phrase drill correct errors?

_____ If child can read fluently (greater than 70 WCPM) then readminister maze passage by guiding child to read aloud and select the correct maze answer for practice to 13 correct, then readminister the maze passage. If score is greater than 13, begin intervention using maze materials.

(cont.)

Assess Instructional Level for Math

Student: _____ Date: _____

Expected Grade-Level Skill: _____

	During in-class screening	During can't do/ won't do	Percentage attempted items correct > 90%?	Accurate? Can child explain or draw picture?
Digits correct/ 2 min.				

Prerequisite Skill 1: _____

Digits correct/2 min. with incentives	Percentage attempted items correct > 90%?	Accurate? Can child explain or draw picture?

Prerequisite Skill 2: _____

Digits correct/2 min. with incentives	Percentage attempted items correct > 90%?	Accurate? Can child explain or draw picture?

Prerequisite Skill 3: _____

Digits correct/2 min. with incentives	Percentage attempted items correct > 90%?	Accurate? Can child explain or draw picture?

Linking to Intervention

_____ If skill is inaccurate, choose an acquisition intervention.

_____ If skill is greater than 90% accurate but below the instructional criterion, choose a fluency-building intervention at that level of difficulty. When child performance reaches mastery during intervention, move up to the next level of skill difficulty.

_____ You may work on more than one skill at a time, and it is common to use fluency building for one skill while using an acquisition intervention for a different skill.

CHAPTER 3

Selecting Group Interventions
Identifying a Classwide Problem

OVERVIEW

Screening data offer school teams a chance to be strategic about where to allocate additional support and where supports may be pared back. With well-controlled, well-collected screening data, schools can answer questions like:

- Is instruction working for most students in the school?
- Are particular groups of students at risk relative to their classmates? If so, do the groups share common features?

Research tells us that strategic use of student performance data to allocate instructional resources can improve achievement for all students, for subsets of vulnerable students, improve equity of achievement and eligibility decisions, improve accuracy of referral decisions, and reduce the number of students who require special education where rates are inflated. Failing to attend to and strategically use data collected as part of screening and progress monitoring in RTI is one of the most common errors made by implementers. This chapter provides a step-by-step guide to identifying and addressing common schoolwide and classwide learning problems.

In this chapter, we refer to "the team" repeatedly; therefore, some specifics about the team's purpose and who should serve on the team are important to mention. As systems begin to use data to inform instruction and allocate instructional resources in systematic

> **Failing to attend to and strategically use data collected in RTI is one of the most common errors made by implementers.**

and strategic ways, it is important to involve individuals who have the skills to implement effectively and ensure results. The school principal, as the instructional leader, is a pivotal member of the team. The classroom teacher, as the individual who

24

has the greatest opportunity to impact a student's learning, is also a pivotal member of the team. We suggest that teams be organized by grade level, including the school principal, all teachers at a given grade level, the school psychologist, and any other support personnel who can influence the use of instructional resources at the school (e.g., reading specialist, Title I coach, resource teacher, speech and language therapist). The purpose of the team is to evaluate and enhance learning at each grade level. Each meeting should open with a brief presentation of the data to be interpreted and acted upon and should conclude with an action plan. Subsequent meetings should begin with a review of implementation accuracy and progress monitoring data.

STEP 1: SELECT SCREENING TASKS

Before screening occurs, teams must select screening tasks that will yield meaningful data for decision making. If the screening task is too easy, it may fail to identify students and groups of students who need intervention. If the screening task is too difficult, it may overidentify students for intervention. As a rule of thumb, the screening task should reflect a skill that has been taught and that the average-performing student in the class is expected to be able to do to be successful in the instruction that is forthcoming (VanDerHeyden & Burns, 2009). In reading, oral reading fluency data can be used in the primary grades and maze tasks can be used in grades 3–8 (National Reading Panel, 2000). For mathematics, computation probes function well for making screening decisions (Foegen, Jiban, & Deno, 2007).

It is useful for teachers to meet in grade-level teams to select the actual screening probe from among a set of technically adequate measures. Technically adequate measures are those measures that yield reliable, valid, and sensitive scores that can be used to reach valid decisions. The grade-level meeting is a useful opportunity for the teachers to review state standards for learning in the content areas and identify screening measures that will tell them whether most children are thriving in their learning environments and which children require additional support.

From a measurement perspective, some might advocate for selecting a measure based on the teachers' opinions concerning general student proficiency or identifying a measure that will result in an approximately normal distribution (some children will find the task challenging, most will be able to do the task, and for some it will be too easy). This approach is a mistake if users want to evaluate whether classes and grades in general are meeting expected learning standards. The screening task should be selected according to what is expected of the average student, rather than according to what teachers think students are capable of doing well. For example, for screening in mathematics in the fall of third grade, it would be reasonable to select double- or triple-digit subtraction with and without regrouping. This is a skill that students are expected to be able to do in the fall of third grade and a skill they will need to have mastered to be successful in solving word problems and measure-

> **The screening task should be selected according to what is expected of the average student, rather than according to what teachers think students are capable of doing well.**

ment problems that require subtraction. At winter of third grade, mathematics instruction begins to emphasize multiplication, division, and proportions. Hence, subtraction will not be a major focus of instruction going forward, but is a skill that is required for learning more complex mathematical skills in third grade and beyond.

Teachers may prefer to select an easier task than appropriate (e.g., double-digit addition in third grade), which might identify the lowest-performing students in need of intervention in that classroom, but would not verify that the class as a whole is on track to attain expected skills. If the teacher administered an overly easy probe and most students performed above criterion, it would still be possible that the class as a whole was at risk in terms of mathematical proficiency but the data would not indicate a need for instructional change. Moreover, the first purpose of screening is to rule out a classwide learning problem, which cannot be accomplished with data obtained from screeners that are selected without regard to expected standards for student performance at that grade level at that point in the year. The common core content standards are a useful source for identifying screening tasks (Common Core Standards Initiative, 2010).

STEP 2: ENSURE ADEQUACY OF SCREENING DATA

Table 3.1 lists procedural controls for the screening process to ensure that the resulting data are of high quality. On the day that the screening measures are selected, the screening administration procedures should be shared with teachers (i.e., printed administration directions) and the process should be detailed for teachers so teachers know what to expect. If needed, teachers should be trained to administer and score oral reading fluency measures. It is usually helpful to generate a screening schedule for the day so that teachers know when the screening will occur in their classrooms and can be prepared to use about 10 minutes of whole-class time for screening followed by independent seatwork for about 30 to 40 minutes while the teacher reads with each student individually for the oral reading

---

TABLE 3.1. Ensuring the Adequacy of Screening Data

- Select screening task that is tied to expectations for learning at that time of year.
- Select measures that are technically adequate for screening decision (reliable, valid, sensitive).
- Train teachers to administer measures correctly.
- Provide scripted instructions for screening measure administration.
- Provide digital countdown timer for each teacher.
- Provide a trained coach in each classroom to ensure correct administration of screening measures.
- Check scoring reliability for subset of measures in each class every time screening occurs.

fluency measure if that is being used. Digital countdown timers should also be provided to teachers for the screening. Scripted administration directions should be provided to teachers and teachers should be encouraged to read the instructions exactly as printed. The screening materials should be given to teachers on the day of screening. Assigning a coach to each classroom during the screening period is helpful to ensure that screening occurs smoothly, that scripted instructions are followed, that the oral reading fluency probe is properly scored, and that students start and stop working as instructed. Finally, teachers can meet together in a follow-up grade-level meeting to score their data. Scoring in a small group allows coaches to double-check the scoring to ensure that all teachers are scoring the same way.

The scores should be organized by class and by grade and compared to some benchmark. Implementers can organize the data manually using software like Microsoft Excel but it is helpful (and less error prone) to use a Web-based system to organize the school's screening data (e.g., Pearson, 2008; ISTEP, 2011).

STEP 3: EVALUATE SCREENING DATA TO IDENTIFY GRADEWIDE AND CLASSWIDE LEARNING PROBLEMS

Once the data have been entered and organized, each class should be examined to identify classwide learning problems. A classwide learning problem is defined as the median score occurring in the frustration range (VanDerHeyden & Burns, 2009). Gradewide problems are defined as 50% or more of classes in a given grade showing classwide learning problems (see Figures 3.1, 3.2, and 3.3).

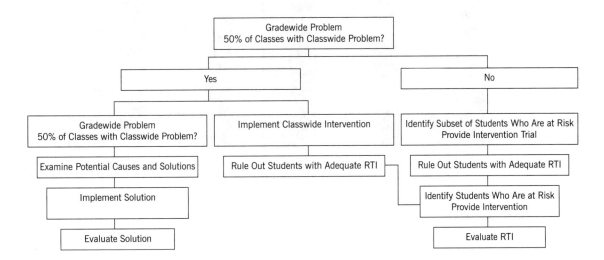

FIGURE 3.1. Classwide problem flowchart. Once the screening data are organized, teams must make a series of interpretations to build a strategy for optimizing instructional effects at Tiers 1 and 2.

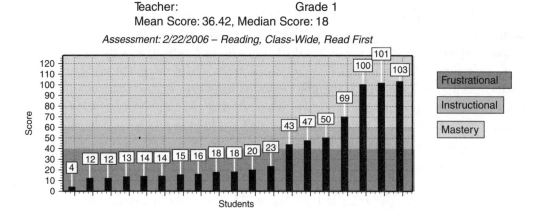

FIGURE 3.2. Example of a classwide learning problem. This classwide screening graph illustrates a classwide problem. The median score is in the frustrational range on a skill that has been taught and is necessary for students to have success in as instruction progresses.

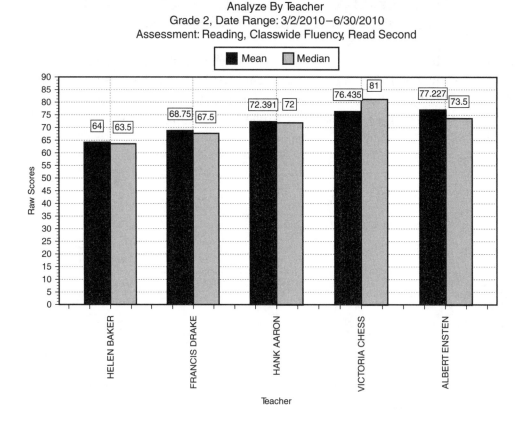

FIGURE 3.3. Example of a gradewide learning problem. This graph shows the mean and median scores on screening for each class at a given grade level. Here all of the classes except for one have a median score that is below criterion. This graph illustrates a gradewide problem.

STEP 4: IDENTIFY PATTERNS IN THE DATA

If a classwide learning problem is detected, then the grade-level team should examine the gradewide data to determine whether a gradewide learning problem is apparent. If there is a gradewide learning problem, the team should ask the following questions:

1. Was the screening task appropriate? Does it reflect what children are expected to be able to do at this time of year to be able to succeed in the instruction that is forthcoming?
2. Were the screening data reliable, sensitive, and led to valid decisions?
3. Was the screening measure correctly administered?

If the answers to the above questions are yes, then the team can examine potential causes of poor performance as follows:

4. Is a research-based core curriculum in place?
5. Is the curriculum being followed with sufficient daily instructional minutes?
6. Is there a calendar of instruction that specifies the date by which essential skills will be mastered during the school year?
7. Is that calendar being followed?
8. Have students mastered the prerequisite skills?
9. Is the instructional environment one in which students are actively engaged, non-instructional time kept to a minimum, and most student responding accurate and, if not, is followed by corrective feedback?
10. Is the gradewide problem isolated to one grade level or is it pervasive? Are there shared features between classes with classwide learning problems (e.g., veteran or first-year teachers, only higher grades with gradewide problems)?

The answers to the above questions should lead to an action plan that includes a system for knowing if the corrective action(s) has been implemented consistently, and includes more frequent progress monitoring of all students within the grade. Once the problem has been remediated, the team can consider steps to prevent the problem from recurring in the future including more frequent screening to permit earlier detection, providing supplemental intervention in the preceding year or semester, revising the calendar of instruction, allocating additional instructional time in the preceding or current year, integrating student assessment data with instruction to ensure that students are mastering expected skills as instruction progresses, changing instructional materials and instructional interactions, and restructuring teacher teams to function as data teams to plan and evaluate solutions to identified learning problems.

If there is a classwide learning problem, the team should ask the following questions:

1. Was the screening task appropriate? Does it reflect what children are expected to be able to do at this time of year to be able to succeed in the instruction that is forthcoming?

2. Were the screening data reliable, sensitive, and did they lead to valid decisions?

3. Was the screening measure correctly administered?

If the answers to the above questions are yes, then the team can examine potential causes of poor performance as follows:

4. Is the teacher adhering to the curriculum?

5. Is the teacher adhering to the instructional calendar and allocating sufficient instructional minutes?

6. Was this class inadvertently (or purposely) tracked?

7. Did students in this class master the prerequisite skills?

8. Are there common or shared features among students performing below benchmark in the class?

9. Is the instructional environment one in which students are actively engaged, noninstructional time kept to a minimum, and most student responding accurate and, if not, is followed by corrective feedback?

As the team answers the above questions, an action plan is built to correct the classwide learning problem. To prevent the problem from recurring in the future, instructional leaders should link identified causes of classwide learning problems to professional development and personnel review activities. Additionally, where classwide problems are detected, more frequent progress monitoring is necessary to ensure that the problem is successfully resolved and to permit earlier detection should the problem recur.

STEP 5: PLAN CORE SOLUTIONS

The solution to the problem will depend on the answers to questions 4 through 8 above. For example, if a grade-level team determines that most of the students struggle with one core aspect (e.g., phonemic awareness), then the teachers could decide to address that aspect of learning more explicitly and frequently, but teachers not adhering to the curriculum would require an entirely different approach. However, any classwide or gradewide problem suggests that student progress has to be more frequently monitored.

Screening data are periodically collected throughout the school year (e.g., three times per year), which is sufficient enough to address the questions listed above. However, if a problem exists, then data must be collected more frequently and perhaps in a more precise manner. For example, if a grade-level team decides that most of the students are demonstrating a difficulty with a component of core instruction such as phonemic awareness for reading, then specific measures of that core instructional area should be added to the assessment system. Moreover, the skills of each student for which there is a classwide or gradewide problem should be assessed much more frequently, perhaps weekly or every other week. Those data could then

> **If a problem exists, then data must be collected more frequently and perhaps in a more precise manner.**

be used to determine whether the problem is improving or if changes to the intervention plan are needed.

STEP 6: PLAN SUPPLEMENTAL INTERVENTION

Classwide learning problems can have a variety of causes (e.g., insufficient time allocated to instruction, inadequate practice materials, prerequisite skills not taught to mastery, poor instruction, low-performing students sent to the same class) that can lead to corrective actions to prevent additional devastating effects to student learning for the whole class. However, when a classwide problem is detected, it is likely that students have accumulated deficits in a number of skills that will be necessary for success in the instructional program. Hence, where classwide learning problems are detected, it can be efficient to use an intervention to supplement core instruction to repair existing skill deficits even as more intensive efforts are undertaken to correct systemic causes of classwide learning problems (e.g., insufficient time allocated to instruction, poor quality of instruction).

The first step in conducting classwide intervention is to identify task difficulty that will work for the majority of students in the class. A logical hierarchy of skills can be developed by the teacher working backward to measure classwide performance on each subsequent skill until a skill is identified that most students in the class perform accurately. Identifying a skill for which most students are accurate is important because error correction is difficult to manage effectively when using peer tutors. If prerequisite skills can be identified, a fluency-building intervention protocol (see Forms 3.1 and 3.2 at the end of the chapter) can be used to efficiently build fluency for the class as a whole. Use of a fluency-building intervention for classwide intervention can be very effective at improving achievement (Codding, Chan-Iannetta, Palmer, & Lukito, 2009; VanDerHeyden & Burns, 2005). Acquisition interventions that must include procedures to deliver accurate corrective feedback immediately following errors and at higher rates (because errors are frequent at that stage of learning) can be more successfully managed using small-group or individual intervention.

The classwide intervention should be viewed as a supplement (add-on) to core instruction rather than as a replacement or substitution for high-quality core instruction. Classwide intervention can be an efficient way to build fluency in foundation or prerequisite skills so that core instruction can be more productive for students (see Figures 3.4 and 3.5). Core instruction may still require troubleshooting to optimize effects (e.g., improve materials, allocate more instructional time, enhance quality of teacher–student interactions). As the classwide intervention is implemented, performance is tracked to determine when to advance the difficulty level of the intervention content.

This fourth-grade class presented above was dysfluent in multiplication facts. As a supplement to core instruction, Ms. Jones decided to conduct classwide intervention 5 days per week using the protocol in Form 3.1. She decided to begin with multiplication facts 0–12 because students understood the concept of multiplication. For example, students accurately answered multiplication problems,

> **The classwide intervention should be viewed as a supplement to core instruction.**

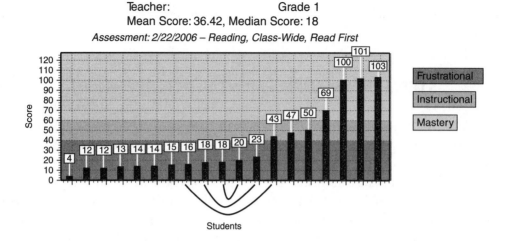

FIGURE 3.4. Arrangement of students into working pairs. Using the classwide screening graph, students can be matched into working pairs for classwide intervention. One way to group students is to link the lowest-performing student with the highest-performing student and continue working your way toward the middle of the graph until all students are grouped into pairs. Teachers can make any necessary adjustments to ensure student pairs work well together. In the example provided here, there are an odd number of students in the class. When this happens, the teacher can use his or her best judgment to match the odd student with a group. Often, the lowest-performing student can be matched with a reading specialist who may be in the room to assist when classwide interventions are implemented. The student could be matched with a student from another classroom. The teacher could be the odd-student's partner and could rotate day to day as a motivator.

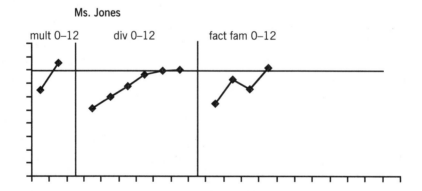

FIGURE 3.5. Classwide progress monitoring data. Each week, the class median score can be tracked to reflect progress. In this example, Ms. Jones's class reached mastery on multiplication facts in 2 weeks. Once the class reached mastery, the materials were changed and students began to follow the classwide intervention protocol working on division facts. In 6 weeks, the class reached mastery. At this point, the materials changed again, targeting fact families for multiplication and division. The classwide intervention continued and in 4 weeks, the class reached the mastery criterion for this skill. Teams can identify a logical sequence of skills matched to grade-level standards and provide classwide intervention as a supplement to ensure mastery of key foundation skills at each grade level.

but often had to count on their fingers and draw sets of hash marks to arrive at the correct answer. Because fourth-grade mathematics instruction included multidigit multiplication with regrouping and work with proportions (decimals, fractions) and factors, Ms. Jones believed that improving fluency in the prerequisite skills would facilitate her Tier 1 instruction.

The intervention required 10–15 minutes per day. Each week, the class median score was tracked to reflect progress. Ms. Jones's class reached mastery on multiplication facts in 2 weeks. Once the class reached mastery, the materials were changed and students began to follow the classwide intervention protocol working on division facts. In 6 weeks, the class reached mastery. At this point, the materials changed again, targeting fact families for multiplication and division. The classwide intervention continued and in 4 weeks the class reached the mastery criterion for this skill. Teams can identify a logical sequence of skills matched to grade-level standards and provide classwide intervention as a supplement to ensure mastery of key foundation skills at each grade level. This intervention protocol can be used equally well to target reading skills.

CONCLUSION

We cannot overstate the importance of identifying classwide problems as the first step in an RTI model or any intervention effort. In order for an intervention to work, it has to be correctly targeted (see Chapter 2), but in order for the skill to generalize into improved educational outcomes, it has to be contextualized within effective instructional practice. If there is a classwide problem, then there could be a number of potential reasons why, but one thing is certain, the students are not benefiting or will not benefit from core instruction. For example, teaching a child to decode a word is often the appropriate intervention target for reading and is not a difficult task. However, if the intervention is not contextualized within effective reading instruction, the student will learn how to decode the word but will not learn how to read!

We have seen the exact scenario described above played out in schools far too often. From our experience, teachers and principals are enthusiastic about implementing interventions to help students, but are much less excited about examining their own practice. Hence, we see groups of children whose reading and math scores increase during intervention, but the number of students

> Teaching a child to decode a word is often the appropriate intervention target for reading. However, if the intervention is not contextualized within effective reading instruction, the student will learn how to decode the word but will not learn how to read!

who pass the state test remains the same or only slightly improves. Whether we like it or not, it always comes back to good core instruction and behavioral management. Identifying and remediating a classwide problem is not difficult and should not be a difficult process. If grade-level teams examine data and address the questions outlined above, then it does not become a judgmental or evaluative process. However, it should be the beginning of any intervention model. Once core instruction is solidly in place, then small-group and individual interventions have a much better chance to work.

Classwide Fluency-Building Intervention

This intervention is designed to **build fluency and increase accuracy** and can be used for prerequisite or criterion-level skills.

Teacher Intervention Protocol (conduct these steps every day):

_____ **Instruct students to find their partner and get out practice materials quickly and quietly.**

GUIDED PEER PRACTICE

_____ **Set timer for 3 minutes and tell students, "Begin practicing."**

_____ **When timer rings, tell students, "Stop. Switch places."**

_____ **Set timer for 3 minutes and tell students, "Begin practicing."**

_____ **When timer rings, tell students, "Stop practicing."**

TIMED INDEPENDENT PRACTICE

_____ Pass out worksheets facedown on students' desks. Tell students, **"Write your name on the back of your paper. Don't turn them over until I tell you to."**

_____ Set timer for 2 minutes. Say, **"On your mark, get set."** Begin the timer, and say, **"Go."**

_____ When the timer rings, tell students, **"Hold your papers up in the air so that I can see that you are no longer working."**

_____ Tell students, **"Trade papers with your partner for scoring. When I call out the answers, mark the answers 'right' or 'wrong.'"**

ERROR CORRECTION

_____ **Call out the correct answers.** Review answers that several students miss.

_____ Tell students, **"Give papers back to their owners now. If you missed problems, write the correct answer under the problem where your partner wrote it. Explain to your partner out loud how you fixed your mistake."**

_____ Tell students, **"Write your score on your progress chart and pass your papers to the front so I can pick them up."**

REWARD/MOTIVATION

_____ Shuffle the papers. **Randomly draw a paper from the stack.** If the score on this randomly selected paper is higher than the randomly selected score from the day before (or the class median if you have calculated it), then deliver a classwide reward (e.g., 5 minutes free time).

Copyright by Amanda M. VanDerHeyden.

Classwide Progress Monitoring

Write the number of words read correctly during 1 minute followed by a slash and the number of errors (number of words/number of errors).

Student name	Current level	Monday	Tuesday	Wednesday	Thursday	Friday	Change level?
							Yes No
							Yes No
							Yes No
							Yes No
							Yes No
							Yes No
							Yes No
							Yes No
							Yes No
							Yes No
							Yes No
							Yes No
							Yes No
							Yes No
							Yes No
							Yes No
							Yes No
							Yes No
							Yes No
							Yes No
							Yes No
							Yes No
							Yes No
							Yes No
							Yes No
							Yes No
							Yes No

Copyright by Amanda M. VanDerHeyden.

CHAPTER 4

Whole-School
Behavioral Interventions

OVERVIEW

As with academic intervention, successful behavior management systems begin at Tier 1. It is critical that the majority of students behave appropriately without intensive individual intervention. As such, whole-school environments must be effective and efficient in the allocation of resources when creating and maintaining supportive school climates (Chafouleas, Riley-Tillman, & Sugai, 2007; Colvin, Kame'enui, & Sugai, 1993; White, Algozzine, Audette, Marr, & Ellis, 2001). For this goal to be realized, the whole-school environment must be organized so that behavioral expectations are communicated clearly, target behaviors are being taught reliably, and behavioral consequences are being used both consistently and appropriately. In line with that goal, this chapter overviews whole-school and classroom evidence-based intervention programs for behavior.

Before moving to discussion of whole-school programs, a general issue should be addressed. At the level of a whole-school intervention program the goal is to be successful with as many students as possible, understanding that some students will eventually require more intense levels of intervention services. As such, it may be acceptable for 85–95% of students in a school to be maintained (in terms of behavior) at the whole-school and classroom levels. Children who experience difficulties that require more intense services in such an environment would then be supported with a more intense individual intervention program. The benefits of this model are clear in that maintaining most students in one intervention program (whole-school/classroom systems) allows for higher levels of resources to be allocated to students with more intense needs. This approach is obviously in line with the general RTI frame-

> The goal is to be successful with as many students as possible, understanding that some students will eventually require more intense levels of intervention services.

work. One of the important implications of this logic is that the whole-school model should be validated at the group level and the types of outcome data collected should be at the system/classroom level. As such, we focus on intervention programs/practices in this chapter that have been documented to work at the school level. In later chapters we focus more on individual classrooms/small groups, as well as developing specific interventions to accommodate the function of individual students with ongoing problem behaviors.

SPECIFIC ISSUES OF BEHAVIORAL INTERVENTION AT THE WHOLE-SCHOOL LEVEL

Considering the scope of a whole-school intervention program, there are a number of challenges that are specifically related to this level of behavioral intervention. These challenges include a need for universal buy-in, high level of staff understanding, versatility of rules and expectations that maximize universal application, intervention feasibility, and multiple levels of outcome data. Each of these challenges are next addressed in brief.

Universal Buy-In

One of the greatest challenges of whole-school behavioral intervention is that the model must be consistently applied in each classroom, in the hallways, in the cafeteria, on the playground, and in all school offices. In addition, there must be a consistent level of behavioral expectations agreed upon by staff in each school location. As such, it is critical that all staff members not only agree to implement the schoolwide behavior program as designed, but also take the time to come to an agreement as to what are the behavioral expectations for the school. It is a given that individual teachers, administrators, and staff will have varying opinions of what is acceptable school behavior. To accommodate differences in expectations, school time must be allocated for a discussion and decision as to what the schoolwide specific expectations are, ideally by considering input from all stakeholders (e.g., administrators, teachers, parents, and other staff). Without this universal buy-in, varied applications of the schoolwide plan are inevitable, and such incongruences have the potential to minimize the program's effectiveness.

There are two primary implications of the importance of schoolwide buy-in. First, as noted above, time must be taken to present the model to staff in an attempt to increase support. This step is critical and should not be rushed. Second, the schoolwide intervention model should

> **Without a universal buy-in, varied applications of the schoolwide plan are inevitable, and such incongruences have the potential to minimize the program's effectiveness.**

have a generally high level of acceptability to stakeholders. Fortunately, intervention/treatment acceptability research has been a mainstay in the intervention extant literature base for decades. One of the original definitions of treatment acceptability was provided by Kazdin (1980) when he suggested that it was the degree to which individuals perceived a treatment to be fair, reasonable, and appropriate. A developed line of research attempted to assess to what extent consumers found specific features of interventions acceptable or unacceptable and when possible those features were modified accordingly (Chafouleas, Briesch, Riley-Tillman, & McCoach, 2009). Since the early 1980s there have been a number of conceptual models examining treatment acceptability and use (Eckert & Hintze, 2000). In one of the initial models, Witt and Elliott (1985) provide a circular model involving four factors: treatment acceptability, treatment integrity, treatment use, and treatment effectiveness. These authors postulated the relationship among these factors to be bidirectional, suggesting that each influences the other. In this model, treatment acceptability was critical as it was the gateway for subsequent use. In an extension of the Witt and Elliott model, Reimers, Wacker, and Koeppl (1987) presented a model that included five components (treatment knowledge/understanding, treatment acceptability, treatment compliance, treatment effectiveness, and environmental disruption). More recently, Chafouleas, Briesch, et al. presented support for a model with four factors (acceptability, understanding, feasibility, and systems support). While there has been some debate about the importance of the treatment acceptability factor in each modeling in regard to subsequent usage, the line of research does consistently highlight the importance of acceptability in terms of early treatment application. In other words, it is important for the consumers to accept the intervention, or it is unlikely that they will ever use it.

Staff Understanding

A second critical issue is that time for training is taken so that all staff members feel confident in their understanding of the intervention and how to carry it out. Without such understanding, educational professionals are likely to be uncomfortable implementing the intervention. As noted above, both the Reimers et al. (1987) and Chafouleas, Briesch, et al. (2009) models of usage included a factor focusing on understanding. In these models, the assumption behind the additional component of understanding is that if a treatment is not understood, then use and effectiveness are likely to be minimal. In addition, the Reimers, Wacker, and Koeppl model was built under the assumption that treatment acceptability cannot be accurately assessed until a treatment was understood. The specific nature of "understanding" an intervention has been best explored in the medical literature (Chafouleas, Briesch, et al., 2009). Specifically, intervention adherence seems to be impacted by the number of intervention steps (De Civita & Dobkin, 2005), how difficult the intervention is to understand (Kazdin, 2000), and the individual's understanding of the intervention purpose (Modi & Quittner, 2006). The primary implication for the role of understanding in treatment acceptability for schoolwide behavior plans is that time must be taken to develop staff knowledge of both the program and the intended purposes of the program. The time spent training staff to maximize understanding should increase

> **Time for training is taken so that all staff members feel confident in their understanding of the intervention and how to carry it out.**

their likelihood to use the interventions initially (assuming high levels of initial acceptability) and also increase program effectiveness through more accurate implementation.

Versatility of Rules and Expectations to Maximize Universal Application

School rules must be developed so that they are applicable in a variety of settings. If rules are too specific in a particular classroom, they are unlikely to be useful in a second classroom, and much less likely to be used in the hallway or cafeteria. As such, it is important to emphasize a global schoolwide rule rather than a specific rule. "Being respectful" or "Making good choices" are general rules that can work in a variety of settings. General rules are also a way to provide a consistent framework for children so that they can predict what is expected across settings. Obviously each global rule might need to be further operationalized for a specific setting, but that is a task that can be accomplished in each setting. It is critical that children understand both the global rules as well as the setting-by-setting application of those rules.

Intervention Feasibility

Perhaps the most challenging aspect of whole-school behavior programs is keeping the model feasible for all school faculty and staff. Discussion of feasibility has been present in the educational literature for decades. For example, Witt and Elliott (1985) developed an instrument called the Intervention Rating Profile–20 with items developed to assess the impact of time, resources, and effort requirements of an education intervention. The rational for including these items was the belief that there is an inverse relationship between time demands and usage. Happe (1983) stated this well when he wrote, "The plan that requires the consulted to become a timer-setting, data-taking, token-counting, head-patting octopus has a very low probability of implementation and maintenance" (p. 33).

In addition to time, the concept of ecological intrusiveness is considered important. Witt (1986) defined ecological intrusiveness as the extent to which behavioral regularities are impacted and altered by the new interventions. In practice, an intervention is ecologically intrusive and unfeasible if introducing it results in less time for instruction, routines, or is disruptive to others (Chafouleas, Briesch, et al., 2009). Even a "brief" intervention can result in a great deal of time lost if it upsets the classroom environment. One final aspect of feasibility to consider is the systems-level factors that either support or impede intervention use. Broughton and Hester (1993) suggested that intervention acceptability can be impacted by the level of administration support. As noted by Chafouleas, Briesch, and colleagues educational professionals are unlikely to use a perceived feasible and effective intervention if they believe it will cause political problems due to a lack of institutional support. The implication of the work on feasibility is clear in terms of schoolwide behavior programs. Such models must be designed so that they minimize the amount of time required and expected levels of staff effort, conform to the behavioral regularities of the school environment, and be supported by overt district and building administration support.

Multiple Levels of Outcome Data (School, Classroom, Child)

The final requirement for a schoolwide behavior plan is a package of assessment methods to provide both screening and formative assessment data at the whole-school, classroom, and individual child level (Chafouleas, Riley-Tillman, et al., 2007). As noted in Chapter 3, screening data offer school teams a chance to determine whether the program is working for most children in the school, and for identification of a system-level problem with the accompanying logical course of action to be taken (see Table 4.1 for an example). In other words, screening data can help determine if there are particular classrooms or groups of student who are exhibiting more problematic behavior (discussed in more depth in Chapter 6). For example, if behavior problems are documented in a variety of locations and classrooms with a range of children, then problems exist at the whole-school level. Intervention focused on a single classroom or with a specific child is likely to be undermined by the larger-system issue. In the case of a specific classroom where there are pervasive behavior problems with a range of students resources should be focused on working with the classroom teacher.

> **The final requirement for a schoolwide behavior plan is a package of assessment methods to provide both screening and formative assessment data at the whole-school, classroom, and individual child level.**

As with academic screening programs there are a number of considerations when selecting a screening system. First, the outcome data should have some general utility. For example, schoolwide behavior plans often rely on office discipline referral (ODR) data because the act of removing a child from a classroom is considered a consistently important outcome. Second, schoolwide assessment methods should have well-documented technical adequacy (i.e., reliability and validity). Finally, while defensible formative assessment is critical for all intervention programs, at the whole-school level care must be taken to consider feasibility. If the data collection system is planned at a level that is considered overly burdensome, there will be a risk the program will be sacrificed over time. This is a particularly important consideration because data collection will need to occur across multiple levels. Thus, it is often a good idea for schools to start by examining existing data sources (Chafouleas, Riley-Tillman, et al., 2007).

EVIDENCE-BASED WHOLE-SCHOOL BEHAVIORAL INTERVENTION PROGRAMS

An excellent example of a whole-school EBI is schoolwide positive behavior supports (SWPBS; Chafouleas, Riley-Tillman, et al., 2007; Horner & Sugai, 2001). While there are a number of SWPBS models, all are focused on developing consistent positive behavioral expectations that are implemented schoolwide. These schoolwide expectations are operationalized by a lead-

TABLE 4.1. Examples of Problem Behavior Presentation with Associated Course of Action

System level of problem behavior	Data presentation	Course of action
Schoolwide	Problematic behavior in a variety of locations in the school (e.g., hallway, cafeteria, and multiple classrooms)	In this situation attention should be focused on developing a more effective schoolwide behavior plan
Classwide or in a single environment (e.g., cafeteria)	Problematic behavior in a single location in the school (e.g., hallway, cafeteria, and multiple classrooms)	Attention focused on the classwide behavior management plan
Small group—multiple locations	Problematic behavior with a specific group of student across a variety of locations	Focused intervention with the group in all affected locations
Small group—single location	Problematic behavior with a specific student in a single location	Focused intervention with the teacher/student in the affected location
Individual—multiple locations	Problematic behavior with a specific student across a variety of locations	Focused intervention with the student in all affected locations
Individual—single location	Problematic behavior with a specific student in a single location	Focused intervention with the teacher/student in the affected location

ership team into clear rules that are taught to students through direct instruction and modeling. Next, the schoowide rules are concurrently posted throughout the school to prompt students to behave in an appropriate manner. One of the

> **One of the most critical core features of SWPBS is consistent enforcement of the positive behavioral expectations by all school staff.**

most critical core features of SWPBS is consistent enforcement of the positive behavioral expectations by all school staff. This combination allows for children to have a consistent set of behavioral expectations that span the entire school, be taught the appropriate behaviors, and practice using consistent expectations across different teachers, administrators, and other educational professionals. Finally, outcome data are collected on both staff implementation of SWPBS and student and staff behavior change. For consistency, we focus on one particular model of SWPBS, positive behavior interventions and supports (PBIS or SWPBIS).

SWPBIS focuses on four key elements: outcomes, data, evidence-based practices, and systems supports (see Figure 4.1; Sugai & Horner, 2002). SWPBIS supports that the outcome should be generally defended by the stakeholders (school staff, parents, and students). Practices are defined as evidence based and driven by applied behavior analytic theory. There is a heavy focus on the collection and use of outcome data to drive educational decisions. Finally, systems supports are defined as policies, procedures, and other practices that

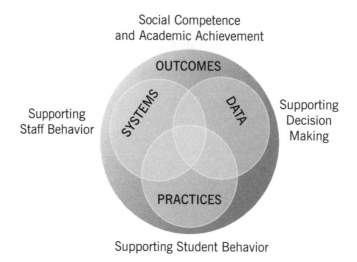

FIGURE 4.1. Four elements of schoolwide positive behavior interventions and supports. From Chafouleas, Riley-Tillman, and Sugai (2007). Copyright 2007 by The Guilford Press. Reprinted by permission.

will lead to long-term implementation. While it is beyond the scope of this book to provide a comprehensive overview of SWPBIS, what follows is a brief orientation to the primary practices in SWPBIS. Readers interested in more information should contact the Office of Special Education Program (OSEP) Center on Positive Behavior Interventions and Supports at *www.pbis.org*.

Schoolwide Behavioral Expectations

The initial component in SWPBIS is the development by school staff of a small number (three to five) of positively stated behavioral expectations (Lewis & Sugai, 1999). These expectations are developed in a PBS framework by the individual school so that they are in line with both the unique needs of each school and the principles of SWPBIS. Punishment-oriented practices and polices are deemphasized as they may increase the occurrence of problem behavior (Hyman & Perone, 1998; Reinke & Herman, 2002). These expectations are typically phrased in a positive manner using simple wording (e.g., respect or be engaged) and then operationalized into specific behavioral definitions for each target environment (e.g., classroom, hallways, cafeteria) and examples and nonexamples of desired behaviors. Finally, school teams develop a behavioral matrix that lists several behaviors in each setting representing the core schoolwide behavioral expectations (see Figure 4.2). For additional examples of a SWPBIS matrix visit the OSEP technical center on PBIS at (*www.pbis.org*). The general goal of consistent schoolwide expectations is to establish a common language in relation to schoolwide behavioral expectations. This process of determining what the core school expectations are, operationalizing these expectations, and introducing them into the target environment should result in all staff members being able to state the expectations as well as provide examples in settings in which they are active.

	Hallway/ Stairway	All Classrooms	Café	Bathroom/ Water Fountain	Bus/Bus Stop/ Walkers	Locker Room	Auditorium	Media Center
PRIDE	☐ Keep hands, feet and objects to yourself ☐ Use a quiet voice	☐ Keep hands, feet and objects to yourself ☐ Use a quiet voice ☐ Enter room quietly ☐ Be considerate of other people's belongings ☐ Be an active listener	☐ Keep hands, feet and objects to yourself ☐ Use a quiet voice ☐ Enter and exit in an orderly manner ☐ Be considerate of other people's belongings ☐ Stand in line as directed	☐ Keep hands, feet and objects to yourself ☐ Use a quiet voice ☐ Allow others their privacy ☐ Wait your turn at the sink or fountain ☐ Take care of school property	☐ Keep hands, feet and objects to yourself ☐ Use a quiet voice ☐ Be considerate of the bus driver and the bus ☐ Wait patiently to get on or off the bus ☐ Share your seat	☐ Keep hands, feet and objects to yourself ☐ Use a quiet voice ☐ Be considerate of other people's belongings	☐ Keep hands, feet and objects to yourself ☐ Use a quiet voice ☐ Stay seated until directed otherwise ☐ Respond to the speaker appropriately ☐ Listen with eyes on speaker	☐ Keep hands, feet and objects to yourself ☐ Use a quiet voice ☐ Enter room quietly ☐ Use media center materials and equipment appropriately
RESPONSIBILITY	☐ Walk facing forward, staying to the right ☐ Follow rules without adult reminders ☐ Walk directly to destination using appropriate route ☐ Have hall passes available ☐ Report all unsafe behavior and vandalism	☐ Respond to quiet signal immediately ☐ Be on time and be prepared ☐ Follow classroom procedures ☐ Report all unsafe behavior and vandalism	☐ Sit in designated areas ☐ Respond to quiet signal immediately ☐ Report all unsafe behavior and vandalism	☐ Walk directly to destination using appropriate route ☐ Report all unsafe behavior and vandalism ☐ Wash and dry hands ☐ Return to class immediately	☐ Have belongings ready to enter and exit ☐ Remain seated at all times ☐ Report all unsafe behavior and vandalism ☐ Follow bus rules at all times ☐ Get on and off bus at correct stop ☐ Stay off private property	☐ Be prepared for gym class ☐ Respond to quiet signal immediately ☐ Report all unsafe behavior and vandalism	☐ Respond to quiet signal immediately ☐ Sit in designated areas ☐ Enter and exit in an orderly manner ☐ Be prompt ☐ Report all unsafe behavior and vandalism	☐ Respond to quiet signal immediately ☐ Follow media center procedures ☐ Report all unsafe behavior and vandalism ☐ Return materials on time
RESPECT	☐ Use polite language ☐ Keep hallways and stairways clean	☐ Use polite language ☐ Do your own work ☐ Do your best work at all times ☐ Keep work areas clean	☐ Use polite language ☐ Keep table and floor clean and place trash into barrels ☐ Leave area as you found it or better	☐ Use polite language ☐ Keep area clean ☐ Throw paper towels in trash cans ☐ Flush appropriately ☐ Keep water fountains clean	☐ Use polite language ☐ Throw trash in waste basket	☐ Use polite language ☐ Leave area as you found it or better	☐ Use polite language ☐ Treat speaker as a welcome guest ☐ Treat furniture appropriately ☐ Leave area as you found it or better	☐ Use polite language ☐ Keep your work area clean ☐ Leave area as you found it or better

FIGURE 4.2. A sample behavioral matrix of expectations within settings. From Simonsen, Sugai, and Negron (2008). Copyright 2008 by the Council for Exceptional Children. Reprinted by permission.

Teaching, Prompting, and Reinforcing Appropriate Behaviors

Once schoolwide expectations and specific behavioral operationalizations have been developed, school staff is expected to teach appropriate behaviors in each setting. This process is formalized at each school in some manner so that time is allocated to ensure that each child has both observed the expectations in each setting (modeled by adults and other children) and have had an opportunity to practice each behavior with corrective feedback (if needed). Once students have demonstrated that they can do the behavior, staff focus should shift to prompting correct behaviors and systematically reinforcing students when they exhibit the correct behaviors.

TABLE 4.2. Example of a Continuum of Rule Violations with Defined Processes for Responses

Severity of infraction	Examples	Level of attention	Process for continued violations
Minor	Disrupting other students, late to class	Teacher managed	Three minor rule violations are treated as a major.
Major	Physical fighting, repeated insubordination/ noncompliance	Office/administrator managed	Three major rule violations result in a referral to the problem-solving team.
District	Illegal drug possession, weapons, vandalism	Board/community involvement	

Note. Based on Chafouleas, Riley-Tillman, and Sugai (2007).

Prompting is accomplished at a building level with the positing of behavioral expectations in all settings. In addition, staff members are trained to seek out opportunities to notice when students are behaving appropriately and reinforce those occurrences as well as positively work with students who are behaving in an inappropriate manner. This process is based on the effective application of behavioral techniques that will be further discussed in the chapters on individual behavioral intervention and generalization programming. The general goal of this practice of SWPBIS is to establish consistent schoolwide practices that are in line with evidence-based practice. SWPBIS schools develop a continuum of consequences to respond to rule-violating behavior (Chafouleas, Riley-Tillman, et al., 2007). Problem behaviors are defined in three levels (see Table 4.2) with clear decision rules (e.g., three repeated minor violations result in a major violation, three major violations result in a referral to a behavior support team).

Data Collection

The final general practice in SWPBIS is the collection of outcome data at the school, classroom, and individual student level. SWPBIS is based on applied behavior analytic ideology and is designed to be driven by data. Consistent with the schoolwide focus of PBIS, data sources are developed at the school/classwide level (e.g., ODR) and for individual children (e.g., check-in, check-out). Researchers have demonstrated that ODRs can be effective in the problem-solving process if a number of key criteria are met. (Horner & Sugai, 2001; Irvin et al., 2006; Irvin, Tobin, Sprague, Sugai, & Vincent, 2004; Sprague, Sugai, Horner, & Walker, 1999; Sugai, Sprague, Horner, & Walker, 2000; Tobin, Sugai, & Colvin, 1996; Wright & Dusek, 1998). Specifically, target behaviors must be clearly defined, a standardized referring processes should be in place, and staff need to be trained in the process and procedures for the efficient analysis and interpretation of ODR data (Chafouleas, Riley-Tillman, et al., 2007).

In a SWPBIS model outcome data are to be used to adapt resource allocation in the school (see Table 4.2). For example, if there are a large number of ODRs coming from one classroom, additional training should be provided to that group of students and the teacher(s) making the referrals. SWPBIS outcome data are also used to document the impact of the program to parents, the school district, and other stakeholders. The goal of this final aspect of SWPBIS is to develop consistent intervention evaluation practices. The use of ODR for the purposes of resource allocation (including strengths and weaknesses) is continued in Chapter 6.

Research Regarding Use of Schoolwide Positive Behavior Intervention and Support

SWPBIS has received a significant amount of empirical support from both educational researchers and schools. There have been many referred journal articles on SWPBIS, which included one randomized clinical trial of SWPBIS (Bradshaw, Reinke, Brown, Bevans, & Leaf, 2008). In addition, the OSEP center on PBIS (*www.pbis.org*) lists several randomized trials that have been completed and are in press in academic journals. In terms of school use of SWPBIS, state/district coordinators report that there are approximately 11,000 schools that meet the following criteria: (1) employees trained directly or indirectly by center collaborators, (2) trained leadership teams were in place, and (3) they have implemented the program for at least 1 year (George Sugai, personal communication, April 28, 2010). Although the total number of 11,000 schools is considerable, there is a variation in the training quality and adherence to a full SWPBIS model. Regardless, there is clearly considerable applied and research support for SWPBIS.

CONCLUSION

As noted in several other places in this book, for an RTI model to be successful, it is essential to develop effective schoolwide interventions for both academic and social behavior success. The effective implementation of Tier 1 intervention strategies maximizes the success of most children and allows educational professionals to allocate additional time and resources only to children who are most in need. When such systems are not in place, Tiers 2 and 3 predictably become overwhelmed by "problem" cases, many of which should have been serviced successfully in Tier 1. Fortunately, the schoolwide social behavior literature has produced a cluster of defensible models under the general title of positive behavior supports and interventions. Educational professionals who are serious about implication of a successful RTI schoolwide model should see this chapter as a brief starting point and seek out addition information from the OSEP technical center on PBIS (*www.pbis.org*).

> **Effective implementation of Tier 1 intervention strategies maximizes the success of most children and allows educational professionals to allocate additional time and resources only to children who are most in need.**

CHAPTER 5

Small-Group Academic Interventions

OVERVIEW

As stated in Chapter 1, there are usually three tiers of intervention within an RTI model. Tier 1 is the most important, but in our experience, Tier 2 will make or break your RTI model. The most effective small-group intervention in the world will not help a student learn how to read unless it is contextualized within effective reading instruction, but an effective Tier 2 model will greatly enhance the effectiveness of Tier 3. Thus, school personnel should focus their efforts on quality core instruction and classwide problems (see Chapter 3) before they begin small-group interventions within an RTI framework. However, they should also establish an effective Tier 2 model before implementing a problem-solving team within Tier 3.

On average, 20% of the student population requires additional support beyond quality core instruction (Burns et al., 2005). Thus, if there are 600 students in the school, then 120 of them would require additional support. Many schools implement a problem-solving team to address the needs of all struggling students, but an effective problem-solving team requires in-depth problem analysis and individualized interventions beyond what can realistically be conducted and delivered for 120 students each year. One goal of effective small-group interventions is to address the needs of most of those students in less intensive format. If the small-group (Tier 2) interventions adequately help 80% of the struggling students, then only 20% of the 120 (24 students) would require additional support, which is less than 5% of the total student population. The likelihood of an effective problem-solving team approach is much higher when addressing 5% of the student population than if attempting to work with 15–20% of the student population.

Tier 2 interventions generally rely on a standard protocol for approximately 15–20% of the student population, but "standard protocol" does not mean that every student receives the same intervention. Instead, low-level analysis is used to determine what category of intervention is needed for a group of students. For example, students who lack decoding skills will receive intervention A and those who lack reading fluency will receive intervention B. We talk extensively in Chapter 2 about using data to determine which intervention is appropriate for individual students. In this chapter we briefly describe an assessment approach to identify the category of the problem, but cover this topic more thoroughly in the second volume of this book. We also discuss the basic tenets of an effective small-group intervention model and provide examples of small-group interventions.

> **"Standard protocol" does not mean that every student receives the same intervention. Instead, low-level analysis is used to determine what category of intervention is needed for a group of students.**

IDENTIFYING THE CATEGORY OF THE PROBLEM

Small-group interventions are designed to be more general than individualized interventions, but should still target an individual skill. The National Reading Panel (2000) identified five areas necessary for reading instruction that could also serve as a heuristic for identifying the category of the problem for reading. After students are identified as struggling readers through general outcome measures such as curriculum-based measures of oral reading fluency or group-administered comprehension measures, then single-skill measures of phonemic awareness, phonics, reading fluency, vocabulary, and comprehension are used to identify the root of the problem for reading. We suggest collecting data in the relevant skill to "drill down." In other words, if a child struggles with reading comprehension, then be sure to screen reading fluency to make sure that the root of the problem is not fluency rather than comprehension—a student cannot comprehend the words if he or she is not reading them. Practitioners should work backward in the sequence (1) comprehension, (2) vocabulary, (3) reading fluency, (4) decoding, and (5) phonemic awareness until they find an acceptable skill and the lowest skill in which a deficit is found would be the appropriate target for a small-group intervention. For example, if a student demonstrated low comprehension, low vocabulary, low fluency, and acceptable decoding, then the intervention would focus on fluency, but the intervention for a student with low comprehension, vocabulary, fluency, and decoding who had phonemic awareness would focus on decoding.

Clearly, reading is a complex process and the aforementioned sequence of skill development will not occur for every child, but it is a common sequence among students who are struggling readers (Berninger, Abbott, Vermeulen, & Fulton, 2006). Therefore, assessing how well a student is progressing through the five skills identified by the National Reading Panel (2000) could provide a useful heuristic for most students who struggle with reading. There are many schools that use one research-based intervention for every student who struggles in reading, but if the intervention focuses on reading fluency and the student does not have adequate decoding skills, then the intervention will not be effective.

Math is similar to reading in some respects, but the research about math interventions is less clear. According to the National Research Council and Institute of Medicine (2009), math proficiency comprises (1) conceptual understanding, (2) procedural fluency, (3) ability to formulate and mentally represent problems, (4) reasoning, and (5) successful application of math to daily activities (Kilpatrick, Swafford, & Finell, 2001). Thus, much like reading, these areas could be a potential heuristic with which to develop small-group math interventions.

An alternative approach to assessing the areas associated with math proficiency could be to assess the skills within a curriculum or benchmark standard sequence. For example, a study that we conducted (VanDerHeyden & Burns, 2009) found that the sequence of skills presented in Figure 5.1 represented an effective development. In other words, if a second-grade student mastered fact families addition and subtraction 0–20, then they were much

Second grade	Third grade
1. Addition facts 0–20 2. Subtraction facts 0–9 3. Subtraction facts 0–12 4. Subtraction facts 0–15 5. Subtraction facts 0–20 6. Mixed subtraction/addition 0–20 7. Fact families addition and subtraction 0–20 8. Two-digit addition without regrouping 9. Two-digit addition with regrouping 10. Two-digit subtraction without regrouping 11. Two-digit subtraction with regrouping 12. Three-digit addition without and with regrouping 13. Three-digit subtraction without and with regrouping 14. Second-grade monthly math probe	1. Addition and subtraction facts 0–20 2. Fact families addition and subtraction 0–20 3. Three-digit addition without and with regrouping 4. Three-digit subtraction without and with regrouping 5. Two- and three-digit addition and subtraction with and without regrouping 6. Multiplication facts 0–9 7. Division facts 0–9 8. Fact families multiplication and division 0–9 9. Add/subtract fractions with like denominators 10. Single-digit multiplied by double/triple digit without regrouping 11. Single-digit multiplied by double/triple digit with regrouping 12. Single-digit divided into double/triple digit without remainders 13. Add and subtract decimals to the hundredths
Fourth grade	**Fifth grade**
1. Multiplication facts 0–12 2. Division facts 0–12 3. Fact families multiplication/division 0–12 4. Single-digit multiplied by double-digit without and with regrouping 5. Double-digit multiplied by double-digit without regrouping 6. Double-digit multiplied by double-digit with regrouping 7. Single-digit divisor into double-digit dividend without remainders 8. Single-digit divisor into double-digit dividend with remainders 9. Single- and double-digit divisor into single- and double-digit dividend with remainders 10. Add/subtract fractions with like denominators without regrouping 11. Multiply multidigit numbers by two numbers 12. Add and subtract decimals to the hundredths	1. Multiplication facts 0–12 2. Division facts 0–12 3. Fact families multiplication/division 0–12 4. Multiply two- and three-digit without and with regrouping 5. Single-digit divisor divided into double-digit dividend with remainders 6. Single-digit divisor divided into double-and triple-digit dividend with remainders 7. Reduce fractions to simplest form 8. Add/subtract proper fractions/mixed numbers with like denominators with regrouping 9. Add/subtract decimals 10. Multiply/divide decimals 11. Double-digit divisor into four-digit dividend 12. Multiply and divide proper and improper fractions

FIGURE 5.1. Sequence of math skills found by VanDerHeyden and Burns (2009).

more likely to master two-digit addition without regrouping. Most math curricula include a sequence of skills much like this one, or the proposed Common Core Standards Initiative (2010; see *www.corestandards.org/*) provide a more general skill breakdown that may be useful.

One approach to identifying the category of the problem could be to assess the skills in the given sequence in backward order until the resulting score falls within the instructional level (14–31 digits correct per minute for second- and third-grade students, and 24–49 digits correct per minute for students in the fourth grade or higher; Burns, VanDerHeyden, et al., 2006). The first skill that represents an instructional level would be the appropriate place to start. For example, if assessments with a fourth-grade student found frustration levels (i.e., below the instructional-level criteria mentioned above) for (1) add/subtract proper fractions/ mixed numbers with like denominators, (2) reducing fractions to the simplest form, (3) single-digit divisor divided by double- and triple-digit dividends with remainders, (4) single-digit divisor divided into double-digit dividend with remainders, and (5) multiply two- and three-digit numbers with and without regrouping, but instructional-level scores for fact families multiplication/division 0–12, then the intervention would focus on multiplication and division facts 0–12 until they were mastered and would then progress to multiplying two- and three-digit numbers with and without regrouping.

There is considerably more research regarding the reading sequence than either of the proposed math sequences. Thus, using a school's curriculum as a guide is as likely to be successful as any other approach, as long as practitioners frequently collect data to monitor the students' progress. As stated above, there will be much more additional information provided about the proposed sequences in the second volume of this book.

TENETS OF AN EFFECTIVE SMALL-GROUP INTERVENTION

Once school personnel decide the appropriate target for the small-group intervention, how then are the interventions actually delivered? The Institute for Education Science (IES) published a practice guide for RTI for reading and concluded that providing intensive intervention within a small-group format for up to three foundational reading skills was the only aspect of an RTI system for which there was a strong research base (Gersten et al., 2008). They further recommended that the groups meet between three to five times each week for 20 to 40 minutes each session. The practice guide for math RTI found strong evidence for (1) providing explicit and systematic interventions that included models of proficient problem solving, verbalization of thought processes, guided practice, corrective feedback, and frequent cumulative review; and (2) including instruction on solving word problems based on common underlying structures (Gersten et al., 2009).

The two aforementioned practice guides provide an excellent and useful overview of effective practices, but do not provide much specificity about implementation. Below we discuss specific aspects of an effective small-group intervention model based on the IES practice guides and a synthesis of small-group intervention research (Burns, Hall-Lande,

Lyman, Rogers, & Tan, 2006). We focus on service delivery, effectiveness, measurement, and cost.

Service Delivery

The delivery of intensive instruction is a complex and multifaceted process that attempts to answer several questions including Who is teaching? Who are being taught? How long is the instructional sequence? Several researchers offer guidance regarding these matters, and from this guidance we draw some common recommendations.

Who Implements the Intervention?

Perhaps the most common question that we receive regarding small-group interventions regards who actually delivers the intervention. The small-group intervention can be delivered by a fully licensed teacher, peer learners, or volunteer tutors. It makes the most sense for a classroom teacher to deliver the small-group intervention, but expertise in the academic area (e.g., reading) is more important than status as the classroom teacher. Although the teacher is the most costly option, there is a higher assurance of instructional quality and consistency with core instruction when the teacher is providing intensive interventions. Moreover, there is a common argument that our most struggling students often receive support from the least-qualified personnel (e.g., paraprofessionals). We suggest that it is highly advantageous for teachers to deliver the small-group interventions and can do so through scheduling daily intervention time in addition to the 90-minute core instructional block. Students may be flexibly grouped during the intervention time and may not receive the intervention from their own classroom teacher, but a teacher is providing the intervention.

> **There is a higher assurance of instructional quality and consistency with core instruction when the teacher is providing intensive interventions.**

Teacher involvement through supervision and/or curriculum and materials development seems critical, but there are other viable options for delivering the intervention. Peer learners who are more highly skilled benefit from teaching others, and less-skilled students can learn via modeling in the "zone of proximal development" (Vygotsky, 1986). Therefore, peer tutors provide an intriguing option for delivering small-group interventions. However, the size of the group is much smaller and usually uses a dyad as opposed to a group. Placing the students in heterogeneous dyads with close teacher supervision could be a way to deliver small-group interventions to more students because one teacher could supervise several dyads (McMaster, Fuchs, Fuchs, & Compton, 2005).

Perhaps the professional most commonly used to implement small-group interventions is an educational assistant or paraprofessional. Certainly there are other options to provide tutoring such as graduate students engaged in research projects (e.g., Vaughn, Wanzek, Linan-Thompson, & Murray, 2007), high school students, or community volunteers. Any of these options can be effective, but only if the intervention is highly scripted and the interventionist is closely supervised by a teacher.

How Big Should the Group Be?

There is a wide range of group sizes within small-group intervention research. A comparison of meta-analyses found that small-group instruction was at least as effective as one-on-one interventions and perhaps more effective and more efficient (D'Agostino & Murphy, 2004; Elbaum, Vaughn, Tejero, & Watson, 2000; Vaughn, Gersten, & Chard, 2000). Thus, groups of 4 to 6 students are probably an optimal combination of effectiveness and efficiency. Younger grades (e.g., kindergarten) might have smaller groups of 2 to 4, and older grades may group children in larger groups such as 8 in middle school but even 10 or 12 for high school. Whatever the ratio, it must be emphasized that these more intensive interventions require closer oversight and involvement of an instructor, and that the group be as large as possible yet still be effective. A group that serves 6 as equally well as 5 should include 6 children to conserve precious resources.

> **Groups of four to six students are probably an optimal combination of effectiveness and efficiency.**

How Long Should the Intervention Run?

There seems to be a confluence of perspectives on the length of time and duration of the reading intervention across various approaches. The range includes daily half-hour lessons over a span of 12 to 20 weeks (e.g., D'Agostino & Murphy, 2004), daily half-hour lessons of one or two 10-week instructional segments (Vaughn et al., 2007), 30- to 50-minute sessions three times each week (O'Connor, Fulmer, Harty, & Bell, 2005), and 30-minute sessions four times/week for 1 school year (Burns, Senesac, & Symington, 2004). Thus, consistent with the IES practice guide recommendations (Gersten et al., 2009), the interventions should probably be approximately 30 minutes in length and should occur three to five times each week.

Providing small-group interventions is one instance in which more is not always better. In order for the intervention to be effective, it has to be highly and correctly targeted and has to be contextualized within effective instruction. Once the intervention session exceeds approximately 30 minutes, then the interventionist is likely no longer engaged in intervention but is instead providing instruction. All students in the school should participate in quality instruction in math and reading, but approximately 20% of them will receive additional support. We are very concerned that RTI will result in a return to tracked approaches to instruction. Although many of us probably fondly remember our "Bluebird" and "Redbird" reading groups as children, there are literally decades of research that shows poorer outcomes for tracked reading groups. We have to be careful that we are not giving "Tier 2 kids" (or "yellow-zone kids") and "Tier 3 kids" (or "red-zone kids") different instruction than "Tier 1 kids" (or "green-zone kids"). In fact, we recommend that school-based personnel avoid using terms like "Tier 2 kids" or "red-zone kids" because they are consistent with a tracking paradigm. There are no "yellow-zone kids" because all students receive quality core instruction, but some may require a Tier 2 intervention to be successful. We have students who receive a Tier 2 intervention, but no "Tier 2 students."

> **Once the intervention session exceeds approximately 30 minutes, then the interventionist is likely no longer engaged in intervention but is instead providing instruction.**

The length of the intervention over time can be best determined by measurement issues. A minimum of 16 data points at two per week are needed in order to provide slopes that are reliable enough to make decisions (Christ, 2006). Thus, a range of 8 to 16 weeks of intervention are likely needed to fully evaluate the effectiveness of an intervention. Practitioners could decide after a shorter time period to modify the intervention or to attempt a different intervention within a tier, but should not change the amount of resources needed to implement the intervention until the effectiveness can be adequately judged. In other words, a grade-level team may decide to move a student from the phonics group to the phonemic awareness group after a short period of, say, 3 to 4 weeks, but they would not abandon the Tier 2 intervention to attempt a Tier 3 intervention unless they have enough data to do so.

Effectiveness

The small-group interventions need to be effective. Practitioners could judge the effectiveness of interventions by looking for the effect size reported in research. Effect size is a simple concept in which the effectiveness of the intervention is estimated with standard deviation units and often reported as Cohen's d or Hedges's g. The mean of the control group is subtracted from the mean of the experimental group, and the difference is divided by the pooled standard deviation. Thus, an effect size of .70 means that the students who received the intervention did .70 standard deviations better than the control group. Essentially, all practitioners have to know is that .80 is generally considered to be a strong effect, .50 a moderate one, and .20 a small effect (Cohen, 1988). Past research on common small-group interventions demonstrated at least moderate effect sizes (e.g., up to .40 and .49, McMaster et al., 2005; .44 to .99, Burns, Dean, & Foley et al., 2004). The focus of small-group interventions should be on efficiency. We want to help as many students as we can within Tier 2, but will do whatever it takes to help a student in Tier 3. Thus, we try to help a large number of students with small-group interventions while also conserving resources for Tier 3, and a moderate effect size (approximately .50) may be sufficient.

Cost

An educational program is considered cost effective if it can generate the same results at a decreased cost, or significantly improved results at the same cost (Hartman & Fay, 1996). For example, delivering services to a student with academic problems and/or behavioral issues in the general education classroom costs approximately 22% of the total cost to deliver services to the same child in a special education classroom for 1 year (Sornson, Frost, & Burns, 2005), which suggests that preventing student difficulties with small-group interventions can have significant cost-savings implications.

A small-group intervention could be considered cost effective if it reduces the need for special education while simultaneously enhancing instructional services and resulting student proficiency for a large group of students in the regular education classroom. Tier 2 has the efficiency advantage over Tier 3 in that more students are served. Thus, initial costs should be weighted against potential cost savings over a period of 5 to 10 years, or longer, assuming the intervention is effective. However, school personnel should be

> **A small-group intervention could be considered cost effective if it reduces the need for special education while simultaneously enhancing instructional services and resulting student proficiency for a large group of students in the regular education classroom.**

highly efficient in selecting small-group interventions. There are a number of commercially prepared interventions that work well for delivering small-group interventions, and purchasing products saves considerable time in developing materials while likely enhancing the consistency of implementation. Many of the commercially prepared interventions with the strongest research base do not cost much money. Thus, practitioners should be weary of the intervention systems that costs several thousands of dollars and should consider whether that intervention program available at *www.amazon.com* for $19.99 would be just as good; in our experience, it often times is.

SMALL-GROUP ACADEMIC INTERVENTION PROGRAMS

School personnel should engage in low-level analysis to determine the appropriate intervention target within Tier 2, and should deliver it within a small group. Thus, small-group interventions are often more broadly focused and not as easy to describe in one or two pages. We refer you to the Florida Center for Reading Research's (FCRR) website (*www.fcrr.org/FCR-RReports/CReportsCS.aspx?rep=supp*) for a list of research-based commercially prepared interventions and a rating as to how well each addresses phonemic awareness, phonics, fluency, vocabulary, and comprehension. After identifying interventions, we recommend that schools create a menu from which grade-level teams can select. An example of a K–12 menu is provided in Figure 5.2. The interventions selected in Figure 5.2 were taken from the FCRR's website and include those that were highly rated for the corresponding NRP area, and for which there is an acceptable research base. For example, there could be multiple intervention groups for students in second grade with those who require remediation in phonics receiving Phono-graphix (McGuinness, McGuinness, & McGuinness, 1996) and those who need help with vocabulary participating in Building Vocabulary Skills (Graves, 2006).

Small-group interventions for math are more difficult to identify because there is no math equivalent of the FCRR. However, given that fluent computation is an important goal for math (National Council of Teachers of Mathematics, 2000; National Mathematics Advisory Panel, 2008), it could be a target for small-group interventions. Students compute fluently when they solve math problems more quickly by recalling the answer than by performing the necessary mental algorithm (Logan, Taylor, & Etherton, 1996). For example, fluent computation can occur when a student can look at $4 \times 3 =$ and quickly recall that the answer is 12 without counting $4 + 4 + 4$. Students with math difficulties frequently

Grade	Phonemic awareness	Phonics	Fluency	Vocabulary	Comprehension
Kindergarten	Road to the Code	Road to the Code	NA	Text Talk	NA
First grade	Road to the Code	Road to the Code	NA	Text Talk	NA
Second grade	Fast Forward Language	Phono-graphix	Six-Minute Solution	Building Vocabulary Skills	Comprehension Plus
Third grade	Fast Forward Language	Phono-graphix	Six-Minute Solution	Building Vocabulary Skills	Comprehension Plus
Fourth grade	NA	REWARDS	Six-Minute Solution	Building Vocabulary Skills	Comprehension Plus
Fifth grade	NA	REWARDS	Six-Minute Solution	Building Vocabulary Skills	Comprehension Plus
Sixth grade	NA	REWARDS	Six-Minute Solution	Building Vocabulary Skills	Thinking Reader
Seventh grade	NA	REWARDS	Six-Minute Solution	Read On	Thinking Reader
Eighth grade	NA	REWARDS	Six-Minute Solution	Read On	Thinking Reader
Ninth grade	NA	REWARDS	Six-Minute Solution	Read On	Questioning the Author
Tenth grade	NA	REWARDS	Read Naturally	Read On	Questioning the Author
Eleventh Grade	NA	REWARDS	Read Naturally	Read On	Questioning the Author
Twelfth Grade	NA	REWARDS	Read Naturally	Read On	Questioning the Author

FIGURE 5.2. Sample intervention matrix for reading.

struggle to quickly recall basic math facts (Geary, Hoard, Byrd-Craven, Nugent, & Numtee, 2007; Hanich, Jordan, Kaplan, & Dick, 2001), and given that the level of analysis that can be conducted with 20% of the population is low, interventionists should focus on determining on what skill they should intervene rather than how to address it. Many students who are not proficient in more advanced math problems lack fluency of the basic skills within them (Houchins, Shippen, & Flores, 2004), and teaching basic or component skills (e.g., single-digit multiplication), usually through repeated practice, led to increased performance of the more advanced skills (Dehaene & Akhavein, 1995; Singer-Dudek & Greer, 2005).

There are commercially prepared interventions that enhance the fluency with which students complete basic math skills. Previous research found that Math Facts in a Flash (MFF; Renaissance Learning, 2003) led to increased math computation skills among classrooms of students (Ysseldyke, Thrill, Pohl, & Bolt, 2005) and among students receiving a Tier 2 intervention for math (Burns, Kanive, & DeGrande, in press). Because MFF is delivered with a computer, a relatively large number of students could participate at one time. Thus, MFF could be a potential small-group intervention for Tier 2 math. However, the fluency-based interventions outlined in Chapter 3 are also plausible for small groups, except here the students would be given the skill in the curriculum sequence at which their score fell at the instructional level. Moreover, many of the interventions for individual students that are described in the subsequent chapters could be modified to work with small groups. Interventionists would only have to take the effective practices outlined in the coming chapters and modify them according to the tenets of effective group interventions. Doing so would make the interventions more efficient, but they may be less effective for individual students within the group.

CONCLUSION

One of the basic facts of small-group interventions is that they will likely work for many students, but not all of them; and that is OK. Teachers and interventionists are dedicated to helping every student, but realizing that their actions will not help every student is extremely hard to accept. Thus, practitioners often engage in high levels of analysis for large groups of children, often with negative results. However, our small-group interventions should focus on categories of problems, and more in-depth analyses are reserved for students for whom the small-group intervention is not successful. We offer evidence-based small-group interventions for increasing reading comprehension on pages 56–59 at the end of this chapter. Fortunately, a well-implemented small-group intervention will help a large proportion of students, as long as it is correctly targeted and implemented in a manner that is consistent with what we know about effective interventions for small groups.

Repeated Reading with Error Correction

Brief Description

The small-group repeated reading intervention combined several approaches and is based on research by Klubnik and Ardoin (2010). This is an intervention for students with adequate decoding skills, but who need to become more fluent. In other words, students should read at least 93% of the words correctly from grade-level (or instructional) material. The groups can vary in size but generally include three to four students.

What "Common Problems" Does This Address?

Because of the close link between reading fluency and comprehension, students need to be able to correctly read approximately 50 to 60 words per minute in order for comprehension to occur. Thus, the intervention is appropriate for a group of students who need additional focused practice to obtain a fluency level at which comprehension can occur.

Procedure

1. Group the students into small groups of three or four.
2. Give each student a copy of a reading passage. The passage should fit on one page and should not include pictures. However, it should be somewhat engaging in topic and writing. Each student should be able to read at least 93% of the words correctly.
3. Have each student read one sentence at a time. For example, Student 1 would read the first sentence, Student 2 the second sentence, and so on. The order is then repeated until the passage is completed.
4. The passage is then read two additional times, with a different student reading first each time so that students have a chance to practice different sentences.
5. The interventionist follows along as the students read the sentences and records errors and which student made them. A word is considered an error if it is incorrectly read, skipped, or read correctly but not within 3 seconds.
6. Each time after the passage is read, the interventionist then corrects student errors. Have each individual student go back to the word and reread it if he or she can. If the student does not read the word correctly within 3 seconds, then say the word for him or her and ask him or her to read the sentence that contains the word two times.
7. After correcting the errors, begin reading the next passage. If the error corrections were from the third and final oral reading, then have the students silently read the passage and ask any questions. The interventionist should then ask a few short comprehension questions to the group and discuss the answers.

(cont.)

Critical Components That Must Be Implemented for the Intervention to Be Successful

The students need to be able to read at least 93% of the words. Thus, errors should be rare, but should not be corrected while the students read. Allow them to finish the passage first. Repetition of the missed words is important, but have them read the words in text by reading the sentence that contains the word rather than just repeating the word in isolation.

Materials

- Enough copies of the text for each student to have his or her own.
- Incentives as needed.

Reference

Klubnik, C., & Ardoin, S. P. (2010). Examining immediate and maintenance effects of a reading intervention package on generalization materials: Individual versus group implementation. *Journal of Behavioral Education, 19,* 7–29.

Manipulation Strategy for Comprehension

Brief Description

The small-group manipulation strategy is a comprehension-oriented intervention designed by Glenberg, Brown, and Levin (2007). It involves using toys and small objects to act out short action statements and can be conducted in a small group of about four students.

What "Common Problems" Does This Address?

A small-group manipulation strategy is appropriate for children who read fluently but who struggle with comprehension. This is a low-level comprehension intervention and is likely appropriate only for young children.

Procedure

1. Write eight action statements from a short narrative story. Be sure that the statements are short and are in the same sequence as the actions appear in the story.
2. Gather small toys or objects that correspond to the action statements (e.g., a toy cow for a story about a cow).
3. Group the students into small groups of three or four and have them sit around a small table.
4. Lay out all of the toys and small objects on the table and name each one.
5. Read the first action statement aloud and act out the statement with one of the toys while saying your thoughts out loud. Be sure to explain why you perform each action.
6. Have each student read one action statement and then act out the statement with a small toy. The student can have a second student participate if needed and desired.
7. After completing all of the statements, ask students some questions about what they read. Also, be sure to ask meta-analytic questions that ask what word told the students what to do.

Critical Components That Must Be Implemented for the Intervention to Be Successful

Because this is a comprehension intervention, metacognition is extremely important. Be sure to model why you selected a particular toy or small object, identifying the action word and explaining how it suggested a specific activity. Moreover, the students should be able to read the short sentences with little assistance.

Materials

- About eight action statements taken from a story written on a sheet of paper in sequential order.
- Enough copies of the sheet of statements for each student to have his or her own.
- A collection of small toys and objects that represent the characters and objects in the statements.
- Incentives as needed.

Reference

Glenberg, A. M., Brown, M., & Levin, J. R. (2007). Enhancing comprehension in small reading groups using a manipulation strategy. *Contemporary Educational Psychology, 32,* 389–399.

Text Previewing

Brief Description

Research by Graves, Cooke, and LaBerge (1983) found that simply having students preview text increased comprehension. They implemented a simple strategy that was developed for narrative text, but could be modified for expository text. The intervention involves three steps. The groups can vary in size but generally include five to eight students.

What "Common Problems" Does This Address?

Previewing is a simple intervention that is quick and easy but is not very intensive. Thus, it is appropriate for students with acceptable reading fluency but who lack comprehension. Moreover, this is probably a good approach for content-area instruction at the secondary level.

Procedure

1. Identify five to eight students who need additional support for reading comprehension and have them sit at one table.
2. Provide each student with a copy of the book or reading passage.
3. The first step in previewing is to engage students with the text, which is done by providing short statements or questions about the text. These statements or questions should highlight the most interesting aspect of the text.
4. Next, briefly describe the major elements of the text.
   a. Describe the setting of the story or the broad context of the expository text.
   b. Describe characters and points of view within a narrative text.
   c. Describe the plot for a narrative text or the major points of an expository text.
5. Finally, write the names of the characters from narrative text or keywords from expository text on 3" X 5" index cards. Then point to each card while reading the name/word.
6. Have each student read the text and discuss various short comprehension questions.

Critical Components That Must Be Implemented for the Intervention to Be Successful

The students should be able to read at least 93% of the words and the text should be about concepts of which they have a basic understanding. Moreover, the interventionist should be sure that all students are paying attention and participating.

Materials

- Enough copies of the text for each student to have his or her own.
- Index cards with words written on them.
- Incentives as needed.

Reference

Graves, M. F., Cooke, C. L., & LaBerge, M. J. (1983). Effects of previewing difficult short stories on low ability junior high school students' comprehension, recall, and attitudes. *Reading Research Quarterly, 18*, 262–276.

CHAPTER 6

Classwide/Small-Group
Behavioral Interventions

OVERVIEW

As discussed in Chapter 3, screening data offer grade-level and problem-solving teams the opportunity to focus support on the environments in which the greatest need exists. While this topic is far more developed for academic interventions, there exists a clear need for schoolwide and classwide screening procedures for behavior problems, as well as subsequent appropriate interventions. This chapter outlines a model parallel to the academic model presented in Chapter 3 focusing both on what tools and practices exist, as well as those that need further development.

STEP 1: SELECT SCREENING TASKS

Unlike academic behavior, social behavior is more relative in nature. For example, consider reading fluency and disruptive behavior. When attempting to estimate a child's reading fluency, it is expected that there be some variability in words read correctly per minute (WCPM) across probes. For example, it is reasonable that a child could read 35 WCPM in the first 1-minute probe, 45 WCPM in the second, and 48 WCPM in the third. Such variability would likely be due to differences in the specific probes or the child's motivation to read quickly. Regardless, it is understood that the child does have some "true score" in terms of reading fluency. It is not reasonable to suggest that he or she would subsequently read 165 WCPM on a similar probe in close proximity to the prior results. Simply put, there is an actual level of reading fluency that can be estimated. In contrast, disruptive behavior operates in a very different manner. First, a child can be universally disruptive one day and essentially nondisruptive the next day. While there is a true score in terms of a child's behavior in a specific interval, that does not carry over to other intervals in the same manner as reading fluency. In addition, what is perceived as disruptive to one teacher might not be disruptive to another teacher. For example, a child who "hovers" above his or her seat might be considered disruptive in one class where a teacher is insistent that all children have their bottom touching the seat, whereas he or she is considered to be behaving appropriately with another teacher who is comfortable with children being generally in the area of their seat. Behavior ratings are more relative to rater and context than academic ratings. Although there are some consistencies across rater and rating period, ratings of behavior problems that exist in the context of a particular environment are evaluated based on perceptions of an educational professional. As such, the types of screening applications that we utilize in relation to behavior are based on teacher perception and are to be interpreted in reference to that teacher/environment. The general process of selecting appropriate behavior assessment tools follows four general questions outlined by Chafouleas, Riley-Tillman, et al. (2007):

> **The types of screening applications that we utilize in relation to behavior are based on teacher perception.**

1. Why do you need the data?
2. Which tools are best matched to assess the target behavior?
3. What decisions will be made using the data?
4. What resources are available to collect the data?

In the current discussion, we are focused on using behavior data for screening purposes to identify schools, classrooms, groups, or individuals who are considered at risk for behavior problems. Because data are used to identify problems, screening assessments should have predictive power, which is the ability to reliably and accurately identify those at risk for future difficulty (Chafouleas, Riley-Tillman, et al., 2007; Good, Simmons, & Kame'enui, 2001). Moreover, screening measures should be brief enough so that they can be repeatedly administered to a large population.

There are four categories of social behavior assessment with potential utility for screening: office discipline referral (ODR), systematic direct observation (SDO), behavior rating scales, and direct behavior rating (DBR). What follows is a brief overview of these methods in relation to screening purposes. Readers interested in a more comprehensive overview are referred to Chafouleas, Riley-Tillman, et al. (2007) or the forthcoming second volume of this book.

Office Discipline Referral

SWPBIS uses ODR data as a behavior screener. ODR is the systematic use of the process of children being referred to the main office (or other relevant location) for a specific behavior problem. In order for this process to be useful from an assessment standpoint the ODR is instrumented into a specific school form that includes all relevant information (e.g., see Form 6.1 at the end of the chapter). When ODRs are implemented with fidelity, use a consistent form, and resulting data are collected, inputted, and evaluated to inform specific decisions, those data can have a number of useful features. ODR data are typically presented in a graphical format and provide a range of information across the spectrum of whole school to individual child as to where and when children are being referred for misbehavior. For example, Figure 6.1 provides an example of the number of ODRs for each classroom over the course of an academic year. Figure 6.2 provides a drill down examination of one class-room (Grade 2, Class 3) with what seems to be abnormally high rates of misbehavior. Such presentations can be used to identify areas of need in the school or in a specific classroom.

Strengths of ODR in reference to screening include an ODR's availability, utility for various decisions, and ease of use. Of specific importance is the extant literature base sup-porting that ODR data can be useful for decision making when done correctly (Horner & Sugai, 2001; Irvin et al., 2004, 2006; Sprague et al., 1999; Sugai et al., 2000; Tobin et al., 1996; Wright & Dusek, 1998). Despite these strengths, Chafouleas, Riley-Tillman et al. (2007) note some weaknesses that include the potential for excessive demands on staff, a focus on rule violation, difficulty in maintaining fidelity of implementation, and a potential for misinterpretation of outcome data. Regardless, ODRs clearly are an option to consider for schoolwide behavioral screening.

Systematic Direct Observation

SDO is a method that provides accurate assessments of a target child's or a group of chil-dren's behavior in a specific environment over a defined period of time. SDO is the process of having an external observer watch a class for a defined period of time while recording information. SDO has been classically defined by five characteristics outlined by Salvia and Ysseldyke (2004):

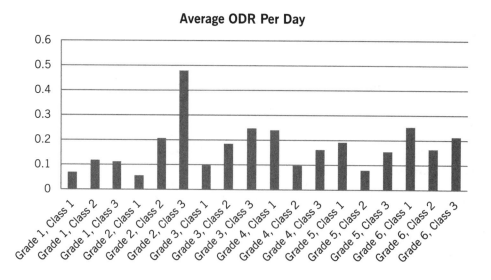

FIGURE 6.1. Example of ODR data for a whole school presented by classroom.

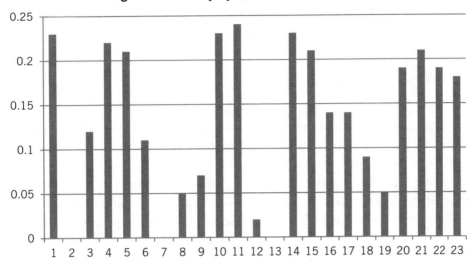

FIGURE 6.2. Example of ODR data for a classroom presented by student.

1. The purpose of SDO is to measure specific target behaviors.
2. Target behaviors are operationalized.
3. Data collection procedures are standardized in order to promote accurate observation devoid of observer opinion.
4. The time and place for the observations are carefully selected and documented with data.
5. Data are inputted, scored, and summarized in a standard manner.

When the five characteristics listed above are in place, SDO has a number of significant strengths that include its ability to directly describe and evaluate a behavior, its use as a flexible instrument, and usefulness as a general progress-monitoring tool. These strengths culminate into a method that results in the creation of highly reliable and accurate outcome data (Hintze, Volpe, & Shapiro, 2002).

Unfortunately, SDO has a number of weaknesses that include difficulty with behavior operationalization, reactivity (the result of an outside observer being present in the classroom at the time of rating), and the potential for observer drift (Chafouleas, Riley-Tillman, et al., 2007). In addition, SDO procedures take a good deal of time to implement and are difficult to use when monitoring low-frequency behaviors. Consider that a trained observer must be available to conduct all observations. Although a 30-minute observation does not seem like a great deal of time, if five observations per classroom are required and there are 21 classrooms in a building (e.g., three per grade in a K–6 building), the total observation time will be 3,150 minutes (or 52.5 hours). Considering it will take the observer(s) time to schedule observations, walk from class to class, and then record/analyze the data, it is highly unlikely that schools will want to, or be able to, allocate the necessary resources to do an

SDO-based schoolwide screening (which would likely need to be repeated several times a year). As a result, SDO procedures are not a likely choice for universal screening applications unless significant resources are available.

Behavior Rating Scales

Behavior rating scales are common behavior assessment tools that require a teacher or other educational professional to rate a child on a number of questions based on his or her past experience with the target child (Kratochwill, Sheridan, Carlson, & Lasecki, 1999). The logic behind behavior ratings scales is compelling in that the format takes advantage of the rater's experiences with the child and the strengths of a rating scale format (multiple questions that focus on a behavioral construct like hyperactivity). As a result, behavior rating scales have a number of strengths including high levels of reliability, usefulness with low-incident behaviors, and usefulness for some evaluative decisions (Chafouleas, Riley-Tillman, et al., 2007). In addition, behavior rating scales are often touted to be useful for screening purposes.

Unfortunately, the feasibility issues in relation to conducting brief repeated behavior screenings on a schoolwide level are one of the major limitations of behavior rating scales. Even the most widely used brief rating scales consist of a rather large number of questions. For example, the Behavioral and Emotional Screening System (BESS) teacher form (of the BASC-2 Behavioral and Emotional Screening System; Kamphaus & Reynolds, 2007), which is designed to be a brief scale, has 27 items. Although the BESS can clearly be used for an individual child, or even a small group of children, use for all children in a classroom would result in hours of work for the rater (likely the teacher). Even the relatively short Attention Deficit Hyperactivity Disorder-IV (ADHD-IV) behavior rating scale (DuPaul, Power, Anastopoulos, & Reid, 1998), which is focused on behaviors consistent with a diagnosis of ADHD, is unlikely to be used feasibly as a repeated measure for an entire class. Such short measures do have potential for some progress monitoring purposes, but they are not feasible when they are used as repeated screening tools (see Angello et al., 2003, for a review).

Direct Behavior Rating

DBR is a class of behavior assessment that is a hybrid of both rating scale and direct observation procedures (Chafouleas, Riley-Tillman, & Christ, 2009; Chafouleas, Riley-Tillman, & McDougal, 2002; Riley-Tillman, Chafouleas, Briesch, 2007). Specifically, a DBR involves procedures and instrumentation that entails having a rater use a specific form to quantify his or her perception of directly observed behaviors immediately after he or she has observed the behavior for a predetermined period of time. For example, a teacher might use a 0–10 scale to rate how long John was academically engaged during a reading period. This method of behavior assessment has been noted as highly acceptable to both teachers and school psychologists (Riley-Tillman, Chafouleas, & Eckert, 2008; Chafouleas, Riley-Tillman, & Sassu, 2006).

The defining characteristics of a DBR are noted in the name. DBR is "direct," in that the rater is required to complete the rating after the observation interval. DBR focuses on specific "behaviors" that have been selected for the individual case. Finally, DBR involves "rating" a child in a standardized manner. As noted in the previous example, it entails a defined observation interval (e.g., a period, or half a day) that is immediately followed by a rating completed by a person such as a teacher who is naturally in the context.

DBR results in formative data rating of student behavior in specific times and places, which can be aggregated to allow for comparisons for initial identification of potential risk. An example of a single-item scale DBR (DBR-SIS) is presented in Form 6.2 at the end of the chapter. The features of this DBR form have been established from a line of research that has considered a variety of issues including a review of the rating scale literature (Christ & Boice, 2009) and a line of psychometric studies examining a variety of issues such as scaling, wording, and observation duration (Chafouleas, Riley-Tillman, et al., 2009; Chafouleas, Christ, Riley-Tillman, Briesch, & Chanese, 2007; Riley-Tillman, Chafouleas, Sassu, Chanese, & Glazer, 2008; Riley-Tillman, Christ, Chafouleas, Boice, & Briesch, 2010; Riley-Tillman, Chafouleas, Christ, Briesch, & LeBel, 2009), along with ongoing conceptual development (Chafouleas et al., 2002; Christ, Riley-Tillman, Chafouleas, & Boice, 2010; Riley-Tillman et al., 2007).

Research on DBR applications has found that DBR and SDO data converge and visual analysis profiles are consistent (Briesch, Chafouleas, & Riley-Tillman, 2010; Chafouleas, Riley-Tillman, et al., 2009; Chafouleas, McDougal, Riley-Tillman, Panahon, & Hilt, 2005; Riley-Tillman, Chafouleas, Sassu, et al., 2008; Riley-Tillman, Methe, & Weegar, 2009). It has also been established that reliable estimates that correlate with behavior rating scales can be established in 7 to 10 ratings by the same rater (Briesch et al., 2010; Chafouleas, Kilgus, & Hernandez, 2009; Christ et al., 2010, Riley-Tillman, Chafouleas, Sassu, et al., 2008). A recent investigation considered the capacity of DBR-SIS to be used specifically as a screening instrument. In this study, K–9 teachers in three geographical regions completed DBR-SIS (disruptive behavior, academic engagement, and respectful), the Student Risk Screening Scale (SRSS; Drummond, 1993), and the Behavior Assessment System for Children–2 (BESS; Kamphaus & Reynolds, 2007) in a 3-week spring assessment period. Preliminary results supported the use of DBR-SIS for screening purposes (Chafouleas, Kilgus, Riley-Tillman, Jaffery, & Welsh, 2011). Additionally, teachers suggested that DBR-SIS was highly usable in the screening application. It is important to note that this pilot study requires longitudinal replications as only one screening period was utilized. This is critical as other work has indicated that average DBR-SIS ratings change over the course of the school year (Chafouleas, Kilgus, et al., 2009).

> **Teachers suggested that DBR-SIS was highly usable in the screening application.**

Behavior Screening Tools Overview

As noted at the start of this chapter, schoolwide behavior screening processes are not as developed as academic screening models. This lack of development can be most clearly seen in the absence of an agreed-upon behavior screening method in the extant literature base. A review of the options suggest that ODR and DBR have the potential to be useful for screening applications but with noted limitations (defined weakness of ODR and limited research on DBR screening applications). Behavior rating scales and SDO have clear utility for targeted applications (e.g., smaller high-risk groups) but don't appear to be likely candidates for repeated schoolwide screening. It is clear that research on each of these classes of assessment will continue, and in time that work should provide a more concrete solution for schools looking to do schoolwide behavior screening. It is reasonable to suggest at this time though, that any identified solution will likely involve using a variety of methods for specific screening applications.

STEP 2: ENSURE ADEQUACY OF SCREENING DATA

Once data methods have been selected, it is important to ensure that the measures are implemented with integrity. As noted in Chapter 3, implementers should introduce procedural controls to the screening process. The selected method, including procedures and a schedule (if appropriate), should be shared with teachers and, if needed, training sessions should be scheduled to establish requisite skill. For example, if ODR data are being utilized, then the rate at which teachers correctly complete a school ODR form should be collected to ensure procedural integrity. If a method like DBR is selected using a seasonal screening, the materials should be provided to teachers on the week of screening to minimize loss. In such a case, support staff should be available so that the process runs smoothly and any abnormalities in the administration can be noted. Regardless of the method, the scores should be organized by class and by grade for analysis. As with academic data, implementers can organize the data manually using software like Microsoft Excel, but it is helpful (and less error prone) to use a web-based system to organize the school's screening data (e.g., School-Wide Information System [SWIS]).

STEP 3: EVALUATE SCREENING DATA TO IDENTIFY CLASSWIDE OR SMALL-GROUP SOCIAL BEHAVIOR PROBLEMS

Once the data have been entered and organized, each class should be examined to identify classwide behavior problems. Unlike academic screening data there is no current consensus as to what would define a classwide, gradewide, or schoolwide problem. This is clearly one area of social behavior assessment and intervention that is ripe for future research. As such, a team will need to review the data and consider if abnormally high levels of social behavior difficulty exist in specific classrooms or with groups of children. Using visual analysis techniques, teams should consider locations or groups with higher levels of misbehavior. Looking back at Figures 6.1 and 6.2 we can see an example of using ODR data for this process. In Figure 6.1 it is rather clear that one classroom (Grade 2, Class 3) has abnormally high daily rates of ODR. Specifically, that classroom has almost twice the daily ODR rates of any

	Direct Behavior Rating (DBR)		
Students	**Average Disruptive Behavior**	**Average Academic Engagement**	**Average Respectful Behavior**
1	1.4	7.5	10.0
2	0.3	9.7	10.0
3	0.5	9.1	10.0
4	0.4	9.4	10.0
5	0.0	10.0	10.0
5	0.0	10.0	10.0
6	0.2	9.6	10.0
7	2.6	5.8	4.0
8	0.0	9.0	10.0
9	0.0	10.0	10.0
10	0.0	10.0	10.0
11	0.0	9.2	10.0
12	0.2	9.6	10.0

FIGURE 6.3. Example of DBR data for screening purposes. These DBR data were collected in a 2-week spring screening. Data presented are the average of 6–10 ratings on students by the classroom teacher. From Chafouleas, Riley-Tillman, Christ, Kilgus, and Jaffery (2011).Reprinted by permission of the authors.

other single classroom, and more than double the average classroom mean rate of .17 ODR daily. When the data is examined at the classroom level in Figure 6.2, it does not appear that one child is particularly problematic; rather most of the children in class are seemingly misbehaving. In this case, there appears to be a classwide problem and as such resources should be allocated at that level.

In contrast the screening data in Figure 6.3 suggest that the problem is not classwide but rather an issue with a few select students. This example from Chafouleas, Riley-Tillman, Christ, Kilgus, and Jaffery (2011) of DBR data was collected in a 2-week spring screening. Data presented are the average of 6–10 formative ratings on students by the classroom teacher. Looking at the data, ratings of Student 7 were consistently out of the class range for all three behaviors. In addition, attention should be given to the academic engagement and disruptive behavior ratings of Student 1. While there are no simple metrics for identifying if it is a classwide or small-group/individual student issue, visual analysis of data and a problem-solving approach should help guide a team to the most logical hypothesis.

STEP 4: IDENTIFY PATTERNS IN THE DATA

If there is a classwide or small-group behavior problem, the team should first review the quality of the screening data to ensure that they are appropriate for decision-making purposes. We suggest that the team ask the following questions:

1. Was the screening task appropriate?
2. Were the screening data reliable, sensitive, and did they lead to valid decisions?
3. Was the screening measure correctly administered?

If the answers to the above questions are yes, then the team should consider potential causes of reported behavior issues. The first "cause" that should be considered is the teacher perception of students' behavior. As noted at the beginning of this chapter, behavior assessment is typically accomplished through the ratings of an observer. SDO is the one method of behavior assessment that attempts to negate observer perception, but unfortunately it is not likely to be feasible for schoolwide behavior screening. As a result, unlike academic assessment where a child's reading fluency should be consistently rated regardless of who is doing the assessment, it is understood that when using social behavior assessment, a prob-

> **When using social behavior assessment, a problem behavior to one rater (e.g., music teacher) might be considered an acceptable behavior to another rater (e.g., gym teacher).**

lem behavior to one rater (e.g., music teacher) might be considered an acceptable behavior to another rater (e.g., gym teacher). As such it is important to differentiate whether the case at hand is due to behavior problems that are considered serious only to the current teacher or to the larger schoolwide community. Questions along this line would include:

- Are there supporting data to suggest that there are serious social behavior issues in the target classroom or with the target student?
  - If yes, then consider a classroom or individual student intervention.
  - If no, consider if the rater's behavioral expectations are *unrealistic* or simply *inconsistent* with the whole school program.

For example, an *unrealistic* expectation exists when a teacher demands that the students in his or her class be on task 100% of the time. Although a robust goal, being on task 100% of the time is impossible for children (as well as adults!) An example of *incompatible* teacher expectations is that of a teacher who expects the students in his or her class to remain quiet in the hallway while, at the same time, the schoolwide expectations for hallway behavior allow for students to talk quietly while in that setting. This teacher expectation is clearly possible, but it is not in sync with schoolwide standards. In either case, the team will need to meet with the teacher and review behavioral goal setting. If the data suggesting a classwide or small-group "problem" are considered by the team as the result of unrealistic teacher expectations, then the team should meet with the teacher and discuss more realistic behavioral expectations. If the data suggesting a behavior "problem" are considered the result of incompatible teacher expectations, then the team/teacher meeting should focus on discussing behavioral expectations in the context of the larger school. It may be beneficial to have a school administrator attend the meeting to consider whether the schoolwide program needs to be altered.

If the reported classwide or small-group behavior problems are considered to be more than unrealistic or incompatible with teacher expectations, the next step is to understand what function is at the root of the behavior problem. Specifically, four general categories of classwide/small-group social behavior problems should be addressed:

1. Is the teacher adhering to the schoolwide social behavior program?
2. Is the class currently working on academic materials at the instructional or mastery level?
3. Is there a classwide behavior skill deficit?
4. Is the reinforcement system in the classroom punishing appropriate behaviors and/ or reinforcing inappropriate alternative behaviors?

As the team answers the above questions, an action plan is built to correct the classwide/small-group behavior problem. If the answer to Question 1 is no, then the team should work with the teacher to make the classroom consistent with the schoolwide program. If the answer to Question 2 is no, then the focus of the intervention should be redirected to academic goals. Simply put, children who are not learning will be frustrated and will eventually misbehave. Solving the academic issues will either end the behavioral problem or open the opportunity for subsequent behavior intervention. It is likely that even if academic problems are addressed, problematic behavior repertoires have developed and these behaviors will need attention. Questions 3 and 4 address whether the classwide or small-group problem is an acquisition or proficiency issue. Appropriate interventions should be applied for each problem area (each area is described in depth in Chapters 8 and 10, respectively).

> **Children who are not learning will be frustrated and will eventually misbehave.**

As with academic classwide/small-group issues, school leadership should link identified causes of problems to professional development and personnel review activities. If identifiable teacher skill deficits exist, then professional development activities should be scheduled to eliminate those deficits. Additionally, when classwide and small-group problems are detected, frequent progress monitoring should be scheduled in the respective environment in order to document intervention effectiveness. Doing this will provide teachers an opportunity to detect reoccurrences of problem behavior.

STEP 5: PLAN CORE SOLUTIONS

Extending from Chapter 4, one core solution is to consider the use of SWPBIS at the secondary level. The effects of using SWPBIS measures like check-in/check-out have been well studied (see *www.pbis.org*). In addition, there are a number of classwide or small-group intervention strategies such as classwide antecedent modifications, improving group behavior with randomized group contingencies, response cost raffle, and good behavior game. These strategies are presented in intervention brief format (see pages 73–82 at the end of the chapter). These and other group intervention practices should be selected according to the

> **Group intervention practices should be selected according to the type of behavior problem and then tracked with appropriate outcome data, with the primary goal of decreasing the scope of the classwide problem.**

types of behavior problem and then tracked with appropriate outcome data, with the primary goal of decreasing the scope of the classwide problem. In addition, each intervention is consistent with both schoolwide and individual interventions that are discussed in Chapters 8, 10, and 11.

STEP 6: PLAN SUPPLEMENTAL INTERVENTION

When a classwide problem is detected, it is likely that students have accumulated deficits in a number of problematic behaviors that can lead to future behavioral (and/or academic) issues. Hence, when classwide behavior problems are noted and immediately remediated, the team should also consider whether there are other behavioral or academic issues that may require additional intervention to correct systemic causes of classwide/small-group behavioral problems (e.g., instructional match issues, poor quality of instruction, or classwide behavioral skill deficits).

CONCLUSION

As noted in the overview to this chapter, while the identification of classrooms in need of intervention is critical for both academic and behavioral issues, screening procedures have been considerably less developed in reference to behavioral difficulties. This chapter provided a parallel to the academic model presented in Chapter 3 with the goal of focusing both on what tools and practices exist as well as on those that need further development. Although this model should provide educational professionals with a starting point, it is also evident that educational researchers need to continue to develop the necessary tools and practices for schoolwide behavior screening.

Office Discipline Referral

Behavior Incident Report

Student _____

Grade _____

Date _____

Time _____

Homeroom Teacher _____

Referring Staff _____

Location

☐ Classroom   ☐ Bathroom

☐ Hallway   ☐ Bus

☐ Classroom   ☐ Assembly

☐ Cafeteria   ☐ _____

☐ Library

Problem Behavior	**Possible Motivation (Check one)**	**Administrative Decision**
Minor (Give to Homeroom Teacher) ☐ Inappropriate Language ☐ Defiance ☐ Classroom Disruption ☐ Misuse of Property ☐ Teasing ☐ Tardy ☐ Out of Assigned Area ☐ Other _____	☐ Obtain Peer Attention ☐ Obtain Adult Attention ☐ Obtain Items/Activities ☐ Avoid Peer(s) ☐ Avoid Adult ☐ Avoid Task/Activity ☐ Unclear ☐ Other _____	☐ Loss of privilege ☐ Time in office ☐ Conference with student ☐ Parent Contact ☐ Individualized instruction ☐ In-school suspension (__hours/ days) ☐ Out of school suspension (__ days) ☐ Other _____
Major (Give to Office Staff) ☐ Repeated Noncompliance ☐ Physical Aggression ☐ Harassment ☐ Stealing ☐ Tobacco or Banned Substance ☐ Off Campus w/o Permission/ Truant ☐ Dress Code ☐ Other_____	**Others Involved (Check one)** ☐ None ☐ Peers ☐ Staff ☐ Teacher ☐ Substitute ☐ Supervisor ☐ Bus Driver ☐ Other _____	**Comments/Descriptions**

Signatures

_____ Referring Staff Person   Date _____

_____ Administrator   Date _____

_____ Student   Date _____

_____ Parent/Guardian   Date _____

Reprinted from Chafouleas, Riley-Tillman, and Sugai (2007).

Direct Behavior Rating Single-Item Scale

Three Standard Behaviors

Date:	Student:	Activity Description:
M T W Th F	Rater:	

Observation Time:	Behavior Descriptions:
Start: _____ End: _____ Check if no observation today	**Academically engaged** is actively or passively participating in the classroom activity. For example: writing, raising hand, answering a question, talking about a lesson, listening to the teacher, reading silently, or looking at instructional materials. **Respectful** is defined as compliant and polite behavior in response to adult direction and/or interactions with peers and adults. For example: follows teacher direction, prosocial interaction with peers, positive response to adult request, verbal or physical disruption without a negative tone/connotation. **Disruptive** is student action that interrupts regular school or classroom activity. For example: out of seat, fidgeting, playing with objects, acting aggressively, talking/yelling about things that are unrelated to classroom instruction.

Directions: Place a mark along the line that best reflects the percentage of total time the student exhibited each target behavior. Note that the percentages do not need to total 100% across behaviors since some behaviors may co-occur.

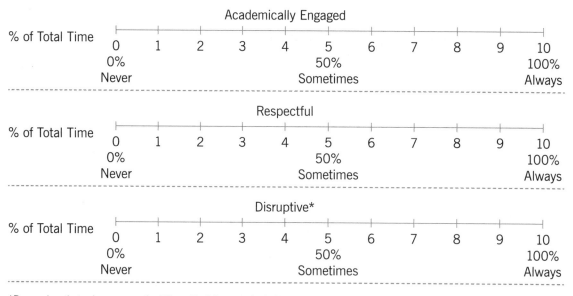

*Remember that a lower score for "Disruptive" is more desirable.

Classwide Antecedent Modifications

Brief Description

This intervention can have a behavioral or academic focus depending on the modifications made. Developing and teaching a child explicit classroom rules will address problem behaviors where the function is that the child has not learned the desired behavior. Setting appropriate task demands and structuring the class to increase interest should help when the function is that the child does not want to do the task or the task is too hard.

The context of the environment in which behaviors occur is not usually considered when analyzing a child's behavior. Instead, more attention is typically given to the consequences following that particular behavior (especially when it is a disruptive behavior being analyzed). While consequences of behaviors matter, what occurred *before* the problem behavior should also be considered when creating an intervention. Altering the antecedent of the target behavior has the substantial advantage of being proactive. As such, with appropriate modifications of the antecedents, a problem behavior (e.g., disruptive behavior or task demand refusal) can be avoided. This intervention brief presents a series of classwide antecedent alterations that will change typical antecedents of problem behaviors to antecedents that prompt appropriate behaviors. See Kern and Clemens (2007) for an excellent thorough review of this classwide intervention.

What "Common Problems" Does This Address?

This classwide intervention is appropriate for settings where there are classwide behavior problems (e.g., disruptive behavior or task refusal). In such settings, antecedents that typically produce problem behavior (e.g., academic task demands that are too difficult result in students "acting out" and refusing to do academic activities) are altered and transformed into antecedents that produce appropriate behavior (e.g., appropriate academic task demands or choice of task sequence = increase of time on task) will greatly reduce problem behavior and increase academic engagement.

Procedure

1. Set classroom rules.
   a. Develop, model, and post clear classroom rules.
      i. If some children don't have the skill to follow a rule, try using direct instruction to teach the skill.
   b. Reinforce (e.g., praise or token) appropriate behavior as quickly as possible; minimize reinforcement (e.g., remove attention) for inappropriate behavior.
   c. Have a consistent classroom schedule.
2. Appropriate task demands.
   a. All instructional material should be appropriate for the students' current level.

(cont.)

3. Structure the class to increase interest.
   a. Use a brisk pace with ample opportunity for student response.
      i. Consider classwide response system such as choral responding or response cards to increase classwide response opportunities.
   b. Include easy tasks along with more difficult tasks.
   c. Allow for student choice.
   d. Use high-interest materials/topics.

Critical Components That Must Be Implemented for the Intervention to Be Successful

- Clear development of classroom rules.
- Identification of student instructional level.
- Appropriate task demands.
- Accurate selection of reinforce(s), and high-interest material.

Materials

- Reinforcers as necessary.

Reference

Kern, L., & Clemens, N. H. (2007). Antecedent strategies to promote appropriate classroom behavior. *Psychology in the Schools, 44,* 65–75.

Improving Group Behavior with Randomized Group Contingencies

Brief Description

The primary purpose of this intervention is to increase the likelihood that a group of students (or one target student within a group) continues to act appropriately. This package can be used for a small group of students or an entire class. This intervention is appropriate after all of the target behaviors (appropriate behaviors—e.g., capacity to sit in seat for at least 30 minutes, raise hand) for the classroom have been learned and demonstrated by each member of the group, or it can be used to teach appropriate or disruptive behavior rules to a population of students (this intervention incorporates teaching rules of behavior). It provides an effective and feasible way to teach and maintain appropriate group behavior.

Randomized group contingencies is a classic evidence-based intervention with articles dating back to the early 1970s (e.g., Axelrod, 1973). This intervention employs a contingency-based reward system designed to alter a group of students' behavior. The special component of this intervention is that it relies on students working together as one group to earn a reward. By working together, it is implied that students rely on each other. This interdependence takes place when students learn how to self-monitor their own behavior, peer monitor each others' behavior, and learn how to motivate one another. When using an interdependent group reinforcer, students have to rely on one another to gain access to the reward.

This intervention brief (based on Kelshaw-Levering, Sterling-Turner, Henry, & Skinner, 2000) has suggestions and guidelines for two different types of intervention: a reinforcement intervention (increasing appropriate behavior by rewarding it) and a punishment intervention (reducing inappropriate behavior through removal of potential reward). Standard practice is to try a reinforcement intervention first. A reinforcement intervention like this one increases the likelihood of positive behavior change because it teaches students how to behave as the teacher wants them to by placing emphasis on their appropriate choices. A punishment intervention, on the other hand, teaches students what a teacher does not want them to do. It is possible to teach students appropriate classroom behavior while simultaneously punishing inappropriate behavior but it is not recommended. Choosing a groupwide intervention to reduce inappropriate behavior naturally places the students' focus on what not to do (inappropriate behavior) instead of practicing what to do (appropriate behavior). In short, although a punishment intervention is presented, it is not recommended as a first attempt at a groupwide behavioral intervention.

What "Common Problems" Does This Address?

Provides motivation for students who engage in inappropriate classroom behavior and who are otherwise unmotivated to behave appropriately. It may also create classwide accountability for behavior that results in peer support of one another instead of tattling/picking on each other. It can reduce disruptive classroom behavior.

(cont.)

Procedure

1. Create proactive classroom rules that describe the behavior the teacher desires for the students to engage in. In other words, make a chart that tells them *what to do* instead of what *not* to do in the classroom.
2. Display the chart with the proactive classroom rules on it.
3. Remove any other behavior-related charts that do not directly reflect upon/reinforce the proactive classroom rules chart.
4. Make a list of potential reinforcers for the class and have the class create their own list of reinforcers. When feasible and reasonable, include students' requests for reinforcers in the teacher list of reinforcers. Don't forget that reinforcers can be nontangible items like a pass to read to kindergarteners, a pass for a computer lab instructional experience during typical lecture-learning time, bring-a-soda-to-class day, or a groupwide "get-out-of-quiz" pass (with an alternative, fun backup assessment of the same skills that would be assessed in the quiz).
5. Create a contract that includes the specific expectations for group behavior in order to earn the rewards. This includes any "warnings" students may receive and any consequences for inappropriate behavior. Also include the schedule of reinforcement (i.e., how often, what times) so they will have a chance to earn a reward for good behavior and what they can do to "start over" if their reward goal is not reached (reinforcement schedule). Have the students read and sign the contract. Display the contracts or store the contracts where they can be referenced at any time.
6. Demonstrate (with a teacher or student model) the desired classroom behavior and its opposite (undesired classroom behavior) so that students can be very clear about what the expectations for behavior are. Assess the students to make sure that *all* of them are capable of demonstrating the appropriate behavior or *not* engaging in undesired behavior (i.e., accommodate for maturity level or level of disability).

Option 1: Reinforce Appropriate Behavior

1. Locate the reinforcers list for students (see "Procedures" for instructions on how to do this).
2. Place the reinforcers on small pieces of paper, fold them, and place them in a jar or hat.
3. Create an ending number of points (behavior goal) that represent the number of appropriate behaviors the class is expected to engage in (i.e., class must have at least 60 or more appropriate behaviors = class must receive 60 or more points).
4. Display the behavior goal clearly in the classroom.
5. Explain to the class which behaviors are considered appropriate.
6. Provide examples of appropriate behavior (demonstrations of what to do) and nonexamples (demonstrations of disruptive behavior).
7. Explain the rules.
   a. Every time one student in the group engages in an appropriate behavior the teacher will put a point on the board.
   b. This game will last for *X* number of minutes (periods, subjects, etc.).
   c. The class will earn a mystery reward at the end of the game time if they earn at least the goal number of points posted clearly in the classroom.
8. At the end of the game period, the teacher tallies all of the points.
9. If the goal is met, the teacher allows a student who has behaved appropriately during the allotted game time to draw a mystery reward from the jar or hat.
10. The teacher immediately distributes the mystery reward to the entire group of students.

(cont.)

Option 2: Design Contingencies (Behavior Requirements) for the Reduction of Inappropriate Behavior (Punishment of Inappropriate Behavior)

1. Locate the reinforcers list for students (see "Procedures" for instructions on how to do this).
2. Place the reinforcers on small pieces of paper, fold them, and place them in a jar or hat.
3. Create a starting number of points (behavior goal) that represent the number of disruptions the class is allowed to engage in (i.e., class must have 36 or fewer disruptive behavior episodes = class must receive 36 or fewer points).
4. Display the behavior goal clearly in the classroom.
5. Explain to the class which behaviors are considered disruptive.
6. Provide examples of disruptive behavior (demonstrations of what *not* to do) and nonexamples (demonstrations of appropriate behavior).
7. Explain the rules.
   a. Every time one student in the group engages in a disruptive behavior the teacher will put a point on the board.
   b. This game will last for *X* number of minutes (periods, subjects, etc.)
   c. The class will earn a mystery reward at the end of the game time if they do not exceed the goal number of points posted clearly in the classroom.
8. At the end of the game period, the teacher tallies all of the points.
9. Teacher allows a student who has behaved appropriately during the allotted game time to draw a mystery reward from the jar or hat.
10. If the goal is met, teacher immediately distributes the mystery reward to the entire group of students.

Alternative Method of Tallying Points

1. *For the reduction of disruptive behavior,* have two clear jars prepared: one with as many marbles or tokens as the goal number of disruptions in it, the other an empty jar. Each time a student engages in an inappropriate behavior, have that student transfer a marble or a token from the goal jar to the other jar. If there are still marbles at the end of the game, the group wins their mystery reinforcer.
2. *For the increase of appropriate behavior,* have the same jars set up, except for the empty jar, which should be labeled as the goal jar. The other jar should have the goal number of marbles/tokens in it as well as "bonus tokens" in case the students behave in a consistently appropriate way (beyond the set goal). When the students all behave appropriately, the teacher (or a randomly selected student) should transfer a marble from the marble jar to the goal jar. Once all of the marbles are transferred, class has earned their mystery reinforcer.

Critical Components That Must Be Implemented for the Intervention to Be Successful

- A list of rules that inform students about what they are supposed to be doing must be posted so that everyone has quick access to the behavior guidelines that exist within the classroom.
- There must be access to powerful reinforcers (things that the students will *clearly* work for).
- All of the rules and the counterrules (nonexamples) must be modeled to the students before the start of the intervention.

(cont.)

Critical Assumptions/Problem-Solving Questions to Be Asked

This intervention has the following assumptions:

- The class has been systematically observed and disruptive behaviors are specifically identified prior to implementing the intervention.
- The percentage of students engaging in disruptive behavior must not represent more than 33% of the targeted classroom population.
- Rewards/reinforcers must motivate at least 90% of the entire class to change their behavior (they must be powerful). One really great way to help resolve this is to have students draw three different rewards from the hat/jar and let the student who drew it select the reinforcer.
- The class is capable of working together to achieve the rewards (they have the skills needed to cooperate with each other).
- Reinforcement schedule is consistent (the teacher always reinforces the students immediately and often enough that the demand does not outweigh the reward).
- Teachers need to ask themselves: Are all of my students capable of successfully engaging in the appropriate/desired/required behavior?
  - If yes, continue with the intervention as described.
  - If no, implement an intervention that targets skill building for students *before* implementing this intervention. Otherwise it will fail as a classwide intervention.

Materials

- Classroom rules chart.
- Classroom rules contract.
- Reinforcers list.
- Jar (Opaque) or hat.
- Small pieces of paper.

References

Axelrod, S. (1973). Comparison of individual and group contingencies in two special classes. *Behavior Therapy, 4,* 83–90.

Kelshaw-Levering, K., Sterling-Turner, H. E., Henry, J. R., & Skinner, C. H. (2000). Randomized interdependent group contingencies: Group reinforcement with a twist. *Psychology in the Schools, 37,* 523–533.

Note. The lead student developers on this brief were Shannon Brooks and Shomara Reyes, psychology graduate students at East Carolina University.

Response Cost Raffle

Brief Description

The response cost raffle is an evidence-based intervention with a number of empirical demonstrations of effectiveness from which this brief was developed (e.g., Witt & Elliott, 1982; Proctor & Morgan, 1991). This behavioral intervention was designed to decrease the frequency of classwide inappropriate behavior. It works because it motivates students to reduce their instances of inappropriate behavior through the use of negative punishment (taking away reward opportunities for students who misbehave). This intervention involves giving an entire class of students raffle tickets at the beginning of a predetermined instruction time. If a student engages in inappropriate behavior during the predetermined time, the teacher must remove one raffle ticket for each inappropriate behavior that occurred. When the teacher removes the raffle ticket(s), he or she also removes opportunities for students to earn prizes by taking away their reward-winning opportunity (e.g., raffle ticket) when they engage in inappropriate behavior.

What "Common Problems" Does This Address?

Problems that arise from students engaging in inappropriate behavior during instructional time. It is intended to reduce behaviors including (but not limited to) off-task behavior, inappropriate vocalizations, out-of-area movement (being out of seat while engaging in disruptive behavior), noncompliance, and failure to complete class assignments.

Procedures

1. Create and explain classroom rules. Make sure they are displayed clearly and focus on what the desired behavior is (vs. what *not* to do).
2. Make a list of potential reinforcers for the class and have the class create their own list of reinforcers. When feasible and reasonable, include students' requests for reinforcers in the teacher's list of reinforcers. Don't forget that reinforcers can be nontangible items like a pass to read to kindergarteners, a pass for a computer lab instructional experience during typical lecture-learning time, bring-a-soda-to-class day, or a groupwide "get-out-of-quiz" pass (with an alternative, fun backup assessment of the same skills that would be assessed in the quiz).
3. Explain to the class which behaviors are considered disruptive.
4. Provide examples of disruptive behavior (demonstrations of what *not* to do) and nonexamples (demonstrations of appropriate behavior).
5. Explain the rules.
   a. Every student in the class will receive five cards/raffle tickets with the student's name on them.
   b. All students must keep their cards on their desk.
   c. Every time one student engages in a disruptive behavior the teacher will remove his or her card from his or her desk.
   d. This game will last for *X* number of minutes (periods, subjects, etc.).
   e. The students who still have cards/raffle tickets at the end of the instructional period will be entered into a raffle for a prize.
6. The teacher will randomly draw a raffle card and immediately reward the student whose name is listed on the card.

(cont.)

Critical Components That Must Be Implemented for the Intervention to Be Successful

A list of rules that inform students about what they are supposed to be doing must be posted so that everyone has quick access to the behavior guidelines that exist within the classroom. There must be access to powerful reinforcers (things that the students will *clearly* work for). All of the rules and the counterrules (nonexamples) must be modeled for the students before the start of the intervention. Finally, students should have an opportunity to demonstrate the target behaviors with immediate, specific, and accurate feedback. Other important considerations include:

- Earned rewards must be delivered immediately.
- Students must have shown their ability to demonstrate the desired classroom behavior.
- If a student has not demonstrated that he or she is able to successfully exhibit the desired classroom behavior, teach the student how to demonstrate the appropriate behavior *before* implementing this intervention.

Materials

- Classroom rules chart.
- Index cards.
- Raffle prize list.
- Large envelope/shoe box.

References

Proctor, M. A., & Morgan, D. (1991). Effectiveness of a response cost raffle procedure on the disruptive classroom behavior of adolescents with behavior problems. *School Psychology Review, 20,* 97–109.
Witt, J. C., & Elliott, S. N. (1982). The response cost lottery: A time efficient and effective classroom intervention. *Journal of School Psychology, 20*(2), 155–161.

Note. The lead student developer on this brief was Shannon Brooks, a psychology graduate student at East Carolina University.

Good Behavior Game

Brief Description

The name may be a little misleading because this intervention is focused on the reduction of inappropriate behavior using reinforcers already found within the classroom environment. It is best used for the population of teachers who aren't comfortable providing positive social praise. This intervention is designed as a competition for two opposing groups of students. The teacher gives a list of "do not" rules and criteria for a reward. The teacher counts every time each team violates one of the rules. The team with the least amount of violations wins.

What "Common Problems" Does This Address?

A high frequency of inappropriate behavior regularly exhibited by a group of students. It is assumed that this behavior is being positively reinforced. This classic intervention was developed by Barrish, Saunders, and Wolf (1969) to reduce inappropriate behavior without the use of positive social reinforcement and contrived reinforcers (such as candy, pencils, etc.).

Procedure

1. Create a list of "do not" rules that will prompt the students to engage in positive behavior.
    a. Examples (the reciprocal positive behaviors are listed in parentheses).
        i. Do not speak without permission from the teacher (raise your hand and wait for the teacher to call on you before you speak).
        ii. Do not talk to your friends during class (listen to the teacher and work quietly).
        iii. Do not sit on top of desks or in the floor (sit on your chair).
        iv. Do not use a loud voice (use a quiet voice at all times).
2. Divide group of students into two competing groups and assign them a team name/number. Write their team names on the board—it is where you will be tallying each team's violation of the rules.
3. Explain the "do not" rules.
4. Explain the criteria for winning.
    a. Example of criteria:
        i. The team with the least amount of violations wins. If each team has fewer than 5 violations, both teams will win; if one or both teams have fewer than 20 violations for the week, they will win additional privileges.
    b. Examples of privileges (you can offer more than one for winning):
        i. Team victory pendants.
        ii. Go to the front of the lunch line (one team) or go to lunch early (two teams).
        iii. Choose which activity will be completed during an enrichment period.
        iv. Free time during one of the enrichment periods.
        v. Go to the playground a few minutes early.
        vi. Sit at the front of the class.
        vii. Eat lunch with the teacher (or with their favorite friends).
        viii. Do not have to sit in assigned seats.

(cont.)

c. Tell the students how long they are playing the game (math class, whole day, etc.).
d. Keep track of the number of rule violations the students engage in by tallying them on the board where everyone can see.
e. Reward the team with the least amount of points.

Critical Components That Must Be Implemented for the Intervention to Be Successful

- A powerful incentive needs to be chosen so that it will motivate all students to play the game.
- The "do not" rules need to be written so that they exactly reflect the opposite of the appropriate behavior that the teacher would like to have exhibited (e.g., "Sit in your seat" would translate into "Do not stand up or get out of your desk without permission").
- Also, the team that did not win must not be allowed to partake in the activities (e.g., instead of having free time they have to complete worksheets).

Critical Assumptions/Problem-Solving Questions to Be Asked

Although the intervention is used to reduce the occurrence of inappropriate behavior, the teaching of an alternative appropriate behavior is not naturally embedded in this intervention. This game was originally designed to be carried out for one teaching period (Math, English, etc.). Because of the nature of the game the behaviors that change in this environment may not generalize into other environments naturally.

Reference

Barrish, H. H., Saunders, M., & Wolf, M. M. (1969). Good behavior game: Effects of individual contingencies for group consequences on disruptive behavior in a classroom. *Journal of Applied Behavior Analysis, 2,* 119–124.

Note. The lead student developer on this brief was Shannon Brooks, a psychology graduate student at East Carolina University.

CHAPTER 7

Academic Acquisition Interventions

Skill acquisition matters. Children must acquire any core academic skills at some point in time. Although some children walk into the door with core reading, mathematics, and writing skills, others do not. Regardless of the initial skill level of a child, all will need direct instruction in a range of academic skills across their formative schooling. Accuracy also matters. Before a student can become proficient in any skill, he or she must first complete it accurately. Most teachers and interventionists would likely agree with the previous statements, but it is not unusual for instructional practices to contradict them. For example, many classrooms across the country have students complete a "math minute" in which they work on math problems for 1 minute and try to complete more problems than they completed the previous day. This is a fluency-building activity (see Chapter 9) and if the students are accurate in the skill but complete the problems slowly, then it is a great activity. However, if they complete less than 90% of the problems correctly, then the instructional activity may actually do more harm than good. Repetition in a skill leads to long-term retention. Remember, practice makes permanent, only perfect practice makes perfect. Thus, building accuracy in any skill is the first step to mastery.

Acquisition interventions are those that use modeling, closely guided practice, and immediate feedback to initially teach a skill and then increase the accuracy with which a task is completed. Although the aspects of an acquisition intervention are intuitively aligned with rote academic tasks such as word recognition and math facts, they also apply to more metacognitive skills such as reading comprehension because there are specific subskills involved in reading for understanding. For example, students can be taught explicit steps in identifying the main idea or in finding relationships from which inferences are made.

It is somewhat common in schools to ask: "Has the child learned the skill?" We believe the better question is "How well has the child learned the skill?" or more technically, "How accurately can the child produce the acquired skill?" Research has consistently demonstrated that increasing accuracy can lead to growth over several weeks in reading (Burns,

> It is somewhat common in schools to ask: "Has the child learned the skill?" We believe the better question is "How well has the child learned the skill?" or more technically, "How accurately can the child produce the acquired skill?"

2007), math (Codding, Archer, & Connell, 2010), and writing (Burns, Ganuza, & London, 2009). Moreover, increasing accurate responding among students who struggle to complete basic skills has consistently led to improved behavioral outcomes such as time on task (Beck, Burns, & Lau, 2009; Burns & Dean, 2005; Gickling & Armstrong, 1978). We have consulted with high school teachers about struggling students in their classrooms, and almost 100% of the time at least one of the referring problems, if not the primary problem, was homework completion. In our experience, it was often the case that students who were not completing homework did not know how to consistently complete the work. Thus, our intervention frequently involved short instructional sessions in the required task before completing the homework assignment, which just about always increased the homework completion rate. Students should be able to complete at least 90% of any required task accurately before they complete the task independently, which means that homework (or independent practice) should not be assigned unless the teacher or interventionist knows with some confidence that the student can complete the task with high accuracy. Below we discuss the characteristics of interventions that increase the accuracy with which academic tasks are completed.

SPECIFIC ISSUES OF ACADEMIC ACQUISITION INTERVENTIONS AT THE INDIVIDUAL LEVEL

Practitioners are constantly bombarded with claims of "research-based" interventions. We recently synthesized several meta-analytic studies to determine what exactly makes an academic intervention consistent with the research base. We found that academic interventions with strong effects consistently (1) correctly targeted the student's deficit, (2) provided explicit instruction in the skill, (3) provided an appropriate level of challenge, (4) allowed for sufficient repetition for the skill to be retained, and (5) utilized immediate corrective feedback (Burns, VanDerHeyden, & Boice, 2008). As stated in Chapter 2, students should be able to read 93 to 97% of the words correctly to successfully interact with written text (Gickling & Thompson, 1985) and just about all other academic tasks require approximately 90% known items for it to be successfully completed (Burns, 2004). Thus, these high percentages should be considered as defensible goals when implementing an acquisition intervention, which addresses the appropriate level of challenge criterion of a research-based academic intervention. Repetition and feedback are considered in more detail when individual interventions are discussed, but research has clearly demonstrated the importance of both (Hattie, 2009; Szadokierski & Burns, 2008). Below we discuss how to analyze an

> Academic interventions with strong effects consistently (1) correctly targeted the student's deficit, (2) provided explicit instruction in the skill, (3) provided an appropriate level of challenge, (4) allowed for sufficient repetition for the skill to be retained, and (5) utilized immediate corrective feedback.

academic task to correctly target the intervention, what explicit instruction entails, and the characteristics of effective feedback.

Task Analysis

We discussed using assessment data to determine in which phase of the learning hierarchy the student is functioning. However, interventionists must also determine what skill is the most appropriate for intervention before assessing in which phase the student is for that skill. In other words, what critical academic skill(s) is a child missing? The National Reading Panel (2000) provides a useful heuristic for reading interventions with their five areas of effective instruction, phonemic awareness, phonics, fluency, and vocabulary/comprehension. Interventionists should implement the process of test down to teach up, which was described in Chapter 6. After determining which reading area is most appropriate for intervention, the interventionist can then use accuracy and fluency data (Chapter 2) to narrow down the intervention options.

Individual interventions for math can also be identified by using the categorical assessments described in Chapter 2. After determining the appropriate objective or category for the intervention (e.g., single-digit multiplication, double-digit addition, double-digit subtraction with regrouping), interventionists should then determine whether the deficit is procedural or conceptual. Conceptual knowledge is the understanding of the relationships that underlie math problems, and procedural knowledge is the understanding of the rules and steps to actually solve the problems (Hiebert & Lefevre, 1986). It is somewhat unclear which type of knowledge develops, but the two are clearly interrelated (Rittle-Johnson & Siegler, 1998; Rittle-Johnson, Siegler, & Wagner, 2001) and are necessary for math proficiency (Kilpatrick et al., 2001).

A recent meta-analysis found negligible mean effects for math interventions that were focused on the underlying concept, which was "a complex puzzle of findings, open to multiple interpretations" (Baker, Gersten, & Lee, 2002, p. 66). The small mean effects may have occurred because many students cannot complete the problem quickly enough to solve it (Geary et al., 2007; Hanich et al., 2001) but might understand the underlying concept. Ongoing research has found that first identifying whether the student conceptually understands the problem enhanced intervention effectiveness (Burns, 2011).

Rivera and Bryant (1992) discuss active and passive approaches to identify procedural errors in math. Simply examining errors in written work (passive) may give clues about procedural understanding. For example, a student who subtracts 25 from 42 and gets 23 (instead of 17), likely recognized that he or she could not subtract 5 from 2 in the one's column, so simply subtracted 2 from 5. In this example, the student understands the concept of subtraction but does not know how to regroup. If a visual examination of student work does not suggest an intervention target, then the interventionist could simply give the student another problem like the target problem and ask him or her to think out loud as he or she completes it, or to teach the student how to complete the problem (active). Doing so will likely result in the student verbally stating the error or at least giving sufficient clues as to what the error is.

Procedural understanding and errors are relatively easy to detect in written work, but conceptual errors are often difficult to observe (LeFevre et al., 2006). Thus, interventionists could assess conceptual understanding with an interview protocol. We suggest asking the student to draw a picture that goes with the problem and then complete the task. After doing so, ask the student the following questions, which are based on Buschman and the National Council of Teachers of Mathematics (2003): (1) How did you figure this problem out? (2) How did you find the answer? (3) Please explain your figure/picture to me, (4) What do these (lines, dots, circles, etc., as appropriate) mean and how did they help you solve the problem? (5) How does the picture show the problem? and (6) How did you check to see whether you were correct? Moreover, asking students to judge whether or not items are correctly completed can provide information about conceptual understanding (Canobi, Reeve, & Pattison, 2002, 2003; Cowan, Dowker, Christakis, & Bailey, 1996). One way to do that would be to provide examples of the same mathematical equation, with one correct answer and one incorrect answer (e.g., $2 \times 5 = 10$ and $2 \times 5 = 7$), and asking the child to circle the correct answer.

Explicit Instruction with Modeling

Effective teachers provide explicit and detailed instructions of the new material and skills (Rosenshine & Stevens, 1986), which is especially important for students who lack prerequisite skills (Billingsley & Wildman, 1990; Burns et al., 2008; Rosenshine, 1986). Thus, the first step of explicit instruction is that new material should be presented in a step-by-step manner with clear and detailed instructions and explanations, and one small step is mastered through guided, and eventually independent, practice before the next small step is taught. Guided and independent practice usually take the form of "I do" (presentation of materials), "we do" (guided practice), and "you do" (independent practice) presentations. For example, when teaching the sound for the letter combination *ch*, the interventionist would ensure student attention and then model the sound while showing and pointing to *ch*. Next the interventionist would visually present *ch* and ask the student to say the sound with him or her. Finally, the interventionist would show *ch* again and ask the child to say the corresponding sound by him- or herself. This "I do—we do—you do" approach is the basis for explicit instruction and for acquisition interventions.

> **Guided and independent practice usually take the form of "I do," "we do," and "you do" presentations.**

Guided practice is also an important aspect of explicit instruction and generally involves a high number of interventionist questions and student responses. The purpose of guided practice is to correct errors, provide feedback, provide sufficient practice for students so that they will be able to work independently, and allow reteaching of material if necessary (Rosenshine, 1986). It is also important to continuously check for understanding during guided practice. Thus, students are provided with individual practice of the skill with monitoring (i.e., "you do") immediately after the skill is modeled.

Immediate Corrective Feedback

Feedback is the component of instruction that ensures that the child acquires the target skill by reinforcing a correct response and nothing else. There are several characteristics of feedback that influence its effectiveness including frequency, immediacy, and content or accuracy. Feedback is important at all stages of learning, but when children are first learning a skill (acquisition stage of learning), responses will be hesitant and often incorrect, and feedback must be immediate. Independent practice of the skill during the acquisition phase is counterproductive and actually gives the student a chance to practice the skill incorrectly. The content of the feedback at this stage should be correct and quick, and delayed error correction would be inefficient and ineffective. Effective teachers have a system for tracking student responding when they are teaching a new skill and ensuring that students have made the correct discrimination before moving into independent work.

CONCLUSION

Until a student completes a task accurately, interventionists should not care about how quickly the task is completed. The first task is to increase accuracy to 90% for most tasks and 93% for reading tasks. There are many interventions that can increase accurate responding for an academic task, but they all correctly target the foundational deficit, explicitly teach the skill with modeling, and provide immediate and corrective feedback. We offer evidence-based individual academic acquisitions interventions on pages 88–110 at the end of this chapter. Students should never be allowed to practice any academic skill incorrectly. Practice is important, but practice does not make perfect; practice makes permanent, and incorrect practice leads to incorrect learning. Many interventionists and teachers have been in the difficult position of trying to achieve "unlearning" with a student who learned the steps to a math problem incorrectly. Perfect practice makes perfect and is best accomplished with acquisition interventions.

Letter Sounds: Letter-Sound Boxes

Brief Description

Many teachers and interventionists are familiar with the Elkonin boxes that are frequently and effectively used to teach phonemic awareness. This intervention is based on the same idea, but is used to teach letter sounds. It is preferred to other approaches because it contextualizes the letter sounds. The intervention basically involves teaching letter sounds by placing letters in boxes where the sound is heard.

What "Common Problems" Does This Address?

This is a phonics intervention that teaches letter sounds. Therefore, it is appropriate for students who have demonstrated phonemic awareness, but who need to learn letter sounds. Do not attempt this intervention if the student does not recognize that words are made of sounds. Moreover, the students should also be able to identify initial and ending sounds. For example, the student should be able to tell you that the word *top* begins with the sound for *t*, but does not know what letter makes that sound.

Procedure

1. As with any intervention of explicit items, begin with an assessment of what the student knows and only teach what he or she does not know, but use what he or she has already learned to support the process.
2. If the student does not know any letter sounds, begin by teacher him or her five sounds. Letter sounds are categorized as either continuous or stop sounds. Continuous sounds blend into one another, but stop sounds have a definitive beginning and end. The letters with continuous sounds are *a, e, i, o, u, f, l, m, n, r, s, v,* and *z,* and letters with stop sounds are *b, c* (pronounced as "k"), *d, g, h, j, k, p, q, t, w, x,* and *y.* It is best to start with continuous sounds, but be careful not to teach similar sounds consecutively (e.g., *m* and *n,* or *b* and *d*). Be sure to include at least one consonant in the first five.
3. The first five letters are taught with explicit instruction, which involves the following process: "The letter is _____ and it makes the _____ sound. What sound does _____ make?" A correct reply is followed with "Good, _____ makes the _____ sound." Start over again if the student does not make a correct reply within 2 seconds. Be sure to make the appropriate sound without adding sounds. For example, *t* is not pronounced "tuh" and *d* is not pronounced "duh." It is also best to use all lowercase letters at this point.
4. Next, have the student think of words that start with the sound and spell the word with magnetic letters as he or she says it.

(cont.)

5. After learning five letters, you can begin to teach the remaining sounds with boxes. Use three-letter words and create boxes like the ones shown below.

6. Small portable whiteboards and magnetic letters work very well for this. Teach one letter at a time and prepare five words that contain the target letter plus two letters that have already been taught.

7. Model the skill first by saying a word that contains the target letter and two letters already taught. Then say, "I hear the _____, _____, and _____ sounds in the word _____. The (target) sound comes first." Then hold up the target letter and say, "The letter is _____ and it makes the _____ sound. What sound does _____ make?" A correct reply is followed with "Good, _____ makes the _____ sound." Start over again if the student does not make a correct reply within 2 seconds. Again, be sure to make the appropriate sound without adding sounds to it.

8. The interventionist then says, "I hear the _____ sound first, so I am going to put the letter _____ in the first box. I hear the _____ sound second, so I'll put the _____ letter here. Finally, I hear the _____ sound last, so I'll put the _____ letter at the end." Remember, the second and third sounds are letters that the student has already learned. Then, the interventionist says the sounds individually while pointing at the letters and then reads the connected letters as the word.

9. The second example is done together. The interventionist says, "Now let's do another word together," then says a second word that starts with the target letter and includes two letters that the student has already learned. The interventionist then asks, "What sounds do you hear in _____? The letters that make those sounds are _____, _____, and _____" while holding up each magnetic letter as he or she says them. Give the student the letters and ask him or her to say the sounds one at a time while putting the letter in the corresponding open box. Have the student read the word when finished. Provide immediate feedback and verbal reinforcement if correct, or immediately correct if incorrect and return to Step 6.

10. Once the student successfully completes the task with guidance, give him or her independent practice by saying three more words with the target and learned sounds, giving him or her the letters that correspond to the sound and having him or her place them in the boxes. Do not always have the target sound occur first, because then the student could simply learn to put the specific letter first without considering its sound. Provide feedback as you go.

Critical Components That Must Be Implemented for the Intervention to Be Successful

- In order for this intervention to work, the interventionist must clearly model each letter and corresponding sound.
- The objective is to successfully pair the sound with the visual stimulus, so do so as often as you can.

(cont.)

- Using the other letters that the student already knows allows for opportunities to be successful while contextualizing the letter to make it more interesting.
- Magnetic letters and whiteboards work quite well and students tend to enjoy using them.
- Do not forget to teach continuous sounds first, keep similar sounds separated, and use lowercase letters.

Materials

- Small plastic magnetic letters.
- A small personal whiteboard to which the magnetic letters can adhere.
- A dry-erase marker to make the three boxes on the whiteboard.
- Five words that contain the target letter and two of the previously learned letters.
- Reinforcers as needed.

References

Blackman, B., Ball, E., Black, S., & Tangel, D. (2001). *Road to the code*. Baltimore, MD: Brookes.

Joseph, L. M. (2000). Developing first graders' phonemic awareness, word identification, and spelling: A comparison of two contemporary phonic instructional approaches. *Reading Research and Instruction, 39*, 160–169.

Reading Fluency: Supported Cloze Procedure

Brief Description

The supported cloze procedure (SCP) is an assisted intervention in which an interventionist reads a passage jointly with a student by orally reading every other word. Thus, SCP specifically targets reading accuracy by modeling correct reading of words in the passage.

What "Common Problems" Does This Address?

SCP is appropriate for students who have adequate phonetic skills but who struggle applying those skills to reading text. Students who would likely respond best to SCP are those who accurately read substantially less than 93% of the words from grade-level text. However, it is worth noting again that fluency should be the appropriate intervention target, not phonetics.

Procedure

1. Provide the student with a grade-level (or appropriate current skill-level) text of substantial length to engage in meaningful reading, but not too long so as to overwhelm the student. One-page probes work quite well for this task.
2. Ask the student to orally read the passage while the interventionist follows along.
3. Any word that the student does not read correctly within 2 minutes is verbally provided by the interventionist by saying, "That word (pointing to the word) is (state the word). What word is that?" If the student replies correctly, then the interventionist states, "Yes, that word is (state the word). Good." The interventionist replies to an incorrect response by starting the error correction procedure all over again.
4. After the student reads the passage, the interventionist states, "This time we are going to read the passage together. Start at the beginning and you will read the first word, then I'll read the second, then we'll alternate back and forth until we read the entire passage. Any questions?"
5. The student then reads the first word, the interventionist reads the second, then they alternate every other word until the passage is complete. However, the interventionist models fluent reading and avoids robotic-sounding speech.
6. Any student error is corrected with the standard error correction outlined in Step 3.
7. After completing the passage, the two start over again on the same passage, but this time the interventionist goes first, followed by the student. Thus, every word on the passage is modeled by the interventionist and read by the student.
8. (Optional) After reading the passage together a second time, the student could be asked to read the passage again independently.

(cont.)

Critical Components That Must Be Implemented for the Intervention to Be Successful

In order for this intervention to work, the interventionist must clearly model each word. He or she must also model fluent reading. It is easy to engage in word-by-word robotic-sounding phrasing, unless the interventionist moves the pace at a comfortable yet relatively rapid rate. Moreover, this intervention is only used until accuracy improves, at which time SCP ends and a different intervention in which prosodic reading is modeled begins. Because this is an accuracy intervention, we suggest that it not be timed.

Materials

- One copy of one grade-level reading passage, preferably all on one page.
- Reinforcers as needed.

Reference

Rasinski, T. V. (2003). *The fluent reader: Oral reading strategies for building word recognition, fluency, and comprehension.* New York: Scholastic.

Comprehension: Predicting

Before we discuss acquisition interventions for reading comprehension, we must first discuss for whom reading comprehension interventions are appropriate. Most of the reading comprehension problems in the elementary grades are not actually comprehension problems; they are fluency deficits. Consider for a moment a child who reads in an inaccurate and slow manner. As that child struggles to read each word two separate issues arise. First, he or she gets through rather little text. Second, most of his or her attention is placed on simply reading. In such a case, the child logically has little capacity to attend to the content of the text. In technical terms, reading fluency is a "behavior cusp" that allows for the opportunity to access information through reading comprehension. To provide some specific guidance, previous research found that at the elementary level, students need to read approximately 50 to 60 WCPM for comprehension to occur (Burns, 2002, Burns et al., 2011). Thus, if a student is reading less than 50 WCPM, he or she will not understand what he or she reads, and should be first taught better fluency before addressing comprehension.

Brief Description

Prediction is an intervention to explicitly teach students how to identify the main idea *before* they read. According to schematic activation theory (Piaget, 1971) students can more easily understand information if they have a cognitive structure from which to work as they learn and is an effective strategy to enhance basic reading comprehension.

What "Common Problems" Does This Address?

Prediction is a reading comprehension intervention. It is a good first intervention for students who struggle to identify main ideas or for students with very low comprehension skills.

Procedure

1. Present the student with a reading passage or section of a book. This can be done with narrative or expository text, but it might be easier to start with expository writing.
2. Model looking at the title, scanning the major headings, and examining illustrations to use as clues to predict what the story is about before reading. Have the student follow along with his or her copy of the text.
3. The interventionist then models predicting by stating what he or she thinks the reading will be about and why he or she thinks that.
4. The student then reads the story orally to determine whether the prediction was correct.
5. Give the student a second reading passage.
6. Ask the student to examine the title, major headings, and illustrations to determine a prediction about what the story will be about.
7. Have the student write down (or state if he or she is not currently writing fluently) a prediction and share it with the interventionist. Discuss why the student made that prediction and give feedback as to whether it is a good one or not.

(cont.)

8. Read the text together to determine whether the prediction was accurate.
9. Verify that the student made an accurate prediction or work with the student to modify the prediction so that it is more accurate.
10. Give the student a third reading passage or section of a book and ask the student to examine the title, headings, and illustrations, and then to write down his or her prediction.
11. Ask the student to read the passage to determine whether his or her prediction was correct.
12. The student then reports to the interventionist whether the prediction was correct and how he or she knows it is.
13. Verify that the student made an accurate prediction or work with the student to modify the prediction so that it is more accurate.
14. Repeat steps as needed until the student makes accurate predictions.

Critical Components That Must Be Implemented for the Intervention to Be Successful

In order for this intervention to work, the interventionist must clearly model his or her thought processes and ask about those of the students. Reading comprehension must be made observable in order to successfully intervene.

Materials

- Multiple copies of at least three reading examples of sufficient length and difficulty for the student's age and reading level. Single-page probes rarely work. Thus, interventionists may likely use multiple copies of a textbook (e.g., social studies book).
- Paper to write down predictions.
- Reinforcers as needed.

References

Burns, M. K., Tucker, J. A., Hauser, A., Thelen, R., Holmes, K., & White, K. (2002). Minimum reading fluency rate necessary for comprehension: A potential criterion for curriculum-based assessments. *Assessment for Effective Intervention, 28,* 1–7.

Burns, M. K. & Kowoka, H., Lim, B., Crone, M., Haegele, K., Parker, D. C., Petersen, S. & Scholin, S. E. (2011). Minimum reading fluency necessary for comprehension among second-grade students. *Psychology in the Schools, 48,* 124–132.

Palinscar, A. S., & Brown, A. L. (1984). Reciprocal teaching of comprehension-fostering and comprehension-monitoring activities. *Cognition and Instruction, 1,* 117–175.

Piaget, J. (1971). Biology and knowledge: An essay on the relations between organic regulations and cognitive processes. Chicago: University of Chicago Press.

Comprehension: Find the Main Idea

Brief Description

Finding the main idea is also a reading comprehension intervention in which students engage as they read. It teaches how to find information in text as they read.

What "Common Problems" Does This Address?

Finding the main idea is a reading comprehension intervention, but is especially useful for students who do not correctly identify the main ideas in reading and who struggle to extract ideas from the text.

Procedure

1. Present the student with a reading passage or section of a book. This can be done with narrative or expository text, but it might be easier to start with expository writing. The reading sample should also include reading comprehension questions that address main ideas.
2. The interventionist and student orally read a short reading sample together.
3. The interventionist then states the main idea and how he or she determined what it was.
4. Next, the interventionist reads the first comprehension question and then points to where the answer can be found in the text while orally reporting how he or she knew to look there.
5. The student is then asked to read the second comprehension question aloud and to point to where in the text the answer could be found.
6. Correct answers are reinforced. If the answer is incorrect or not given, then the interventionist points to a general location where the answer can be found (e.g., the page) and provides increasing assistance (e.g., the section on the page, the paragraph, then the sentence) until the student responds correctly.
7. The student continues to respond to the questions until he or she correctly demonstrates the skill.
8. A second passage is then orally read by the student as the interventionist follows along.
9. The student then states the main idea and how he or she determined what it was, with appropriate feedback from the interventionist.
10. The student then reads each comprehension question orally and points to where the answer can be found, again with gradually increasing assistance as needed and appropriate reinforcement and feedback.
11. After completing the task with guided assistance, the student then reads a third sample and independently points to where the answer is located for each corresponding comprehension question.

Critical Components That Must Be Implemented for the Intervention to Be Successful

In order for this intervention to work, the interventionist must again clearly model his or her thought processes and ask about those of the student. Remember, the desired response is first to find the information before actually answering the question.

(cont.)

Materials

- Multiple copies of at least three reading examples of sufficient length and difficulty for the student's age and reading level. Single-page probes rarely work. Thus, interventionists may likely use multiple copies of a textbook (e.g., social studies book).
- Highlighting tape or other fun yet nonpermanent approaches to identify small pieces of text within a book.
- Reinforcers as needed.

Reference

van den Broek, P., Lynch, J. S., Naslund, J., Ievers-Landis, C. E., & Verduin, K. (2003). The development of comprehension of main ideas in narratives: Evidence from the selection of titles. *Journal of Educational Psychology, 95,* 707–718.

Comprehension: Teaching Inferential Questions

Brief Description

One of the most difficult aspects of comprehension for many students involves answering inferential questions because they require students to identify the relationship between two objects or events in a passage. Some relationships are explicitly stated in the text, but some have to be inferred from the information provided. Therefore, students should be taught to answer inferential questions on the basis of a stated relationship and those for whom the relationship is inferred.

What "Common Problems" Does This Address?

Students are taught to answer inferential questions that are often included on state accountability tests. However, the strategy for teaching students how to identify relationships will also enhance overall reading comprehension.

Procedure

Students are first taught to answer questions based on the stated relationship, then ones for which the relationship has to be inferred.

1. Present the student with a reading passage or section of a book. This can be done with narrative or expository text.
2. Start by asking a comprehension question.
3. Determine where in the text the information is to answer the question. This should be a skill that has already been learned and should not need to be modeled.
4. Orally state the rule that is provided in the text (e.g., "The more milk you drink, the stronger your bones") and the question for which the rule is required to find an answer (e.g., "Chris drank one glass of milk. Jeff drank three glasses of milk. Who is more likely to have stronger bones?").
5. The interventionist then states the correct answer and orally demonstrates how he or she used the rule to answer the question.
6. Provide a second question and have the student find where the answer is in the text.
7. Ask the student to state the rule and the relevant question while providing feedback. If the response is correct, ask the student to explain how he or she decided that was the appropriate rule.
8. Have the student answer the question with appropriate feedback and oral reinforcement.
9. Provide the student with three more questions to answer based on stated rules within the text. The questions may be based on relationships that you have already used. Provide feedback and oral reinforcement as appropriate.
10. Now that the student can use relationships to answer questions, teach the process for using inferred relationships by modeling one with a different passage.
11. Start by saying, "Some questions can only be answered by using information that we knew before we started or that was provided somewhere else in the text."
12. Orally state the appropriate question (e.g., "What do you think Nicole will choose for dinner, chicken and vegetables or a McDonald's hamburger?") and then state, "What information do I

(cont.)

need to know?" and make a list of relevant information. In this example, the interventionist might state something like, "What does Nicole like to eat?" "What has she eaten before?" and "Are there any rules that we can find based on the information?" The text stated that Nicole had oatmeal and a banana for breakfast and a salad for lunch.

13. The pieces of information provided in Step 12 would be written down and a list of rules would be created. For example, we could infer that because she has eaten healthy foods, therefore, Nicole likes healthy foods.

14. The rules identified in Step 12 would be applied to the question to see whether an answer can be determined (e.g., Nicole likes healthy foods, so she will probably eat chicken and vegetables).

15. Give the student a different question based on the rules to answer the question while providing feedback and asking questions such as "How did you decide that?"

16. Read a different question from the same reading passage that also relies on inferential knowledge and a rule not stated.

17. Ask the student, "What information do you need to know?" and have him or her make a list of relevant information. Provide verbal reinforcement for correct answers and immediate corrective feedback for incorrect responses, but remember that there will be few incorrect responses. As long as it is remotely relevant, then it is information to include.

18. Have the student create a list of rules, which might only be one or two.

19. Ask the student to apply a rule from Step 18 to the question to see whether an answer can be determined.

20. Ask the student to use the rule to answer the question. Then ask metacognitive questions about how he or she determined which rule to use.

21. Give the student another short passage with three to five inferential comprehension questions without stated rules and ask him or her to answer the questions.

22. Observe the student to provide corrective feedback, oral reinforcement, and to ask metacognitive questions.

Critical Components That Must Be Implemented for the Intervention to Be Successful

This is often a difficult skill for struggling readers to learn. Make the steps explicit, clear, and observable. Think out loud every chance you can to model your thought processes. From our experience we have seen that students often develop silly and funny rules or use the rules to give funny answers. In the example above, the student could have said that Nicole would pick the fast-food option because it tastes better or that she likes bad-tasting food. Allow them to be silly while providing corrective feedback. Perhaps say something like, "You may not like how it tastes, but some people might and besides, food tastes differently to different people. What else is true about what Nicole ate?"

Materials

- Relatively short passages, written at an appropriate level, that include three to five inferential questions for each. It is best if both the interventionist and student work from the same copy.
- Paper and pencil with which to write down information.
- Reinforcers as needed.

Reference

Carnine, D. W., Silbert, J., Kame'enui, E. J., & Tarver, S. G. (2004). *Direct instruction reading* (4th ed.). Upper Saddle River, NJ: Merrill Prentice-Hall.

Math Computation: Incremental Rehearsal

Brief Description

Incremental rehearsal (IR) is a flash-card technique to teach students basic math facts. The goal of IR is to increase accurate responding for students who do not correctly complete math facts.

What "Common Problems" Does This Address?

IR is a well-researched intervention, but it is quite intensive and should only be used for students who experience difficulty retaining basic rote information. Moreover, IR of basic math facts can lead to accurate completion of more advanced skills such as multidigit multiplication and story problems. However, IR is a procedural intervention and should only be used if the student demonstrates sufficient conceptual understanding of the skill. Below are the procedures for implementing IR with basic multiplication facts, but it could be used with any type of math fact.

Procedure

1. The first step is to assess which math facts the student knows and does not know. Write the target (or all) single-digit math facts each on an index card (without the answer). It is best to orient the problem the same way that the facts are taught in the classroom (vertically or horizontally).
2. Present each individual math fact to the student and ask him or her to give the answer. All facts for which the correct answer is stated within 2 seconds are considered known, and those not answered correctly or the response comes after 2 seconds are considered unknown.
3. Place eight of the known facts in a pile.
4. Present the first unknown fact to the student while orally stating the fact and the corresponding answer. Next, ask the student to orally restate the fact. For example, the interventionist would say, "4 times 4 equals 16. Now you say it," and would then point to the numbers as the student says them aloud.
5. If the fact is repeated correctly, then the interventionist says, "Good, 4 times 4 equals 16. Every time you see this, you can say 4 times 4 equals 16, or just say the answer, which is 16." If the student does not repeat it correctly, then the interventionist restates it again.
6. Rehearse the unknown fact in the following sequence: First unknown, first known; first unknown, first known, second known; first unknown, first known, second known, third known; first known, second known, third known; fourth known; first known, second known, third known; fourth known; fifth known; first known, second known, third known; fourth known; fifth known; sixth known; first known, second known, third known; fourth known; fifth known; sixth known, seventh known; and first known, second known, third known; fourth known; fifth known; sixth known, seventh known, eighth known.
7. After completing the rehearsal sequence with the first unknown fact, that first fact is then treated as the first known, the previous eighth known is removed, and a new unknown fact is introduced. Thus, the number of cards always remains nine.
8. Start over again at Step 1 with a new unknown fact.
9. Continue individually adding in and rehearsing unknown facts. Each time the fact that was just rehearsed becomes the first known, and the previously rehearsed facts stay in the pile as known.

(cont.)

10. Continue adding in unknown facts until three errors occur while rehearsing one fact. Errors need not only occur on the fact currently being rehearsed. Any incorrect response or a response that exceeds 2 seconds counts as an error. It is not unusual for the student to start making errors on previously taught facts or even facts that he or she knew before the sequence began.
11. After finishing the sequence described in Steps 1 through 10, shuffle all of the cards and present each one more time just to assess whether the fact was actually learned.

Critical Components That Must Be Implemented for the Intervention to Be Successful

The critical aspect of IR is the high repetition while providing an appropriate level of challenge. Many people probably think of "drill and kill" when they think of flash cards, which have a deservedly negative connotation. However, including the known facts in the process provides the student opportunities to be successful and to be reinforced. Moreover, presenting the item that you want him or her to learn, removing it, and presenting it again and again while gradually increasing the length of time in between presentations is an effective way to move a newly learned fact from working memory to long-term memory. Thus, the order of the known facts is completely irrelevant. Interventionists should feel free to shuffle the order as often as they like. However, the order of the unknown facts is important. The student will see the first unknown fact eight times, then seven more while rehearsing the second fact, six more during the third fact, and so on. Recent research indicated that there was not much gain in retention after the twentieth repetition, which suggests that the order of formerly unknown facts can be rearranged after the student rehearses it 20 times. If the student seems bored, then it is too easy and known facts should be removed, but do not go below five. If the student does not retain at least 90%, then more repetition is needed and known facts should be added, but never go above nine.

Materials

- Blank index cards to write the facts on or commercially available math flash cards. Just be sure that the orientation of the card is the same as how the math facts are presented in the classroom.
- Reinforcers as needed.

References

Burns, M. K. (2005). Using incremental rehearsal to practice multiplication facts with children identified as learning disabled in mathematics computation. *Education and Treatment of Children, 28*, 237–249.

Codding, R. S., Archer, J., & Connell, J. (2010). A systematic replication and extension of using incremental rehearsal to improve multiplication skills: An investigation of generalization. *Journal of Behavioral Education, 19*, 93–105.

Tucker, J. A. (1989). *Basic flashcard technique when vocabulary is the goal.* Unpublished teaching materials. School of Education, University of Chattanooga, Chattanooga, TN.

Math Concepts: Part–Part–Whole Activity

Brief Description

Conceptual interventions are often conducted without using written numbers, which are abstract and arbitrary (e.g., "Why does '3' equal (o o o)?" Because we say it does. There is literally no other reason). Computation is simply putting together or separating sets. This can be modeled with manipulative objects by grouping or dividing them. The example we provide below focuses on addition, but it could be done with multiplication, subtraction, and division with only minor, and hopefully obvious, modifications.

What "Common Problems" Does This Address?

This intervention is appropriate for students who have number sense but who do not understand the concept of the given computation operation.

Procedure

1. Assemble a group of small objects that come in different colors (e.g., checker pieces, painted lima beans, rocks, colored paper clips, Legos, Bingo chips).
2. Say, "Today we are going to learn how to (add, subtract, multiply, or divide)."
3. Place a number of objects in front of the student that represent the desired sum (e.g., 10).
4. Say, "I'm going to take these (name of objects) and place them into two groups." Then count the number of objects in each group and state the resulting equation while calling it a number sentence (e.g., "These 4 objects and these 6 objects make 10 objects. That is a number sentence: 4 plus 6 equals 10").
5. Ask, "What is the number sentence?" Praise a correct response and correct an incorrect one.
6. Ask the student to make two different groups, count how many are in each group, and say aloud how many objects are in each group. Then say with him or her, "Let's say the number sentence together: _____ plus _____ equals _____." Give corrective feedback and oral praise as appropriate.
7. Next, give the student the same total number of objects, but with two colors and ask him or her to separate them into two different groups. After separating them, ask the student to count the objects and say the appropriate number sentence with praise and corrective feedback as appropriate.
8. Once the student can complete the previous step correctly and without assistance, give him or her a different total number of objects with two colors (e.g., six red checkers and eight black checkers) and ask him or her to separate them into two groups and state the number sentence. Praise and give corrective feedback as needed.
9. Finally, give the student a larger set of objects that are all one color and ask him or her to make two groups with the objects while saying the number sentence. Give corrective feedback for incorrect responses and return to Step 4. Praise correct responses and restate the numbers sentence to him or her (e.g., "Yes, 9 plus 9 equals 18. Great job.").
10. Have the student continue to create different sets with the same number of objects while stating the number sentence until he or she does so correctly three consecutive times.

(cont.)

Critical Components That Must Be Implemented for the Intervention to Be Successful

This intervention is *only* appropriate for conceptual understanding. Once the concept has been learned, the student should then be taught the abstract symbols that correspond to it and the procedure for completing it. Providing manipulative items as a tool to solve the problem after the student understands the concept usually slows down the student's computation and often does not improve student skill or performance. Make the activity fun by using objects that appeal to the students or grouping them in a fun way. The games Connect Four or Mancala work well.

Materials

- Colored objects.
- Perhaps fun grouping items such as Connect Four game, Mancala game, large rubber bands, and so on.
- Reinforcers as needed.

Reference

VanDeWalle, J. A., Karp, K. S., & Bay-Williams, J. M. (2010). *Elementary and middle school mathematics: Teaching developmentally* (7th ed.). Boston: Allyn & Bacon.

Math Word Problems: Self-Regulated Strategy

Brief Description

Self-regulated strategy is an intervention that relies heavily on modeling and corrective feedback. It has been shown to be effective for improving word problem solving in elementary-level students identified as having learning disabilities or mild disabilities (Cassel & Reid, 1996). Strategy instruction sessions are typically 35 minutes long and should occur two to three times per week. Students should receive instruction in identifying and learning the meaning of cue words and phrases commonly found in word problems (e.g., How many more, how many less?) if they do not already have this skill.

What "Common Problem" Does This Address?

The self-regulated strategy instruction is effective for improving the word problem-solving skills of students who struggle with math. It is appropriate for students who have knowledge of basic math facts but have difficulties solving word problems that use those facts. Previous research found that self-regulated instruction increased the accuracy with which elementary-age students completed math word problems, and that 95% of student errors were due to incorrect operation selection rather than difficulties in solving or reading the problem (Case, Harris, & Graham, 1992).

Procedure

Operations should be taught separately (i.e., focus on one operation, such as addition, rather than multiple operations simultaneously). Addition is used as an example in the procedures outlined below.

1. Administer a probe with seven basic addition facts and seven word problems using those facts. Discuss any student frustration with the word problems and ask him or her to commit to learning to use the strategy.
2. Read through the following six-step problem-solving strategy and provide a copy of the list to the student. Be sure to discuss why and how each step is used to solve word problems.
   a. Read the problem out loud.
   b. Look for important words and circle them.
   c. Have the student generate a list of things that he or she could say to him- or herself as the student looks for important words and phrases. These are the student's self-generated instructions.
   d. Draw pictures to help tell what is happening.
   e. Write down the math sentence.
   f. Write down the answer.
3. Model the strategy and self-instructions by thinking aloud. Think of questions and answer them using self-instruction statements that relate to defining the problem (e.g., "What am I being asked to do?"), planning (e.g., "How can I find that information? I can use the strategies"), the use of the strategies (e.g., "I need to find the important words"), self-evaluation (e.g., "Did I find the information I was asked for?"), and self-reinforcement (e.g., "That's right! I did a good job").
4. After modeling, have the student generate and record additional self-instructions for his or her list. Ensure the student has at least one statement for each of the five categories in Step 3.

(cont.)

5. Have the student rehearse the six-step strategy until it is memorized.
6. Throughout the process of instruction, remind the student to use the strategy and self-instructions in the classroom and discuss when doing this may be helpful. Have the student take the strategy and self-instruction lists with him or her and have his or her teacher initial the pages.
7. Practice applying the strategies with the student. Gradually fade the use of the strategy and self-instruction lists. Provide feedback as needed, but withdraw feedback as the student progresses. Administer assessments similar to the word-problem section of the baseline assessment. When the student reaches six of seven items correct, move to the next stage of instruction.
8. The student should independently use the strategy and self-instruction lists to solve word problems.

Critical Components That Must be Implemented for the Intervention to Be Successful

In order for this intervention to work, students must first understand and be somewhat fluent in the basic computation operations. They must also have sufficient reading skills to understand the word problems. Because this is an acquisition intervention, modeling and immediate corrective feedback are important, as is modeling of your own thoughts when you demonstrate the strategy.

Materials

- Computation probes with facts and word problems.
- A list of steps.
- A list of self-instruction statements.
- Reinforcers as needed.

References

Case, L. P., Harris, K. R., & Graham, S. (1992). Improving the mathematical problem-solving skills of students with learning disabilities. *Journal of Special Education, 26*, 1–19.

Cassel, J., & Reid, R. (1996). Use of a self-regulated strategy intervention to improve word problem-solving skills of students with mild disabilities. *Journal of Behavioral Education, 6*, 153–172.

Note. The lead student developer on this brief was Katherine Pratt, a graduate student in the PhD School Psychology Program at the University of Minnesota.

Math Facts: Cover–Copy–Compare

Brief Description

The development of basic math computation skills is a prerequisite to solving complex computations. Cover–copy–compare (CCC) was first observed to improve math fact fluency by Skinner, Turco, Beatty, & Rasavage (1989) but has since varied slightly in implementation procedures (e.g., Stone, McLaughlin, & Weber, 2002; Poncy, Skinner, & Jaspers, 2007). The essential pattern is that the student views a problem including the answer, copies the problem and answer from memory, compares, and revises; small procedural differences do not necessarily change the empirical or theoretical foundation of the intervention.

What "Common Problem" Does This Address?

CCC increases math fact fluency, but it involves working from a model and providing immediate feedback. Thus, it is probably appropriate as an acquisition intervention for students who understand the underlying concept, but who do not complete math facts with high accuracy or fluency.

Procedure

1. Collect baseline fluency data using a progress monitoring measure.
2. Using blank paper, create a two-column table with enough space in the rows to record math facts. In the left column, list appropriate math facts (with answers). Each row in the right column should have three empty circles. Each student should also receive a piece of paper to cover the problems when necessary.
3. Instruct students to study the first problem in the left column, cover it with their paper, copy it into the right column, and check their answer.
4. If students are correct, they should proceed to the next problem. If incorrect, students should start over by studying the uncovered problem. Regardless of initial accuracy, students should say the correct math fact three times out loud before moving on.
5. Monitor progress throughout the intervention.

Critical Components That Must Be Implemented for the Intervention to Be Successful

This is an easily implemented intervention that can be appropriate for individual students or small groups. However, in order for this intervention to work, students must rehearse the correct answer three times before moving on to the next problem. Thus, the interventionist should closely monitor to be sure that students are following the correct sequence.

Materials

- CCC worksheets with two columns, the model in the left column and three small circles in the right column.
- A pencil.
- Reinforcers as needed.

(cont.)

References

Poncy, B., Skinner, C. H., & Jaspers, K. E. (2007). Evaluating and comparing interventions designed to enhance math fact accuracy and fluency: Cover, copy, and compare versus taped problems. *Journal of Behavioral Education, 16*, 27–37.

Skinner, C. H., Turco, T. L., Beatty, K. L., & Rasavage, C. (1989). Cover, copy, and compare: A method for increasing multiplication performance. *School Psychology Review, 18*, 412–420.

Stone, S., McLaughlin, T. F., & Weber, K. P. (2002). The use and evaluation of copy, cover, and compare with rewards and a flash cards procedure with rewards on division math facts mastery with a fourth grade girl in a home setting. *International Journal of Special Education, 17*, 82–91.

Note. The lead student developer on this brief was Pete Nelson, a graduate student in the PhD School Psychology Program at the University of Minnesota.

Writing: Letter Formation

Brief Description

This intervention is essentially explicit instruction in letter formation that uses high modeling. It is based on cover–copy–compare (CCC; Skinner, McLaughlin, & Logan, 1997) and shown to be effective in increasing correct letter formation among early elementary-age students (Burns, Ganuza, & London, 2009).

What "Common Problems" Does This Address?

Explicit instruction in letter formation is an important early skill for writing. It falls under the broad category of mechanics of written instruction, which is often an area in which students who do not enjoy writing struggle. This intervention is especially useful for students with poor penmanship.

Procedure

1. Use five samples of the student's writing to determine letters that the student does not correctly form. It is best to use existing samples of writing as a more authentic assessment. Letters that are incorrectly formed or difficult to decipher three times are good candidates for intervention.
2. Practice the letters one at a time.
3. Write the letter only slightly larger than usual. Present it to the student and state the name of the letter. Ask the student to restate the letter name and reinforce correct answers (e.g., "Good, that letter is *t*") or correct incorrect replies.
4. Have the student lay a piece of paper over the model and trace it.
5. Cover both the model and the traced letter and ask the student to write the letter from memory.
6. Compare the freehand letter to the original model. If the student correctly wrote the letter, then reinforce him or her and move on to Step 7. If he or she did not form the letter correctly, then go back to Step 3.
7. After correctly forming the letter from memory, have the student write the letter five more times with the model being left in view.

Critical Components That Must Be Implemented for the Intervention to Be Successful

Although correctly forming letters is important, practicing doing so may not be an inherently enjoyable activity. Many students enjoy being successful, so be sure to orally reinforce the desired behavior. Frequently say, "Good job," "Great," "Excellent," and so on. After completing the above sequence, immediately provide an opportunity for the student to write something meaningful and fun (e.g., a letter to a relative or someone famous, a story) so that he or she can practice using the letter in context.

(cont.)

Materials

- Samples of the students writing.
- Tracing paper on which the student can trace letters.
- Writing paper to practice the letters. Use the same paper that is used to teach penmanship in class.
- A pencil for the student and a dark marker to write the letter dark enough to be traced. There is no research showing that larger pencils are better for teaching handwriting to young children, so a normal-size pencil will be fine. However, using larger pencils is acceptable too.
- Reinforcers as needed.

References

Burns, M. K., Ganuza, Z., & London, R. (2009). Brief experimental analysis of written letter formation: A case demonstration. *Journal of Behavioral Education, 18*, 20–34.

Skinner, C. H., McLaughlin, T. F., & Logan, P. (1997). Cover, copy, and compare: A self-managed academic intervention across skills, students, and settings. *Journal of Behavioral Education, 7*, 295–306.

Writing Composition: Planning and Story-Writing Strategy

Brief Description

The mechanics of writing are important, but good composition is what truly defines good writers. This intervention involves having the student pick an idea, organize his or her thoughts (i.e., develop a writing plan), and write and say more, which can be remembered by the acronym POW.

What "Common Problems" Does This Address?

It is often difficult to get struggling writers to write enough to assess their writing skills. This intervention can help alleviate that difficulty because it makes writing a step-by-step process rather than an overwhelming idea.

Procedure

1. Start by having the student brainstorm ideas about which to write. It usually helps to provide him her parameters from which to pick (e.g., "Today we are going to write about summer").
2. Have the student brainstorm a list of topics and ask questions or give cues (e.g., "Take your time and an idea will come") as needed to keep the brainstorming going. The interventionist should first model thinking out loud and brainstorming for a different but related topic.
3. Have the student cross off any ideas that are less appealing to him or her and then select a topic from those that are left.
4. Model how to organize your thoughts into an outline or framework. Do not use a typical outline format with its confusing roman numbers, just list three main ideas—one at the top of the page, one in the middle, and one at the end. Then write indented supporting ideas underneath each one.
5. After modeling how to organize your thoughts, ask the student to organize his or her thoughts in the same manner. Be sure to give feedback as you go so that the student uses the correct process and be sure to give frequent oral reinforcement.
6. The last phase of the strategy is difficult to model because it involves actually writing. The interventionist would then describe his or her thought processes and would discuss how he or she could answer who, what, where, when, why, and how for the writing assignment. He or she would also model how to decide whether the writing makes sense and is complete.
7. The student would then start writing while the interventionist provides liberal and immediate feedback that focuses on content rather than penmanship, spelling, or punctuation. He or she should also make encouraging statements and comments about how fun writing can be when you know what to do.
8. Provide the student with a cue card that contains the acronym POW and what each letter stands for. During the very next writing assignment, work with the student again but do not provide any modeling; just give immediate corrective and encouraging feedback. Repeat the steps above as needed.

(cont.)

Critical Components That Must Be Implemented for the Intervention to Be Successful

Although a different aspect of writing than forming letters, composition may be a frustrating task for students who struggle with writing. Thus, provide frequent encouraging statements and reinforcement. Successful writing itself can be enjoyable to the student, so be sure to reduce reinforcement as he or she learns the skill. Additionally, the thought processes involved in writing are not observable but are extremely important. Therefore, interventionists need to explicitly and frequently model what they are thinking.

Materials

- Writing paper.
- A pencil.
- Reinforcers as needed.

References

Harris, K. R., Graham, S., & Mason, L. H. (2003). Self regulated strategy development in the classroom: Part of a balanced approach to writing instruction for students with disabilities. *Focus on Exceptional Children, 35*(7), 1–16.

Harris, K. R., Graham, S., Mason, L. H., & Friedlander, B. (2008). *POWERFUL writing strategies for all students.* Baltimore, MD: Brookes.

Lienemann, T. O., Graham, S., Leader-Janssen, B., & Reid, R. (2006). Improving the writing performance of struggling writers in second grade. *Journal of Special Education, 40*, 66–78.

CHAPTER 8

Behavioral Acquisition Interventions

OVERVIEW

Think back to the most recent student with whom you worked who was reportedly displaying a "behavior" problem. Did the teacher or individual referring the child specifically note that the child had previously exhibited the appropriate behavior? Was it made clear that the child knew specifically when to do the correct behavior? In the authors' experiences, it is likely that these two issues were not focused on to the extent necessary as it is often assumed that a child can do, and knows when to do, the appropriate behavior. Unfortunately, in many cases children literally have not acquired the skill to exhibit the correct behavior, or do not know when they should engage in a specific behavior. Such cases are particularly frustrating to both the teacher and child as the core issue, a skill deficit, is not understood. As such, the child is frustrated as he or she does not know what to do, and the teacher is frustrated as he or she does not know why the child will not exhibit the appropriate behavior. These cases should be treated in a similar manner to the academic acquisition interventions presented in Chapter 7. Because there are unique features of reading, mathematics, and written expression acquisition interventions, in this chapter we explore some of the issues related to behavioral acquisition intervention.

SPECIFIC ISSUES OF BEHAVIORAL ACQUISITION INTERVENTION AT THE INDIVIDUAL LEVEL

While this book it not meant to be an applied behavioral analysis text, there are several key issues that should be addressed when considering behavioral acquisition interventions (as will be the case in the chapters on behavioral fluency and generalization interventions). At the most basic level, there are two stages when training a child to do a specific behavior that can be identified by asking, "Does the child know what to do?" and "Can the child do the behavior?" Each of these questions are next addressed.

Does the Child Know What to Do?

In the previous chapters on behavior intervention a rather common theme has emerged—it is critical that there be a clear presentation of schoolwide and classwide rules. While it must seem redundant, at the individual child level this issue should be again reconsidered before moving on. Many times a child "can" do a behavior, but he or she simply does not know when to do it, or more likely, he or she does not think to do the correct behavior when necessary. In such situations teachers or other educational professionals should first attempt to "prompt" the correct behavior. While the term *prompting* has an extensive behavioral history, at this stage we are simply referring to some teacher action that initiates the child to try the desired behavior. The prompt can be oral (a teacher says, "Please raise your hand"), physical (the teacher walking over to the child and gently raising the child's hand for him or her), or visual (a teacher pointing to the posted rule on the wall). Each of these prompts can be thought of as a simple reminder that is similar to a note left to remind someone to "send in the rent" or "give the dog medicine." Such notes increase the likelihood that the reader will remember what he or she should do, and thus does the correct behavior. Most of us carry a device such as a smartphone or PDA that is set up to automatically remind us with such prompts. These little reminders are very much a part of all of our lives and are rather essential to prompt correct behaviors.

> **Many times a child "can" do a behavior, but he or she simply does not know when to do it, or more likely, he or she does not think to do the correct behavior when necessary.**

Prompts assume both that there are some understood behaviors (established rules and expected regularities in a classroom) and that the target child knows how to do the behavior. It is illogical to prompt a child to follow a rule if such a rule does not exist. "Active teaching of classroom rules" is an example of an intervention strategy to help children understand what to do. Assuming that a child can do a behavior, and there is a clear rule in place, the prompt then provides an initial reminder. If the child does the desired behavior, then it is at least understood that the child has the behavior in his or her repertoire, and the goal would be to help increase the fluency of the desired response. This issue is discussed in more depth in Chapter 10. However, if after a reasonable number of reminder prompts the child does not exhibit the behavior, then the second question of "Can the child do the behavior?" should be addressed.

Can the Child Do the Behavior?

Consider as an example a child entering into a classroom at the beginning of a school day. In each class, there is an expected routine that a child will not know until it is demonstrated and corrective feedback is given. With any academic behavior, it is not assumed that a child will be able to demonstrate the correct behavior until it is explicitly instructed. This same logic can be applied to common behavioral expectations such as how a child asks for help in a class (e.g., does the child raise his or her hand or walk up to the teacher?), answers a question (e.g., is calling out allowed, or must a child raise his or her hand?), or in more complex situations how he or she should deal with frustration or embarrassment. In any of these events it is critical to ask, "Does the child have the required behavior in his or her repertoire?" If the teacher's answer to this question is "No," or "I am not sure," then it is essential to demonstrate the skill to the child in some manner, and provide opportunities for the child to try it out with corrective feedback provided if an error is made. For example, if a child does not have experience raising his or her hand when he or she would like to respond to a classwide question, it is not assured that he or she will simply figure it out from observing other children in the classroom. While some children pick up modeled appropriate behavior, other children will need more explicit instruction. This is consistent with the overview of the first step of a positive behavior intervention and support (PBIS) model where focus is given to teaching children key behaviors for classroom success.

Demonstrate

When working with a child in this phase of acquisition, several techniques are logical. One of the primary methods in which to initially aid a child in the acquisition of a new behavior is for that behavior to be modeled. Specifically, modeling is the act of allowing the target child to see another child, or an adult, engage in the desired behavior in an overt manner. For modeling to be successful it is critical that each step of a behavior is observable and that the child has the requisite ability to engage in the behavior. To do this process effectively, a behavior should be broken down into smaller behaviors. Consider, for example, a first-grade student who is having difficulty entering the classroom in the morning. There are likely a number of steps that must be accomplished to successfully complete this whole behavior. The child must enter the room with some defined level of decorum. If there is a coat closet in the room, he or she may need to take off his or her coat and put it in the correct place. After this step, there is likely a common morning activity that is done at the desk or in a group. Depending on how complex this morning ritual is, there may be a number of additional steps to consider. While many children can observe this multistep process, a child who is having difficulty should have the opportunity to observe each step of the more complex behavior repertoire.

> **For modeling to be successful it is critical that each step of a behavior is observable and that the child has the requisite ability to engage in the behavior.**

A classic example of this strategy is the use of contingent observation demonstrated by Porterfield, Herbert-Jackson, and Risley (1976). In this study, "sit and watch" was demonstrated to be effective in reducing disruptive behavior in a day care setting. The contingent observation intervention used by Porterfield and colleagues was described as a four-step procedure as follows. First, when a child exhibited disruptive behavior, caregivers were to describe why the behavior was inappropriate and an appropriate alternative. The caregiver would then move the child to the edge of the activity and instruct him or her to observe appropriate behavior. After a short period of time the caregiver would then ask the child if he or she was ready to rejoin the activity and knew how to engage in the correct behavior. If the child indicated in some manner that he or she was ready to rejoin, he or she was directed to do so, if the child did not, he or she was allowed another short observation period prior to another opportunity to rejoin the activity. Finally, after rejoining, the caregiver would immediately praise appropriate behavior when demonstrated. In addition to reducing disruptive behavior, the intervention was considered acceptable to both parents and the teachers. Another similar example can be seen in a study by White and Bailey (1990) in which they experimentally examined the impact of a sit-and-watch behavior on two elementary classrooms and found a dramatic reduction in the rate of disruptive behavior. Specifically, students who were disruptive were removed from the activity for 3 minutes and were seated in a place where they could watch other students' appropriate behavior. In addition, a response cost procedure was included so that children placed in sit-and-watch lose some privileges. This intervention provides an excellent method of using modeling to help with behavioral acquisition. An intervention brief (see pages 116–117) based on these studies is provided at the end of this chapter.

Prompt and Feedback

Once children have had the opportunity to observe the behavior broken down into manageable units, they should next have the opportunity to attempt the behavior themselves in a repeated manner with corrective feedback as needed. Students practice the behavior by being prompted. It is important that the teacher prompt the child to try out the behavior immediately after the demonstration period so that he or she can remember all salient details of the behavior. At this stage, the prompt can be oral, physical, or visual in nature, but it is critical that the child understand what he or she is being requested to do. For example, a teacher may say, "OK, now it is your turn to try" to be quite overt, or when a child is inappropriately calling out, discreetly point to the posted rule to remind the child of the correct behavior. In any event, if the child exhibits the correct behavior when prompted, the teacher should immediately respond in an appropriate manner. For example, in the case of a child who calls out and is prompted by the teacher to do the correct (and recently demonstrated) behavior of raising his or her hand, if the child responds by raising his or her hand, it is critical that the teacher calls on the child. Doing so tells the child he or she is behaving in the correct manner and increases the likelihood that the desired behavior would be repeated. The importance of manipulating consequences to increase behavior fluency is addressed in more depth in Chapter 10.

It is likely that some children will not immediately exhibit the correct behavior; teachers should allow the child to observe and attempt the behavior several times. Moreover, it may be necessary to assist the child with additional levels of prompting with increasingly direct methods of helping the child engage in the correct behavior. For example, holding the child's hand and raising it for him or her, then stepping back and calling on the child is a rather sure way to ensure that a child will accomplish the correct behavior. Or moving a child to his or her correct place in a line is another example of a physical prompt. In cases of using physical prompts teachers should be careful to use a gentle and positive manner.

There are two general approaches when using assistance prompts to initiate a behavior. One method involves the teacher using the minimum necessary level of assistance that will most likely help a child accomplish the behavior. This approach maximizes the likelihood that the correct behavior will be exhibited, but also may use a more significant level of assistance than is necessary. Another approach is to start with minimal prompts (which may prove ineffective) and then escalate the level of assistance until the child exhibits the behavior. This method will likely result in taking more time to start the behavior but will use the least invasive method of assistance necessary. While either method should result in the child attempting the behavior, it may result in the child becoming dependent on a higher level of assistance than necessary. This method, called "most to least," may be desirable if it is essential that a child behave appropriately, but will require the teacher to subsequently use less invasive levels of assistance until the behavior is maintained by typical classroom events.

> **It may be necessary to assist the child with additional levels of prompting with increasingly direct methods of helping the child engage in the correct behavior.**

CONCLUSION

The goal of acquisition interventions is to provide a starting point for the development and use of an appropriate behavior. Children need explicit modeling and prompting to acquire a skill, but the behavior should not be ignored after it is learned. Rather, it is important to immediately begin to increase the proficiency of the target behavior so that the child becomes fluent in the presentation of an appropriate behavior. We offer additional evidence-based individual behavioral acquisitions interventions on pages 118–120 at the end of this chapter. Those issues are focused on in Chapter 10.

Contingent Observation: Sit and Watch

Brief Description

This classic intervention was designed to provide a simple method to aid a child in the acquisition of desired behavior through observing other children behave appropriately. Specifically, using a modified time-out procedure, the student is removed from an activity and instructed in both why he or she was removed and what the appropriate behavior would have been. Then the child is instructed to observe appropriate behavior for a short time prior to reengaging in the activity. Finally, when the child behaves appropriately, he or she is immediately praised. This intervention can be used as a follow-up to the "active teaching of classroom rules" intervention (see page 118).

What "Common Problems" Does This Address?

The goal of this intervention is to assist a child in learning desired behaviors.

Procedure

1. When a child displays an inappropriate behavior, describe it to him or her: "Josh, do not push other children when you want to take a turn at the computer." In addition, describe the appropriate behavior: "Josh, when you want a turn you need to ask the other children and then wait for them to finish up. Remember to keep your hands in your personal space."
2. Next, direct the child to go to the periphery of the activity and instruct him or her to observe other children behaving appropriately: "Josh, please take a turn in the sit-and-watch chair and see how Luke asks Steve to take a turn at the computer and then waits nicely for Steve to finish up."
3. After a brief amount of time (approximately 1–3 minutes) ask if the child is ready to rejoin the group: "Josh, are you ready to try to ask to take a turn at the computer? Remember how Luke asked and then waited nicely for Steve to finish up. Remember to keep your hands in your personal space." If the student indicates that he or she is ready to return and behave appropriately, allow him or her to do so. If the student does not respond or says he or she is not ready, allow him or her to continue to observe. For example: "Josh, sit here and watch until you think that you can ask for a turn properly while keeping your hands in your personal space."
4. When the student returns to the group and displays the appropriate behavior, give praise or some other positive reinforcement as soon as possible: "Josh, I like how you asked to use the computer while keeping your hands to yourself."

Critical Components That Must Be Implemented for the Intervention to Be Successful

- A clear set of rules and desired behaviors must be established prior to implementing this intervention.
- Students should be explicitly taught the purpose of the sit-and-watch procedure. Role playing a situation where use of the sit-and-watch might occur is helpful. Each of the procedures should be implemented in order for this intervention to be successful.
- A child or children who can demonstrate the appropriate behavior.

(cont.)

Additional Procedures

If the child cries for an extended period of time or continues to disrupt the group while in the sit-and-watch space, move him or her to a designated "quiet place." This can be in the same room or elsewhere, as long as the child is unable to make contact with the group. Allow the child to remain in the "quiet place" until he or she calms down and is able to return to the group: "Josh, since you are not sitting and watching, you are going to the quiet place to practice sitting quietly." When he or she is calm, return the child to the sit-and-watch space and proceed through the steps described above.

Critical Assumptions/Problem-Solving Questions to Be Asked

Assumptions: The student is able to demonstrate the ability to perform the desired behavior. Other students are modeling the desired behavior.

Limitations: Children who are unable to recognize desired social behaviors in others may not benefit from this intervention.

Materials

- A "sit-and-watch" space placed within view of group activities.
- A "quiet place" within the classroom (or elsewhere), but as far away from the group as possible.
- A classroom rules chart clearly displayed.

References

Porterfield, J. K., Herbert-Jackson, E., & Risley, T. R. (1976). Contingent observation: An effective and acceptable procedure for reducing disruptive behavior of young children in a group setting. *Journal of Applied Behavior Analysis, 9,* 55–64.

White, A. G., & Bailey, J. S. (1990). Reducing disruptive behaviors of elementary physical education students with sit and watch. *Journal of Applied Behavior Analysis, 23,* 353–359.

Active Teaching of Classroom Rules

Brief Description

This intervention provides a framework to assist teaching the use of modeling practice and feedback to instruction of classroom behavioral expectations. The intervention starts with the explicit display of rules in each classroom environment followed by a review and discussion of the rules with the students. This is then followed by having individual students model the appropriate behavior focused on in the rule. Finally, when children subsequently exhibit the desired behavior, they are immediately praised. This intervention can be followed up with a contingent observation procedure (sit and watch) for children who exhibit misbehavior afterward.

What "Common Problems" Does This Address?

This intervention has been developed to help children learn classroom behavior expectations.

Procedure

1. Display chart with list of classroom rules and provide each student with a copy.
2. Early in the year, set aside a block of time to discuss each rule. It is important to discuss the purpose as well as provide specific examples of appropriate behavior. In this discussion, students should be encouraged to provide their own examples of both appropriate and inappropriate behaviors.
3. At the end of this discussion, explicitly note to the students that they will be observed and that students who follow the rules will be identified and praised.
4. After the discussion, it is critical to identify students who are observing a rule and provide immediate, specific, and positive feedback. For example: "I am so excited that Albert is working on his seatwork quietly!" The purpose of this feedback is to both positively reinforce the student and also provide a model for other children.

Critical Components That Must Be Implemented for the Intervention to Be Successful

- A defined set of rules posted in classroom.
- A specific discussion period in which the rules are fully reviewed using specific examples.
- Immediate and overt and specific and positive feedback for students following rules.

Critical Assumptions/Problem-Solving Questions to Be Asked

Assumptions: Students are able to understand and demonstrate desired behaviors based on clear expectations. If this assumption is not met, it is critical to revise the rules and procedures.

Materials

- A chart with the list of classroom rules.

Reference

Johnson, T. C., Stoner, G., & Green, S. K. (1996). Demonstrating the experimenting society model with classwide behavior management interventions. *School Psychology Review, 25,* 199–214.

Teaching Classroom Procedures: Say It, Show It, Check It

Brief Description

Using this intervention, each classroom rule is presented to students using a three-step process to maximize the likelihood of acquisition. First, the rule is presented to the students. Next, behavioral adherence as well as nonadherence is modeled for each rule. In this phase students have the opportunity to watch and scrutinize each example of adherence and nonadherence. Finally, students have the opportunity to try each behavior and are praised for successful demonstration of adherence behaviors. This intervention is consistent with the PBIS model, and offers an example of how such a model would work in a single classroom.

What "Common Problems" Does This Address?

This intervention has been developed to help children who have not learned the appropriate behavior and are therefore unable to demonstrate it. The current brief was based on the presentation of Rathvon (2008).

Procedure

1. Say:
   a. Present each rule, one at a time to the students. Explain why it is important for the class to follow that rule.
      i. "Our first rule is to come to class on time and sit down at your desk so you are prepared to start the lesson. It is important to come to class on time so that you have the opportunity to learn from the lesson and you don't distract your classmates while they are trying to learn."
   b. Discuss examples and nonexamples of adherence. Students should understand what it would look like if they are following the rule.
      i. "When you are at your desk on time and prepared, working on the assigned lesson when bell rings, you are following this rule. Running to your desk as the bell rings is an example of "not" being ready for class on time.
2. Show:
   a. Demonstrate how to follow the rule. It is also acceptable to have a student model the rule.
      i. "Watch what I would look like if I were to come to class on time and be prepared to learn." Walk into the classroom, put all necessary materials for the day inside your desk, hang up your book bag, and sit quietly at your desk working on appropriate materials. "This is what coming to class on time and being prepared looks like."
3. Check:
   a. Ask students to watch your next demonstration to see whether there is anything wrong with what they watched. This will determine whether students grasp the rule and how to appropriately follow it.
      i. "Watch me now and see you if can find anything wrong with what I am doing." Run into the classroom, throw your book bag on the floor and go over to another student's desk and ask if you can borrow some paper and pencils. Then say, "Did I come on time to class and come prepared to learn?"

(cont.)

   b. Model again how to appropriately follow the rule (or have a student do it). Then ask the students what you did right that showed that you were following the rule.

      i. "Watch what I would look like if I were to come to class on time and be prepared to learn." Walk into the classroom, put all necessary materials for the day inside your desk, hang up your book bag, and sit quietly at your desk working on appropriate materials. "Is this what coming to class on time and being prepared looks like?"

   c. If a student demonstrated appropriate rule following to the class, reward him or her for doing so. Also, reward the class for being able to determine what appropriate rule following and inappropriate behaviors look like.

Critical Components That Must Be Implemented for the Intervention to Be Successful

- This intervention is a wonderful precursor to subsequent behavior management strategies. Applying this intervention alone will not promote rule adherence. Therefore, practice behavior management strategies consistently after implementation of this intervention (i.e., praising rule adherence, explicit consequences for not adhering to the rules).
- This intervention works best when implemented and practiced intensely at the beginning of the school year. However, frequent refresher sessions will be necessary to reteach the students how to properly adhere to classroom rules (i.e., following holiday breaks or other abrupt changes in the school day).
- Minimize the number of rules in the classroom (i.e., three to five) and keep rules and explanations developmentally appropriate.
- Orally present each rule to the class and what the rule would look like in the classroom.
- Explain why each rule is important in the classroom.
- Demonstrate how to adhere to each rule.
- Demonstrate what nonadherence looks like.
- Redemonstrate what proper adherence to the rule looks like and discuss why the demonstration was correct.
- Acknowledge the class for determining what appropriate rule following looks like.

Additional Information

Display the rules in the classroom where they can easily be spotted and referenced. Use caution when carrying out the inappropriate display of the rule portion of this intervention with students who are likely to increase negative behaviors in order to gain peer attention. This intervention also assumes that each student can demonstrate the ability to perform the desired behavior.

References

Rathvon, N. (2008). Say show check: Teaching classroom procedures. In *Effective school interventions: Evidence-based strategies for improving student outcomes* (pp. 81–83). New York: Guilford Press.

Sugai, G., Horner, R., & Lewis, T. (2009). *OSEP Technical Assistance Center on Effective Schoolwide Interventions: Positive behavioral interventions & supports*. Retrieved November 3, 2009, from *www.pbis. org*.

Wolfgang, C. H., & Wolfgang, M. E. (1995). *The three faces of discipline for early childhood: Empowering teachers and students* (pp. 223–225). Boston: Allyn & Bacon.

Note. The lead student developer on this brief was Sarah Raab, a graduate of the MA/CAS School Psychology Program at East Carolina University.

CHAPTER 9

Academic Fluency-Building
Interventions

OVERVIEW

Interventionists frequently underemphasize the importance of ensuring that a student reaches a fluency criterion before concluding that the intervention is complete because they assume that once a skill has been established (meaning the child can perform the skill accurately), the work of the intervention or instructor is done. Research data on human performance tell us otherwise (Johnson & Layng, 1992). Retention and application of learned skills are directly related to level of proficiency (Binder, 1996; Haughton, 1980). Athletes who want to reach and sustain higher levels of performance understand the importance of practice, and academic interventionists could learn from these successful athletes. Students demonstrate high-quality academic performance when they remember and successfully use strategies that they learned during previous instruction and adapt those skills to solve more complex problems. Perhaps one of the reasons skill proficiency is overlooked by many instructors is because of how we measure it. When we teach new skills, we measure quality of the child's performance and that is usually captured by measuring accuracy. When trying to teach a child to perform a skill correctly, it is logical to monitor whether the child's response was correct or incorrect and adjust instruction accordingly. However, the trouble with accuracy as a measurement metric is that once a student reaches 100% accuracy, there is nothing else that accuracy can tell us about the quality of that student's performance.

All teachers understand that one child may respond 100% accurately and have a lower-quality performance than another child who scores 100% accurately but answers confidently, immediately, and can elaborate on and explain the answers. For example, imagine asking two kindergarten students to name all 26 letters by showing them the letters on individual cards. If a student names the letter correctly within 2 seconds of presentation, then it is correct, and if he or she fails to do so, gives an incorrect response, or gives a correct response after 2 seconds, then it is wrong. One student may have no difficulty whatsoever and names

One child may respond 100% accurately and have a lower-quality performance than another child who scores 100% accurately but answers confidently, immediately, and can elaborate on and explain the answers.

each letter in less than 1 second each. Thus, he or she may have accomplished the task, in say, 18 seconds. Her classmate may also name all of them correctly, but he or she has to really think about it and takes just under 2 second each. He or she can name all of the letters correctly, but requires about 45 seconds to complete the task.

Both students received the same score (26 out of 26, or 100% correct), but the quality of the performances and the level of their skill are different. Research tells us we can add a timed dimension to the measurement to obtain more information about the child's proficiency (Binder, 1996). Figure 9.1 demonstrates how responses correct per minute can be used to sensitively reflect a student's progress during intervention even after accuracy has reached a measurement ceiling of 100%.

As noted in Chapter 2, one common cause of intervention failure is selecting the wrong intervention. Ongoing collection of student performance data is a cornerstone of effective instruction in most major policy documents (e.g., National Mathematics Advisory Panel, 2008; National Reading Panel, 2000). Consequently, we see a great deal of student assessment in today's classrooms. One of the authors of this book recently consulted in a kindergarten center and calculated that nearly 15% of the minutes available in a school day were spent conducting student assessment. Assessment is important, but only if it directly improves student learning. The trouble with assessment in most schools is that the resulting data are underutilized and interventions are selected because they happen to be available in the school, are easy to implement, or are familiar to the teacher.

To accelerate student learning, we must know what skills the student can perform and whether the performance is accurate and fluent. Chapters 1 and 2 described how to conduct assessment needed to determine whether a student's skills are accurate and fluent.

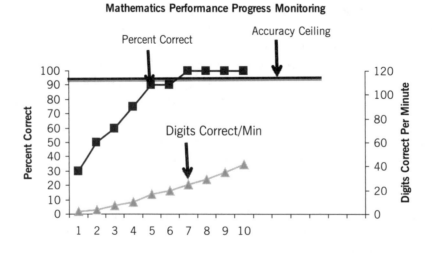

FIGURE 9.1. Monitoring progress with fluency beyond accuracy.

Chapter 7 describes how to plan and deliver acquisition interventions that are designed to establish accurate skill performance (appropriate for skills for which student responding is not yet accurate). The current chapter describes how to build skill fluency to ensure that a child masters a skill before concluding that instruction is complete. That is, once a student has acquired a skill and can perform it accurately, the next stage of instruction should be designed to build fluency.

Fluency-building interventions are indicated when the child's performance is slow but accurate. As discussed in Chapter 2, sampling back through a hierarchy of related sub-skills to identify dysfluent skills provides the instructor or interventionist with a starting place for intervention. Interventions and instructional strategies that are appropriate when building accuracy for a skill (or establishing a new skill) become counterproductive when the student is ready for fluency building and vice versa. Although immediate feedback is critical in acquiring a skill, once a child can respond accurately without adult assistance, it makes little sense to interrupt the child to say that he or she has responded correctly. Similarly, it makes little sense to provide unnecessary cues and prompts or modeling of correct responding. Finally, monitoring accuracy has little meaning because the student cannot ever become more accurate than 100%.

> **Although immediate feedback is critical to acquiring a skill, once a child can respond accurately without adult assistance, it makes little sense to interrupt the child to say that he or she has responded correctly.**

Before further discussing fluency interventions, we need to clarify our use of the term. Unfortunately, "fluency" is used in many different ways within the educational community. The term has become quite common among reading interventionists because the National Reading Panel (2000) defined reading fluency as quick and accurate reading with appropriate expression, and identified it as a critical component of reading instruction. We also recognize the importance of reading fluency and include interventions to address it. However, the purpose of this chapter is to discuss academic fluency, which is the accurate and rapid performance of any academic behavior (Binder, 1996). We attempt to differentiate by referring specifically to reading fluency.

CONTROLLED PRACTICE

At the fluency-building stage of learning, students should be provided with content that is controlled to reflect a level of difficulty for which student responding can remain accurate. The key to effective fluency-building instruction or intervention is to provide uninterrupted periods of sustained, productive practice. Instruction can be segmented into opportunities to respond, or learning trials, that refer to discrete occasions when a task is presented, the child responds, response quality is evaluated, and corrective feedback is provided as needed. The number of these segments that a child experiences during instruction is strongly related to the level of achievement the child attains, even after controlling for risk factors like poverty status (Greenwood, Delquadri, & Hall, 1984; Greenwood, 1991). Stated

> **To improve learning, you want to increase the number of appropriate opportunities to respond, or learning trials, that a student experiences.**

another way, if you want to improve learning, you want to increase the number of appropriate opportunities to respond, or learning trials, that a student experiences during instruction. For most tasks (e.g., spelling, letter sounds, multiplication facts), controlled practice is accomplished by using material in which the student can correctly answer 90% of the items (Burns, 2004), but reading connected text for comprehension requires that the student effortlessly reads 93 to 97% of the words (Gicling & Armstrong, 1978; Treptow et al., 2007).

One word of caution may be important here. When we say "uninterrupted practice periods" we are talking about brief timed intervals of practice that last no longer than 5 minutes for most tasks. When building skill proficiency, it is more effective to offer short intervals of practice as often as possible than to provide long intervals on less frequent occasions even though the total amount of time may be equivalent. Runners who want to increase their speed commonly use interval training where they practice running at a faster speed for short intervals. Over time, this builds their overall speed and ability to sustain a higher speed for longer periods of time. Academic skills function the same way. Logically, shorter intervals are more productive because the quality of responding that can be maintained is much higher because the student does not have to maintain it for very long on any given occasion.

MONITORING PROGRESS

The final phase of any intervention effort should be to evaluate the effectiveness of the intervention, but just like the intervention must match the student's deficit, the assessment data should reflect the intervention. The second book in this series will provide much more information about monitoring student progress, but it is worth briefly discussing here as well. To reflect improvements from session to session, interventionists should monitor responses correct per minute as an indicator of proficiency. This metric retains the accuracy component (you are recording correct responses) but adds a timed dimension to reflect gains in proficiency with time and instruction. Setting a goal for performance and providing small rewards for beating one's last highest score are powerful motivating conditions to accelerate performance during fluency-building instruction. Graphing student progress over time is important to facilitate goal setting and communicate progress to the student. Finally, delayed error correction can be tolerated (because errors should be rare) and can happen following the uninterrupted practice period.

CONCLUSION

One of the most common instruction or intervention errors made in school is failing to ensure that a student reaches a fluency criterion before advancing instructional content or intervention difficulty. Fluent performance is associated with retention of learned skills and the ability to apply the learned skill to solve more complex related problems. Effective fluency-building intervention strategies include strategies to increase practice oppor-

> **One of the most common instruction or intervention errors is failing to ensure that a student reaches a fluency criterion before advancing instructional content or intervention difficulty.**

tunities, strategies to shape more proficient or higher-quality responding, and strategies to maximize motivation. We offer several research-based strategies to build fluent skill performance including response card, flash card, timed trial, incremental rehearsal, word building, word sort, the "ship is loaded" game (to build phonetic awareness) task interspersal, and mystery motivator on pages 126–141.

Increasing Practice Opportunities: Response Card

Brief Description

This intervention is designed to build fluency by increasing student opportunities to respond (Gardner, Heward, & Grossi, 1994). This intervention can be used classwide, in small groups, or individually. Students are provided with a set of printed "response cards" on which answer choices are printed. When the teacher presents the problem, students select the correct card and hold it up for the teacher to see. This allows all students to respond at the same time and therefore makes it possible for students to respond at much higher rates than if they had to take turns. Use of response cards also allows the teacher to scan and ensure that student responding remains accurate during each instructional session. Teachers can use small whiteboards on which students write answers in a modified version of this protocol. Requires approximately 10 minutes each day.

What "Common Problems" Does This Address?

This intervention protocol is useful for building fluency for counting and number naming.

Procedure

Complete these steps every day.

1. Sit with child in a quiet corner of the classroom.

2. Set timer for 3 minutes.

3. Arrange number cards face up in front of the student. Put the number cards in order from lowest to highest, left to right.

4. Shake counters in a cup and pour some or all onto the floor or desk.

5. Ask child to show the card with the number (choose a number between 10 and 20).

6. If the child holds up the incorrect card, say: "Is that a _____ (name the number)? Try again." If the child does not respond correctly, say: "Let's find the _____ (name the number) together" and find the card together.

7. If the child requires assistance to find the correct number card more than once during the 3-minute session, then this intervention is probably too difficult and should be adjusted (either target number naming, or reduce counting difficulty to smaller set sizes until the child can respond correctly before using this intervention).

8. When the timer rings, tell the student to stop working.

(cont.)

Materials

- Digital countdown timer.
- The intervention protocol.
- Number cards 10–20.

Reference

Gardner, R., III, Heward, W. L., & Grossi, T. A. (1994). Effects of response cards on student participation and academic achievement: A systematic replication with inner-city students during whole-class science instruction. *Journal of Applied Behavior Analysis, 27*, 63–71.

Increasing Practice Opportunities: Flash Card Intervention

Brief Description

The purpose of this intervention is to build fluency for basic facts and items that must be committed to memory once a student conceptually understands how to solve a problem. This intervention can be used classwide, in small groups, or individually. Requires approximately 5 minutes each day.

What "Common Problems" Does This Address?

This intervention can be used for skills that must be memorized. So this intervention can be used for addition, subtraction, multiplication, or division facts, for example.

Procedure

Complete these steps every day.

1. Get out flash cards.
2. Set timer for 3 minutes. Present the flash cards and ask the student to give the answer to the problems as quickly as possible. Prompt and correct any missed answers. When the time is up, review missed problems.

Instruct student to do the following:

3. Write name and date on math sheet.
4. Set timer for 2 minutes.
5. Work problems for 2 minutes.
6. When timer rings, stop working.
7. Score your paper with the answer key or teacher's help.
8. Count number of problems you got right. Correct your mistakes.
9. Write score at the top of math sheet.
10. Write score on your progress monitoring chart (see Form 3.2 at the end of Chapter 3).
11. Did you beat your score? Circle "yes" or "no" on the monitoring chart.
12. If you beat your score, choose a reward.

Materials

- Five math probes (i.e., worksheets containing math problems for the target skill).
- Timer.
- Monitoring chart. Review progress and change materials weekly.

Reference

Codding, R. S., Burns, M. K., & Lukito, G. (2011). Meta-analysis of mathematic basic-fact fluency interventions: A component analysis. *Learning Disabilities Research and Practice, 26,* 36–47.

Increasing Practice Opportunities: Timed Trial

Brief Description

This intervention is versatile and can be used to build fluency for tasks that require multiple steps, like more involved mathematics computations, but can also be used to build fluency for simpler operations like math facts. Requires approximately 7 minutes each day.

What "Common Problems" Does This Address?

This intervention is designed to build math operation fluency, but can easily be adapted to work on spelling, reading, or writing skills.

Procedure

Instruct student to complete these steps every day.

1. Get out materials.
2. Write name and date on math sheet.
3. Work all the problems above the line on the worksheet with your teacher's or tutor's help.
4. Set timer for 2 minutes. Use paper to cover the practice problems above the line.
5. Work problems below the practice line for 2 minutes.
6. When timer rings, stop working.
7. Score your paper with the answer key or teacher's help.
8. Count the number of problems you got right. Write the correct answer for the problems you missed.
9. Write score at the top of math sheet.
10. Write score on your progress monitoring chart (see Form 3.2 at the end of Chapter 3).
11. Did you beat your score? Circle "yes" or "no" on the monitoring chart.
12. If you beat your score, choose a reward from your reward menu.

Materials

- Five math probes (i.e., worksheets containing math problems for the problem skill).
- Timer.
- Monitoring chart.

Reference

Ardoin, S. P., Williams, J. C., Klubnik, C., & McCall, M. (2009). Three versus six rereadings of practice passages. *Journal of Applied Behavior Analysis, 42*, 375–380.

Increasing Practice Opportunities: Incremental Rehearsal

Brief Description

Much like many interventions, incremental rehearsal can be used to address different stages of learning. In this example, the intervention is designed to rapidly build fluency for any skill that requires memorization by systematic fading in of unknown with known items. The gradual and systematic addition of unknown items across sessions ensures a high rate of accuracy during responding and therefore a high rate of successful practice. This intervention also reviews previously mastered items within and across sessions to promote retention of previously mastered items.

What "Common Problems" Does This Address?

This intervention is designed to build fluency for sight words. Requires less than 10 minutes each day. Child must know *I, am, to, a*, and *the* to begin this intervention displayed in the List of Words following this form.

Procedure

Complete these steps every day.

1. Sit with child in a quiet corner of the classroom.
2. Say: "I am going to show you some words. When I point to a word, you say it out loud. OK? Let's begin." Point to the first word. This will be a "known" word (e.g., *I* in the List of Words for Incremental Rehearsal). When the child responds correctly, point to the second word. This will be an unknown word (e.g., *little* in the list). If the child does not respond, tell the child, "Say (insert word)."
3. Continue pointing to each word from top to bottom exactly in the order that they are printed. Go through the list of words three times. The order is important—do not mix them up!
4. On the last run-through, keep track of the "unknown" word. Did the child get that word right all three times? Note this on the progress monitoring chart (see Form 3.2 at the end of Chapter 3). This step is very important because it will tell us what to do tomorrow.
5. Complete the sight-word assessment.

Materials

- The intervention protocol.
- Materials for practicing responding (see first day's materials on next page).
- Progress monitoring chart and a weekly progress monitoring probe.

References

Codding, R. S., Archer, J., & Connell, J. (2010). A systematic replication and extension of using incremental rehearsal to improve multiplication skills: An investigation of generalization. *Journal of Behavioral Education, 19*, 93–105.

MacQuarrie-Klender, L. L., Tucker, J. A., Burns, M. K., & Hartman, B. (2002). Comparison of retention rates using traditional, drill sandwich, and incremental rehearsal flashcard methods. *School Psychology Review, 31*, 584–595.

(cont.)

List of Words for Incremental Rehearsal with *Little* as the Target Unknown Word

	Trial 1		Trial 2		Trial 3
	Little		Little		little
	I		I		I
	Little		Little		little
	I		I		I
	Am		Am		am
	Little		Little		little
	I		I		I
	Am		Am		am
	To		To		to
	Little		Little		little
	I		I		I
	Am		Am		am
	To		To		to
	A		A		a
	Little		Little		little
	I		I		I
	Am		Am		am
	To		To		to
	A		A		a
	The		The		the

Accelerating Task Difficulty: Word Building

Brief Description

Word building is a reading intervention designed by Beck (Beck, 1989; Beck & Hamilton, 2000) to improve decoding skills. This intervention directs attention to each grapheme position within a word through a procedure of progressive minimal pairing of words that differ by one grapheme. A grapheme is the letter or letter combinations that represent one phoneme. For example, the grapheme *ph* is represented by the phoneme /f/ in the word *graph*.

What "Common Problems" Does This Address?

This is a phonics intervention that allows students to practice using letter sounds to make words. It is appropriate for children who have learned a high number of sounds, but need additional practice in putting the sounds together to make words.

Procedure

1. At the beginning of each lesson, each child is presented with several letter cards.
2. After creating an initial word with the letter cards, children are then instructed to change a certain letter card (e.g., take away *p* and put *t* in its place) and then to read the newly formed word.
3. As the lesson progresses, instructions will focus the child's attention on different positions in the word form. This is done by holding constant the other letters from the previous word. The following is an example of a word chain, with the new grapheme card (letter) in each trial being capitalized to show the word transformations in each trial: sat, saP, Tap, tOp, toT, Pot, pAt, Sat, sPat, patS, paSt, pat, pOt, poP, Top, Stop.
4. After completing a word-building sequence, each child is administered a brief flash card assessment to determine whether the child could read at least 80% of that lesson's words correctly.
5. If not, word-building activities continue using the same words.
6. Each lesson is concluded with a sentence-reading activity that contains a high proportion of words that had just been decoded. Using the example above, a sentence could read, "Can a sap tap on top pop and stop?" Often the sentence will not make sense, and after the child successfully reads the sentence, the interventionist and child engage in a playful discussion about what the sentence could mean.

Critical Components That Must Be Implemented for the Intervention to Be Successful

In order for this intervention to work, students must receive immediate feedback about the accuracy of their response. In addition, the letter changes occur so that attention is drawn to each position of a word form. Therefore, be sure not to change the same letter placement two consecutive times (e.g., sat and then *h*at).

(cont.)

Materials

- Small cards with letters on them.
- Flash cards with the created words on them.
- Reinforcers as needed.

References

Beck, I. (1989). *Reading today and tomorrow: Teacher's editions for grades 1 and 2*. Austin, TX: Holt.

Beck, I., & Hamilton, R. (2000). *Beginning reading module*. Washington DC: American Federation of Teachers.

McCandliss, B., Beck, I. L., Sandak R., & Perfetti, C. (2003). Focusing attention on decoding skills for children with poor reading skills: Design and preliminary tests of the word building intervention. *Scientific Studies of Reading, 7*, 75–104.

Decoding: Word Sort

Brief Description

Word sorts have become a popular approach for analyzing words to learn decoding skills. It essentially involves having the student sort cards into three stacks according to a graphophonemic component such as a letter or letter-combination sound. There are several advantages of word sorts: they can be done with small or even large groups, are quite straightforward and easy to implement, and can be used with simple letter-sound correspondences to advanced letter combinations commonly taught to older students such as "cracy" (e.g., democracy and aristocracy) and "archy" (e.g., anarchy and hierarchy). There are also a series of word sorts published for various populations (e.g., English-language learners) and skills (e.g., vocabulary and spelling) from the *Words Their Way* series (Bear, Invernizzi, Templeton, & Johnston, 2010) that are quite useful, but this brief addresses the more generic sequence to practice decoding skills.

What "Common Problem" Does This Address?

Word sorts are appropriate for students who can complete the tasks accurately but require additional practice. It is ideal for a student who can identify the correct sounds for the letters with 90% accuracy or higher, but who needs additional practice actually using the sounds to read words.

Procedure

Word sorts are highly flexible and can be easily individualized. The example on page 136 could be used with older students, but simpler sorts could be used as well.

1. Identify three target sounds and find six words that uniquely contain each target sound.
2. Write the words on cards.
3. Select one example of each of the target sounds and place the card on a table in a row ("An*archy*," "Demo*cracy*," and "Punc*tuate*" on the last page).
4. Read each card to the student and point to the target sounds. For example, point to "Anarchy," read the word, point to "archy" and say: "This part sounds like arke. Please say arke as in *anarchy*. Good, *anarchy*." Correct and repeat as needed.
5. Model the task first for the student by completing a second row directly beneath the top row. For example, hold up the word *Hierarchy* and say: "This is *hierarchy*. Does it look more like *anarchy, democracy*, or *punctuate*? I think that it looks most like *anarchy* because it ends in *archy*. This word is *autocracy*. Does it look more like *anarchy, democracy*, or *punctuate*? I think it looks most like *democracy* because it ends in *cracy*. This word is *situate*. Does it look most like *anarchy, democracy*, or *punctuate*? I think it looks most like *punctuate* because it ends in *tuate*." Be sure to say the sounds rather than the letters while pointing to the letters.
6. Give the student three cards with one example of each sound (e.g., "Panarchy," "Theocracy," and "Habituate") and ask him or her to put the cards into the appropriate column according to the target words at the top. Give the student feedback after each one.
7. Give the student the remaining nine cards and ask him or her to sort them into the three columns.
8. Give the student feedback after he or she has sorted the nine cards.

(cont.)

Critical Components That Must Be Implemented for the Intervention to Be Successful

This is a fluency intervention for decoding. Thus, the student should know the sounds being practiced and the other sounds that make up the words.

Materials

- Cards on which to write words.
- Three target sounds with six examples of each sound.
- Reinforcers as needed.

References

Bear, D. R., Invernizzi, M., Templeton, S. R., & Johnston, F. (2003). *Words their way: Word study for phonics, vocabulary, and spelling instruction.* Upper Saddle River, NJ: Prentice Hall.

Joseph, L. M. (2000). Developing first graders' phonemic awareness, word identification, and spelling: A comparison of two contemporary phonic instructional approaches. *Literacy Research and Instruction, 39,* 160–169.

Joseph, L. M. (2002). Helping children link sound to print: Phonics procedures for small-group or whole-class settings. *Intervention in School and Clinic, 37,* 217–221.

(cont.)

Sample Word Sort for Decoding

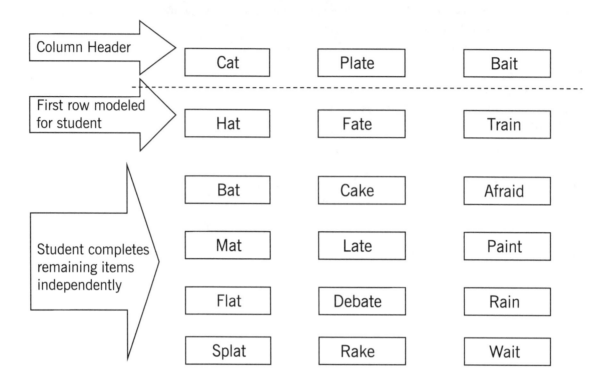

Column Header

| Cat | Plate | Bait |

First row modeled for student

| Hat | Fate | Train |

Student completes remaining items independently

Bat	Cake	Afraid
Mat	Late	Paint
Flat	Debate	Rain
Splat	Rake	Wait

Phonemic Awareness: "The Ship Is Loaded" Game

Brief Description

Phonemic awareness is the knowledge that words are made up of individual sounds. "The Ship Is Loaded" game is an easy way to have students practice manipulating sounds. This activity requires a small group of students who sit in a circle, toss a small soft object (e.g., bean bag), and practice rhyming words.

What "Common Problems" Does This Address?

This intervention is for students who struggle with the basic foundations of reading. Thus, it is likely most appropriate for young children.

Procedure

1. Have four or five students sit in a circle on the floor.
2. The teacher begins by explaining the game and the rules.
3. The teacher then says: "The ship is loaded with" and then selects a single-syllable word with the target sound. For example, *nails* could be used, but it does not need to be a word that is exactly semantically correct (e.g., *holes, mats*, etc. would be fine).
4. Next, the teacher gently tosses the ball to one of the students who then restates the sentence "The ship is loaded with" and then finishes the sentence with a different word that rhymes.
5. If the word rhymes, then praise the student by saying: "Yes, (word) rhymes with nails." If the word is incorrect, then provide positively worded corrective feedback.
6. The student then tosses the object to a different student who states the starting sentence and provides a different ending word that rhymes with the pattern word. Praise each correct response.
7. Continue the game until each student takes a correct turn.

Critical Components That Must Be Implemented for the Intervention to Be Successful

This is designed to build phonemic awareness fluency. Thus, the students should understand the idea of rhyming and be able to do it with some proficiency. It is also very important that this activity be treated as a game with positive feedback and praise.

Materials

- Small soft object such as a bean bag.
- Target words to start the activity.

Reference

Adams, M. J., Foorman, B. R., Lundberg, I., & Beeler, T. (1998). *Phonemic awareness in young children: A classroom curriculum.* Baltimore, MD: Brookes.

Maximizing Motivation to Respond: Task Interspersal

Brief Description

This intervention provides students increased opportunities for success by interspersing simple problems with more challenging "target" problems (Robinson & Skinner, 2002). The simple problems can either be added to the list of target problems (additive interspersal) or can replace a portion of them (substitutive interspersal; Hawkins, Skinner, & Oliver, 2005). Hawkins and colleagues recommend additive interspersal, as it does not reduce exposure to target problems.

What "Common Problem" Does This Address?

The interspersal technique is appropriate for students who correctly complete a high percentage of items but do not recall them quickly enough. Moreover, students' self-efficacy and motivation may increase with opportunities to succeed on the interspersed easier problems (Montarello & Martens, 2005). Thus, the interspersal technique may also help students with low motivation to complete math problems.

Procedure

Similar methods were used across studies that investigated interspersal interventions. These guidelines use interspersal rates shown to be most effective in increasing accuracy, speed, and task persistence for math computation (Hawkins et al., 2005; Montarello & Martens, 2005).

1. Identify the type(s) of problem that is difficult for the student by reviewing student work or through curriculum-based assessments.
2. Next, identify a type of problem that the student has mastered. Problems in this category should be done accurately and quickly. These problems are also referred to as simple or known problems.
3. Create a series of math computation worksheets with known computation problems interspersed at a fixed rate throughout the more challenging problems. When worksheets will be completed during independent seatwork or as homework, the ratio of challenging and known problems should be 1:1 (Hawkins et al., 2005). Every challenging problem is followed by a known problem. If the problems will be read aloud and the student must solve them mentally without showing work, then the ratio of challenging problems to known problems should be 3:1 (Hawkins et al., 2005). Every third challenging problem is followed by one the student has already mastered. A free online application is available for completing this step at *www.interventioncentral.org*.
4. Montarello and Martens (2005) found that adding a tangible reinforcement to interspersal increased the effectiveness of the intervention. If reinforcement is added, students should be allowed a choice of rewards and be aware of the score they must reach to get the reward (Montarello & Martens, 2005).
5. To monitor progress, count total digits correct (TDC) for target problems. Do not count TDC for known problems, as this would inaccurately inflate students' scores (Hawkins et al., 2005). Allow the same amount of work time during intervention (such as 10 minutes) so that results can be compared across sessions (Montarello & Martens, 2005) and improvement can be monitored.

(cont.)

Critical Components That Must Be Implemented for the Intervention to Be Successful

In order for this intervention to work, the students must be able to complete problems with a high level of accuracy. Rehearsing problems that the student does not conceptually understand may eventually impede a student's ability to complete more advanced applications of the math facts. The research is unclear as to how many easy problems should be interspersed, but a ratio of perhaps one target to one easy problem is best for students with low motivation.

Materials

- A list of easy problems that the student can complete quickly and effortlessly.
- A list of target problems.
- Worksheets with easy problems interspersed within the target problems.
- A pencil for the student.
- Reinforcers as needed.

References

Hawkins, J., Skinner, C. H., & Oliver, R. (2005). The effects of task demands and additive interspersal ratios on fifth-grade students' mathematics accuracy. *School Psychology Review, 34,* 543–555.

Montarello, S., & Martens, B. K. (2005). Effects of interspersed brief problems on students' endurance at completing math work. *Journal of Behavioral Education, 14,* 249–266.

Robinson, S. L., & Skinner, C. H. (2002). Interspersing additional easier items to enhance mathematics performance on subtests requiring different task demands. *School Psychology Quarterly, 17,* 191–205.

Note. The lead student developer on this brief was Elizabeth Hagen, a graduate student in the PhD School Psychology Program at the University of Minnesota.

Maximizing Motivation to Respond: Mystery Motivator

Brief Description

This intervention is designed to provide students with the opportunity to earn activity or free time for increasing the number of questions correct during a reading class.

What "Common Problems" Does This Address?

This intervention maximizes motivation for students who need additional practice to become fluent in instructional tasks like reading, writing, and mathematical problem solving.

Procedure

Complete these steps every day.

1. Ask the student to pick out three or four rewards or activities that he or she would be willing to earn for good work during reading class. The interventionist provides a list of possible rewards.
2. At the beginning of the week, construct a mystery motivator chart (see Chapter 10, pages 161–162) using a magic marker "changeables" set. These magic markers are the ones that allow you to make a mark in ink that is invisible until the student colors over it with another marker from the set.
3. Explain to the student that his or her goal is to beat his or her last best score.
4. On the mystery motivator chart, write 0, 3, or 5 minutes in the stars. This is the amount of time the student can earn with the fun activity if he or she makes his or her reading goal. Write more 3's and 5's when first starting this procedure. This ensures that the student will earn activity time quickly.
5. Place the mystery motivator chart on the student's desk during reading class.
6. Remind the student that he or she is given the chance to earn activity time for beating his or her last highest score during the session.
7. Finish the instructional period with a timed test of the task that can be scored as responses correct per minute (e.g., correctly circled words in a maze passage, digits correct per 2 minutes).
8. Correct the student's work. If the student beat his or her last best score, allow the student to color in a star on the mystery motivator chart. The teacher may also reteach any needed steps at this time and guide the student to correct any errors that may have been made.
9. Ask the student to write his or her score on the motivator chart.
10. Give the student the earned activity time as soon as possible.

Critical Components That Must Be Implemented for the Intervention to Be Successful

Be certain that the behavioral expectations are clear and concise. Clarify expectations vividly when writing them. Ask yourself: If a stranger read these expectations would he or she be able to pick out the students who are doing what I expect in my class? Give the student multiple opportunities to be successful.

(cont.)

Materials

- Preferred reinforcing stimuli list.
- Magic markers "changeables" set.
- Reinforcers.
- Mystery motivator chart.

References

Jenson, W. A., Rhode, G., & Reavis, H. K. (1994). *The tough kid tool box*. Boulder, CO: Sopris West.

Moore, L. A., Waguespack, A. M., Wickstrom, K. F., Witt, J. C., & Gaydos, G. G. (1994). Mystery motivator: An effective and time efficient intervention. *School Psychology, 23*, 106–118.

CHAPTER 10

Behavioral Proficiency-Building Interventions

OVERVIEW

In Chapter 8 the primary intervention goal was promoting acquisition of appropriate behavior. Like developing academic skills, the behavioral learning process does not end after a child first demonstrates that he or she has acquired a target behavior. Once the target behavior has been acquired, the focus should be turned to maximizing the proficiency at which the child displays the appropriate behavior. Ideally when a behavioral intervention is implemented, a child will attend to environmental stimuli and respond quickly with an accurate demonstration of the desired behavior. However, establishing rapid and accurate responses to environmental cues sometimes requires mastering several skills. For example, teaching a child appropriate hand-raising behavior involves three steps. First, the child learns how to raise his or her hand. Second, the child learns the appropriate time and place in which to raise his or her hand. Third, the child learns how to wait quietly for acknowledgment from an adult before speaking out loud. The child may learn the first step (how to raise his or her hand) in a short amount of time, but may require a longer period of time to learn the second step (under what conditions it is appropriate to raise his or her hand) and even longer to learn how to demonstrate the third step (how to wait quietly for acknowledgment from an adult before asking a question).

After a behavior is acquired, educational professionals often expect that the child will always demonstrate that behavior appropriately. Unfortunately, appropriate behavior is unlikely to be consistently displayed without the implementation of effective contingency management strategies. In this chapter we focus on individual interventions that are designed to increase the proficiency of desired behavior. When a child has become proficient with a trained behavioral skill, the child can readily and accurately display the behavior

> **Establishing rapid and accurate responses to environmental cues sometimes requires mastering several skills.**

under the right conditions (e.g., raise hand during appropriate times and wait to be acknowledged to speak).

IS THE CHILD READY FOR PROFICIENCY-BUILDING INTERVENTIONS?

The first step in promoting proficiency through behavioral technology is to make sure that the child has already acquired the target behavior. This is a critical step because behavioral proficiency interventions assume the child has the ability to perform the target behavior. If the child cannot perform the target behavior (i.e., cannot raise his or her hand), implementation of a proficiency intervention will not work. If a child has not acquired the target behavior, refer back to the behavioral interventions in Chapter 8.

Educational professionals should also consider whether or not the child has the capabilities to reach goals indicative of behavioral proficiency. For example, an unreasonable goal would be expecting a loud, energetic 3-year-old child to sit quietly for 30 minutes. As with any intervention, it is critical that the behavioral goal be realistic and that it considers the characteristics of the target child. One rule of thumb is to consider what the child readily does before the intervention and what his or her peers who are successful in the classroom readily do. Requiring the child to improve 20% over his or her baseline with the ultimate goal of performing similarly to not-at-risk peers is a good place to start.

> **One rule of thumb is to consider what the child readily does before the intervention and what his or her peers who are successful in the classroom readily do.**

Behaviors Happen for a Reason

Educational professionals often either focus exclusively on the target child or on the problematic behavior that the child is exhibiting. Unfortunately, understanding the reasons why a child is behaving in a particular manner is impossible when the focus is exclusively on the child and his or her behavior.

While a detailed description of a behavior (what it looks like, what it sounds like, how distressing it is to peers, parents, and teachers) is interesting, it unfortunately does not provide enough information to arrive at an effective intervention (Skinner, 1983). A behavior is best understood by considering what happens before and after the behavior is exhibited. Considering the events that precede the behavior (called antecedents) and the events that follow behavior (called consequences) we can begin to understand "why" the behavior is useful to the child or stated another way, what the function of the behavior is. This combination is often referred to as the ABCs (antecedent–behavior–consequence) of understanding the reason for a particular behavior.

Understanding the function of the behavior allows those who want to change behavior to alter the antecedents and consequences to weaken the function as well as teach and reinforce a replacement behavior. When a child is noncompliant during instructional routines, the purpose of behavioral assessment is to understand what function the noncompliance serves for the child. When noncompliance is preceded by a particular task at a certain level of difficulty and followed by escape from that task, then one possible reason for the noncompliance is that it allows the child to escape doing a nonpreferred or difficult task. A difficult task is the discriminative stimulus signaling that noncompliance will be reinforced and escape from the task (e.g., removal from the classroom) is the consequence that reinforces the behavior and makes it more probable in the future.

Knowing the function of the behavior leads directly to interventions designed to (1) weaken the response–reinforcer relationship, and (2) strengthen more adaptive response–reinforcer relationships in the classroom. Accomplishing the above objectives becomes pretty formulaic once the conditions maintaining the behavior are known. Interventionists can train replacement behaviors, prevent the child from obtaining escape when the child is noncompliant, reduce the child's motivation to be noncompliant by reducing task difficulty, and so on. The scientific basis for identifying functions of behavior and building behavioral interventions is called operant conditioning, which has a long and well-established history. As such, it is critical for educational professionals to have a working understanding of the reinforcing and punishing properties of behavioral antecedents and consequences.

ANTECEDENTS TO BEHAVIORS

Antecedents to behaviors are important to understand because they are the events or stimuli in the environment that signal or cue the student that reinforcement will be available for a certain behavior and therefore increase the probability of the occurrence of a behavior. Antecedents help a child identify that demonstrating a particular behavior in a particular situation will result in a particular response. For example, consider two teachers. Teacher A has a history of responding immediately to children when they speak without permission. Teacher B has a history of ignoring children when they speak without permission and will only respond to children who speak when they raise their hand. Students who have experiences with both teachers will be more likely to speak without permission when teacher A is present and less likely to speak without permission when teacher B is present. In this case the antecedent is helping the child discriminate between the two teachers so that he or she knows how to obtain the teacher's attention when he or she wants to speak aloud in class. As we note below, understanding antecedents (the "A" of the ABCs of behavior) lays the foundation for several intervention opportunities.

CONSEQUENCES OF BEHAVIORS

At the heart of understanding the reasons why a child behaves in a particular way is the question "What does the child gain when he or she engages in that behavior?" All behavior is motivated by something. In the most basic terms, children will exhibit a target behavior in order to gain something that is desired or to avoid something aversive. On the flip side, children will not engage in a target behavior if that behavior results in an aversive consequence or if the behavior results in the loss of something that is desired. Consequences of behavior are typically referred to

> **At the heart of understanding why a child behaves in a particular way is the question "What does the child gain when he or she engages in that behavior?"**

as positive reinforcement, negative reinforcement, positive punishment, and negative punishment. Before moving forward it is important to consider these terms. For the purpose of this book we talk about these terms from the perspective of the target child and the person who is implementing the intervention.

Each of these terms begins with a word to describe the action being taken. *Positive* refers to the addition of something. One should not assume that positive means pleasant or good in this case. Rather, the behavioral meaning of positive is based on the notion of addition (adding something to an environment). Alternatively, *negative* refers to the removal of something. The removal of something in this case could be defined as pleasant (e.g., the removal of an unpleasant sensation like hunger) or as unpleasant (e.g., the removal of a desired object like a cell phone).

The second word in each term describes the impact of the addition or removal of the stimulus. *Reinforcement* refers to an addition of something to the environment or removal of something from the environment that increases the likelihood that the target behavior will persist or increase. Although we can predict the reinforcing value of something that may be positive or negative, the designation of whether or not something is reinforcing can only be made after the addition or removal of something results in subsequent persistence or increases in the target behavior. *Punishment* refers to the addition of something to the environment or removal of something from the environment that decreases the rate of a target behavior. In the same way that we do when we designate reinforcement, we can guess as to what consequences would reduce a behavior, but whether something is punishing can only be defined by whether the target behavior decreases or diminishes when the stimulus is added or taken away. If a behavior increased after a consequence, it was reinforced, if it decreased, it was punished. Using these definitions, there are four resulting terms.

Positive Reinforcement

When something has been added to the environment after a behavior has occurred that results in an *increase* in the frequency or intensity of the behavior of interest, we call it positive reinforcement. For example, we may want to increase the likelihood that a student completes his or her homework. This student may be given a sticker each day that he or she brings the completed homework to school. If giving the student a sticker increases the likelihood that he or she will complete homework in the future, then giving him or her a sticker would be a form of positive reinforcement. Remember, when we are discussing behavioral principles, positive does not mean "good," it is simply another word for "adding."

Negative Reinforcement

When something has been taken away from the environment after a behavior has occurred that *increases* the frequency or intensity of the behavior of interest, we call it negative reinforcement. For example, a student may not want to finish his or her homework. The student cries and the parents give him or her a break from homework that they fear is overwhelming the student emotionally. If the removal of homework increases the likelihood that the student will cry again in the future, then the removal of homework would be considered negative reinforcement. Remember, when we are discussing principles of behavior, negative does not mean "bad," it simply is another word for "removal."

Positive Punishment

When something has been added to the environment after a behavior has occurred that results in a *decrease* in the frequency or intensity of the behavior of interest, we call it positive punishment. For example, we may want to decrease the likelihood that a student cries when he or she doesn't want to do math homework. When the student cries, we add more math problems to the homework assignment. If adding more math problems to the homework assignment *decreases* the likelihood that he or she will cry in the future, then adding more math problems to the homework assignment is a form of positive punishment. Remember, when we are discussing behavioral principles, positive does not mean "good," it is simply another word for "adding."

Negative Punishment

When something has been taken away from the environment after a behavior has occurred that *decreases* the frequency or intensity of the behavior of interest, we call it negative punishment. For example, we may want to decrease the likelihood that a student cries when he or she doesn't want to do math homework. When the student cries, we take away access to his or her favorite music or TV show. If taking away access to the favorite music or TV show *decreases* the likelihood that the student will cry the next time he or she is asked to do math homework, then the removal of watching TV or listening to music is a form of negative punishment. Remember, when we are discussing principles of behavior, negative does not mean "bad," it simply is another word for "removal."

When the goal is to increase the occurrence of a behavior, reinforcement (either positive or negative) should be used. When the goal is to decrease the occurrence of a behavior, punishment (either positive or negative) can be used. Changing behavior through the use of reinforcement is a rather straightforward (not easy, but straightforward if implementers are willing to do the work) process that requires one to select an appropriate reinforcer and a suitable schedule of reinforcement.

In contrast, the use of punishment deserves some special cautions. Two possible side effects from punishment include overall behavior suppression and the occurrence of more problematic behaviors when the first problem behavior is punished. At the core of knowing how to decrease problematic behavior is the understanding that all behavior has function. In other words, people engage in behavior in order to achieve a certain result. For example, children shopping with their parents in a grocery store may throw a tantrum to gain candy (attain something desired) or to leave the store (escape from something undesirable).

> **The use of punishment deserves some special cautions.**

While much of the focus of this chapter is on the addition of reinforcement or punishment, it is also important to remove reinforcement for an inappropriate behavior. It should be understood that as any displayed behavior is by definition reinforced, said reinforcement needs to be removed or the behavior will likely continue. The technical term for the systematic removal of reinforcement from a previously reinforced behavior is *extinction* (Cooper, Heron, & Heward, 2007). There are a number of issues that should be addressed when considering extinction procedures. First, there are likely a number of reinforcing variables (both positive and negative) supporting a problematic behavior. For example, a child seeking attention from the teacher could also receive attention from peers for a disruptive verbal outburst in the classroom. Removing one source of attention will not likely result in extinction. Second, when reinforcement is removed it is typical to observe a behavioral phenomenon called an "extinction burst." This burst is noted by an increased frequency and intensity of the problem behavior as the child tries to access the desired reinforcement. This burst tends to be rather short lived if reinforcement is not provided. A good example of an extinction burst can be seen when an individual at a soda machine inserts money but no soda is returned. It is typical for the person to repeatedly push the button, and then escalate physical contact with the machine (e.g., hitting or rocking the machine) before quickly deescalating as he or she realizes that the desired reinforcement (a tasty beverage) will not be accessed. Finally, it is not unusual for a child to exhibit "spontaneous recovery" and exhibit the behavior after it has ceased for a period of time. It seems this is an attempt to see whether the old means of obtaining desired reinforcement might work again. If the behavior is reinforced, it can pick up at preextinction levels, so it is important for teachers to be prepared and not respond (Cooper et al., 2007).

In addition, when trying to extinguish a problem behavior it is important to identify what the child is obtaining from engaging in the target behavior (its function) and establish a replacement behavior (a desired behavior) that serves the same purpose as the undesired behavior. For example, if a child is speaking out of turn to obtain his or her teacher's attention, having the teacher simply ignore the behavior (removing the teacher's attention) will usually result in the child engaging in some new behavior (usually more undesirable) in order to obtain the teacher's attention. When a new desired behavior is not taught, chances are that the child will try something that is more problematic to achieve the same results that the original behavior did (an extinction burst as described above). For example, the child might call out louder, or more often, or in a more profane manner in order to obtain his or her teacher's attention. In school environments, learning and social development are ideal replacement behaviors. Teaching students new ways to have behavioral success in the classroom is an investment that can produce enduring and profound returns for the

> When a new desired behavior is not taught, chances are that the child will try something that is more problematic to achieve the same results that the original behavior did.

student. It is fundamentally unfair and unproductive to punish misbehavior without a plan for training more adaptive replacement behaviors. When using punishment, a replacement behavior should be monitored along with the behavior to be punished. If the replacement behavior does not increase while the punished behavior decreases, then the intervention should be stopped and adjusted.

COMMON REASONS WHY CHILDREN MISBEHAVE

Now that a working understanding of the ABCs of behavior has been established we explore common reasons why children engage in inappropriate behavior. We next describe four general reasons why children misbehave.

Inappropriate Behavior Is Positively Reinforced

In this situation, the child has a history of receiving reinforcement for engaging in inappropriate behavior. Despite the annoyance it may cause for a teacher or parent, children often obtain what they want from engaging in problematic behavior. If they do not get what they want from engaging in problematic behavior, they will cease to engage in it. This is not to say that children know why they engage in appropriate behavior or that they consciously choose to be "annoying." Rather, children are taught by the adults and circumstances in their lives how to behave in order to attain what they desire or need. We suggest that adults should accept the reality that they are responsible for the consequences children experience in most situations. Consider the following example. A parent is on the phone and asks the child to wait quietly while he or she finishes the conversation. For a few minutes the parent ignores the child's pleas for attention. The child's behavior escalates into a tantrum. Once the tantrum begins, the parent speaks to the child and hangs up the phone. Although the parent did not intend to reinforce the inappropriate behavior, the child gained what he or she wanted from the tantrum, that is, the parent's undivided attention. Keep in mind that for most children favorable attention is better than unfavorable attention, but any attention is better than no attention. To help the child learn to engage in appropriate behavior, an intervention that incorporates differential reinforcement is necessary.

Differential reinforcement interventions typically have three steps. The first step involves defining an alternative replacement behavior that will replace the inappropriate behavior but serve the same purpose for the child (i.e., the child will still get what he or she wants or needs). Second, the appropriate replacement behavior must be reinforced in the same way that the inappropriate behavior was reinforced. Third, the inappropriate behavior must no longer be reinforced. Once this three-step process has been correctly implemented the child will gain access to the reinforcing consequence for engaging in the appropriate behavior. There are several types of differential reinforcement processes (Cooper et al.,

2007). Two of these processes include differential reinforcement of incompatible behavior (DRI) and differential reinforcement of alternative behavior (DRA). These two methods are similar in that they both set up the differential reinforcement model so that an appropriate behavior will allow the child to access the desired reinforcing consequence. They are different in that they are based on the relationship between the problem behavior and the alternative replacement behavior. In the case of DRI, the replacement behavior is selected so that it is impossible for the child to exhibit both the problem behavior and the incompatible behavior concurrently (e.g., out-of-seat and in-seat behavior). With DRA, the responses are not incompatible and both behaviors can occur simultaneously (e.g., raising hand and calling out).

Alternatively, some differential reinforcement models don't focus exclusively on teaching a replacement behavior. For instance, a third type of differential reinforcement is differential reinforcement of other behaviors (DRO). In this model, a child will receive something he or she desires when he or she does *not* engage in the targeted inappropriate behavior. It is important to remember that a DRO intervention may be hard to implement because it requires implementers to refrain from concurrently reinforcing other problem behaviors. As such, reinforcement should be delivered only when the problem behavior and no other significant problem behaviors occur during the intervention period. The final option for differential reinforcement interventions is differential reinforcement of low or high rates of behavior (DRL or DRH, respectively). DRL sets goal levels of behavior that are advanced as a child's behavior improves. For example, if a child speaks out of turn at least five times in 1 hour, the initial goal of obtaining a reinforcing consequence might be set at speaking out of turn only four times in the hour. If the child meets that goal, the reinforcing consequence is delivered. Once the child can reach the initial goal of four times in 1 hour consistently, the goal for the target behavior can be reduced to three times, two times, and so on until the inappropriate behavior has been eliminated. With this model an adult can take small steps to eliminate a child's inappropriate behavior by reinforcing the incremental steps required to extinguish the undesired behavior.

Inappropriate Behavior Is Negatively Reinforced

In this situation a child is engaging in an inappropriate behavior because he or she has learned that engaging in that behavior when the aversive stimulus is present results in the removal of the aversive stimulus. Behavior that results in the removal of something undesired is often referred to as "escape" behavior because the child misbehaves so that he or she can escape something aversive. A common example of escape behavior is that of a child begins to yell or throw things when he or she is asked to do something he or she doesn't like (e.g., worksheets) and as a result the child is sent to the principal's office (thus escaping the worksheet). In this example the task demand (completing a worksheet) is acting as an aversive stimulus prompting misbehavior that results in the child being removed from the aversive task or environment. Although being removed from class might be associated with some other aversive stimuli (e.g., punishment at home), if the child repeatedly engages in a specific inappropriate behavior that results in the removal of an undesired task or removal of the child from the environment, then the child's misbehavior suggests that the child would rather be removed from his or her environment than complete the aversive task or activity.

Interventions that are aimed at decreasing inappropriate "escape" behavior are typically developed to make the class activity less aversive and/or remove the opportunity to escape. Once a previously aversive activity is no longer aversive the child will no longer have a reason to misbehave. Note that changing a child's behavior through this process will not produce instantaneous results because the child's previous experiences have taught him or her that the best way to get out of doing something is to engage in an inappropriate behavior. This process can be accelerated by refusing to let the child leave the room or by sending the aversive task with the child if he or she is allowed to leave the room. By making the child complete the activity regardless of his or her behavior or location, the child learns that he or she cannot get out of doing an aversive activity by engaging in inappropriate behavior. Removing the function of an inappropriate behavior while minimizing the aversive components of an unwanted task related to that behavior will eventually result in the reduction of inappropriate behavior.

Occasionally, when a disruptive behavior is maintained by negative reinforcement, the child will have arranged the environment so that he or she is able to successfully avoid ever contacting the aversive stimulus. For example, a child may know that something unpleasant (e.g., a difficult academic task demand) is upcoming, and act out in a manner such that he or she is removed from the class prior to the demand being made. In another example, a child feigns sickness to stay home to avoid a confrontation with another child that he or she knew was planned for that day. In either example, the child has used his or her behavioral history to predict the likelihood of an aversive event and avoided the situation before it occurs. This practice not only avoids the event but also reduces stressful thoughts about the event.

Appropriate Behavior Is Positively Punished

Sometimes children learn that engaging in appropriate behavior leads to aversive consequences. While it seems unlikely that an appropriate behavior would be positively punished, consider what happens when a child correctly raises his or her hand and is ignored by the teacher. In a short amount of time the child will start to experience physical discomfort (which is the addition of something aversive). In another situation a child might attempt to work on an assigned academic task that he or she does not currently have the skill to accomplish. Unfortunately, the child will inevitably experience an uncomfortable consequence when he or she is unable to correctly do the activity (the addition of a bad grade).

As another common example, teachers often provide students additional work when they complete their assigned work. In this case, added work may be an aversive consequence that inadvertently punishes work completion. In this situation it is not atypical for a child to engage in another inappropriate behavior in order to escape the aversive consequence. If the new inappropriate behavior is reinforced, the child has learned a new way to misbehave to avoid what he or she does not want (e.g., embarrassment, discomfort). In another case, a child may withdrawal or disengage to avoid an aversive consequence. In either instance, it is critical to identify what is punishing and stop delivering positive punishment for appropriate behavior.

Appropriate Behavior Is Negatively Punished (Resulting in a Loss of Something Desired)

The fourth common reason for a child to behave inappropriately is that a child learns that he or she will lose something desirable by engaging in appropriate behavior. For example, if a child appropriately raises his or her hand but is not called on, the teacher may be both positively punishing (the addition of some physical discomfort while raising his or her hand) and negatively punishing (he or she also did not have the opportunity to respond to the initial question) the appropriate behavior of hand raising. A child in this situation will quickly learn alternative behaviors (e.g., calling out an answer) so that he or she can receive the desired consequence (opportunity to respond to the question). Interventions that are designed to change negative punishment of positive behavior incorporate methods that remove negative punishment from the demonstration of appropriate behavior. In perhaps a similar but better example a student waits quietly to be called on (because teacher says that is the expectation) but instead the teacher allows the child who is out of line, talking out, and so on to go first.

Two issues are important to note when considering the common reasons children engage in inappropriate behavior. First, children can engage in disruptive behavior for multiple reasons at the same time. For instance, it is possible for a child's behavior to be both positively reinforced and positively punished at the same time. The ways in which children learn how to engage in certain behavior patterns may be sequenced so that punishing desirable behavior may result in the child learning an undesirable behavior but not having it detected until the undesirable behavior has surfaced. Cases in which multiple behaviors are simultaneously taught may require a series of several interventions in order to fully meet the need for each behavior. It is important to note that we purposefully focused on the reasons why children engage in inappropriate behavior rather than the reasons why children engage in appropriate behavior because problematic behavior is usually at the core of interventions designed to change behavior. Regardless, the principles of behavior change can be flipped and presented with a focus on creating positive behavior if such a flip in focus provides useful information. To accomplish this, simple replace "inappropriate" with "appropriate" and vice versa when referencing the four categories above.

REINFORCEMENT SELECTION PROCEDURES

Not surprisingly, reinforcement-based interventions are the most frequently used evidence-based interventions for children who exhibit difficulties engaging in appropriate classroom behavior (Martens, Peterson, Witt, & Cirone, 1986). The success of reinforcement-based interventions depends on accurately identifying reinforcing stimuli (Fantuzzo, Rohrbeck, Hightower, & Work, 1991). Some procedures for identifying reinforcing stimuli include teacher selection of reinforcers, surveys for the students, and forced-choice procedures.

Teacher Nomination of Potentially Reinforcing Stimuli

The most common method is to simply ask a teacher to rank-order five items or activities he or she believes will serve as reinforcers for the designated student's target behavior. Specifically, the item with the most reinforcing properties will be ranked as 1, and the item predicted by the teacher to have the least reinforcing properties is ranked 5. The highest-rated stimuli can then be used in an intervention or as data in a reinforcer assessment study (described below).

Reinforcer Assessment Survey

Another approach to identifying reinforcers is to use a standardized survey. An example of such a survey is the reinforcer assessment survey (RAS; Northup, George, Jones, Broussard, & Vollmer, 1996). The RAS is composed of 42 items that contain seven stimuli for each of six categories (edibles, tangibles, activities, peer attention, teacher attention, and escape) of potential reinforcers. Children are queried on a scale of 0 (*do not like at all*) to 2 (*like a lot*) to assess how much they like each individual item. Scores for the responses are summed, and a preference percentage for each category is calculated. The category yielding the highest percentage is considered to be the most preferred reinforcing category. The primary advantage of this model is that it represents a wide range of stimuli options.

Forced-Choice Stimulus Preference Assessment

Although survey procedures are a nice start when trying to identify reinforcing stimuli, there are more formal assessment methods available. Specifically, Pace, Ivancic, Edwards, Iwata, and Page (1985) designed the forced-choice stimulus preference assessment to more rigorously assess the reinforcement value of items/activities. Forced-choice methods typically begin with a reinforcer survey such as the RAS. The purpose of such a survey is to identify a base of preferred items/procedures that are acceptable for use in the classroom. The 10 highest-rated stimuli are then presented to the student (e.g., as a typed list or as colored index cards with cartoon representations of the activities/items on them). In accordance with findings from previous research, access to each stimulus is typically standardized (e.g., 30-second increment) to equalize saliency of all items and avoid satiation (Northup et al., 1996). Next, in a forced-choice procedure a teacher would present two stimuli to each student and force the student to select one of the two. Typically, every stimulus should be paired with every other stimulus at least once. The number of times a child selects a stimulus is recorded and then divided by the number of times it was presented. Stimuli with a score of 80% or greater are considered "high preferences" (Pace et al., 1985).

Most of the research on forced-choice methods has been conducted with low-incidence populations (e.g., autism). With this in mind, forced-choice stimulus preference assessments may not be as viable as a method of reinforcer selection with typical students (students who do not have low-incidence disabilities).

Assessing Reinforcer Effectiveness

Northup and colleagues (1996) describe a useful method for assessing the reinforcing properties of a stimulus. The process they describe uses curriculum-based assessment (CBA) procedures. These CBAs consist of easy math addition worksheets that are designed to test students at one grade level of difficulty below the student's current mastery level. The use of these probes ensures that the target students can complete the math problems with at least 90% accuracy. In order to gather baseline data, students complete three math probes without reinforcement. Next, the students are asked to complete math probes earning one token for every five math problems completed. Each token provides access to the stimulus that is thought to be reinforcing. After each student completes the worksheets, the average number of accurate digits completed per minute is calculated. Each stimuli's reinforcing properties are then determined by comparing digits correct per minute for baseline probes to digits correct per minute for each of the two reinforcement probes providing a direct test of the reinforcing value of the stimuli (remember, we can only know that a stimulus is reinforcing if when it is provided contingent upon a certain response, that response increases).

MUST A FORMAL ASSESSMENT OF PREFERENCES BE DONE?

The most fail-proof method for identifying reinforcing stimuli is to conduct a reinforcer assessment procedure. However, formal reinforcer assessment procedures may not be viable in many typical educational settings. Among the more practical alternatives, research has consistently demonstrated that forced-choice pairing of preferred stimulus items serves as the best predictor of reinforcing stimuli (Fisher, Piazza, Bowman, & Amari, 1996; Northrup et al., 1996; Pace et al., 1985). Unfortunately, this method is rather time consuming and requires both the generation of a list of stimuli through a survey or interview (with either the individual, teacher, or caregivers) and a procedure in which the actual stimuli are presented in pairs to the individual and the individual has to choose one. Self-report surveys for reinforcement selection are often presented as an alternative to doing forced-choice stimulus preference assessments. Unfortunately, however, research suggests that self-report surveys produce generally inaccurate results (Baer, Williams, Onses, & Stokes, 1985; Guevremont, Onses, & Stokes, 1986; Paniagua & Baer, 1982; Risley & Hart, 1986; Witt, Cavell, Heffer, Carey, & Martens, 1988). Alarmingly and in contrast with evidence-based practice, the most frequent method of reinforcer selection reported in schools is teacher selection (Bergan & Kratochwill, 1990). Although teacher selection is a low-cost way to

> **The most fail-proof method for identifying reinforcing stimuli is to conduct a reinforcer assessment procedure.**

select preferred items for intervention, controlled research suggests that teacher selection is not a defensible approach if you care about efficacy.

It will be important for practicing educational professionals to consider the significance of each case when deciding the required level of rigor needed in the selection of reinforcing stimuli. In higher-stakes cases it is critical to determine the reinforcing properties of stimuli that will be used in interventions. Alternatively, in lower-stakes cases extensive procedures for determining the reinforcing properties of stimuli may not be needed. If educational professionals choose not to utilize assessment procedures, it should be noted that the reinforcement-based intervention simply may work because the selected stimulus is not reinforcing. Thus, interpretation of outcome data from these cases should be tempered. If the intervention does not work and you are not sure about the reinforcing properties of the chosen stimuli, it is imperative that multiple reinforcing stimuli are used in the intervention procedure before determining whether a child responded to the chosen intervention.

SCHEDULES OF REINFORCEMENT

As noted above, another key issue in changing behavior is choosing the schedule of reinforcement or punishment. The consistency and predictability of the presentation of the reinforcing stimulus has an impact on the rate of acquisition of a target behavior and, likewise, the extinction of that behavior. There are four basic stimulus schedules: fixed ratio, variable ratio, fixed interval, and variable interval.

Fixed Ratio

In this reinforcement schedule a reinforcing stimulus is presented after the student has engaged in a target behavior for a set number of times. The ratio can be heavy (e.g., one reinforcing stimulus for each target behavior) or light (e.g., one reinforcing stimulus for 50 target behaviors). A one to one ratio is typically called continuous reinforcement and leads to quick acquisition of a target behavior (Cooper et al., 2007). As such, it is typical to use continuous reinforcement when a child initially is taught a behavior. Behavioral research has indicated that whereas this schedule is effective for behavior acquisition, behavior supported with a fixed-ratio schedule will extinguish quickly once the intervention has ceased. The quick extinction of the target behavior is due to the child learning to expect the reinforcing stimuli after each time he or she has exhibited the behavior a specific number of times. Think for example how many times you would continue to put money into a beverage machine after it did not give you a tasty beverage when you put in the requisite amount.

Variable Ratio

This schedule applies reinforcing stimuli based on rates of the target behavior, but the rates of reinforcement are variable, not fixed. That means that the reinforcement will be delivered after the student has engaged in the desired behavior a variable number of times. As such, a child may receive a reinforcing stimuli after four target behaviors, then after seven target behaviors, then after two target behaviors, and so on. Research has demonstrated that using this method will result in slower acquisition as compared to using a fixed-ratio schedule of reinforcement, but a variable reinforcement schedule is more resistant to extinction (Cooper et al., 2007). In addition, it may be easier for teachers and other educational professionals to use a variable-ratio schedule because it is usually difficult to consistently and accurately observe every occurrence of a target behavior.

Fixed Interval

This schedule of reinforcement involves offering a reinforcing stimulus over a fixed amount of time contingent on the demonstration of appropriate behavior. When using this schedule, no reinforcement is applied when the target behavior is demonstrated during the interval. The most basic example of this schedule is a salaried worker. This method of reinforcement produces a generally low rate of desired behavior during the first part of the interval with the rate of desired behavior increasing as the end of the interval approaches (Cooper et al., 2007).

Variable Interval

The final schedule of reinforcement involves the application of a stimulus after a variable amount of time has passed when the target behavior is present. Although this method predictably results in a slow rate of acquisition, once the behavior has been acquired it is usually demonstrated at a slow and steady rate (Cooper et al., 2007). In addition, the behavior will be less likely to extinguish because the reinforcer is not expected after a set period of time. While this may seem a rather odd schedule, it is logically common in schools. Consider a setting where a student is prompted to follow a particular rule or some consequence will be applied. Although some teachers will adhere to that rule, others will on some days give leniency, whereas on other days they will apply the consequence. The teacher "mood" will vary, and as such application of the rule will as well on a variable interval schedule.

Noncontingent Reinforcement

While the proceeding schedules have focused on the application of a stimulus contingent to the presentation of the target behavior, there are some advantages to the "noncontingent" presentation of reinforcement. Using this method, identified reinforcing stimuli are provided freely to the target child without the demand of a target behavior being presented. The logic behind this method is that children will often exhibit problem behavior to have access to desired consequence. For example, a child may call out to get the teacher's attention, or show aggression in order to be removed from an undesirable location. By providing the reinforcing stimuli prior to the problem behavior, the need for the child to engage in the problem behavior is removed. The method has been found to be effective over a range of situations (Carr, Severtson, & Lepper, 2008). In a recent study, Carr and colleagues examined noncontingent reinforcement (NCR) treatments to document whether they could be classified as empirically supported. In this study the authors concluded that NCR, when presented in a fixed time with an extinction procedure, was a "well-established" treatment. While the effectiveness of this intervention is an attractive benefit, perhaps the most positive advantage is that a teacher does not have to react (or try not to react) to the problem behavior.

CONCLUSION

When the goal of an intervention is to increase or decrease the rate of a target behavior in an educational environment, any intervention will essentially be the alteration of the setting to change either what occurs before, or the consequence of, the behavior. As such, it is critical that educational interventions consider both the ABCs of behavior and the methods for altering the historic pattern into one that promotes the desired child response. For this to occur it is understood that the teacher's behavior must change in order for the child's behavior to change. What now follows is a series of interventions on pages 157–168 that have been found to be effective by altering what happens before, during, and after the behavior (DRI, DRA, NCR, mystery motivator, guided notes, and behavior contracts). While these intervention strategies are a nice starting point, a good intervention team will adapt to the particular case based on the outcome data presented. For example, if a child seems to be responding to a reinforcement-based intervention but in a manner that is not robust enough to satisfy team goals, the reinforcement scheduled could be thickened so that fluency rate increases. Educational professionals with interest in developing increased expertise in behavior intervention should consider text such as Cooper et al.'s (2007) review of applied behavior analysis.

> **The teacher's behavior must change in order for the child's behavior to change.**

Differential Reinforcement
of an Incompatible or Alternative Behavior

Brief Description

Children will continue to engage in problem behaviors that are reinforced. Therefore, it is important to minimize reinforcement for disruptive behavior to reduce disruptive behavior. Unfortunately, simply removing reinforcement often results in an "extinction burst." Data tell us that about 40% of the time, when an adult makes adjustments to the environment to stop reinforcement for a problem behavior (e.g., ignoring disruptive behavior that the child has been exhibiting to obtain adult attention), the child will escalate disruptive behavior in an attempt to bring back the reinforcement. This escalated frequency, magnitude, and duration of the disruptive behavior is called an "extinction burst." Extinction bursts are very problematic in classroom environments. As such, DR interventions have been developed to concurrently remove or reduce reinforcement for the problem behavior while reinforcing a functionally similar replacement behavior. Thus, the problem behavior diminishes while the child is provided with an alternative (more acceptable) means to access the desired reinforcement. To understand DR interventions, consider a child who calls out inappropriately in class for teacher attention. It is understood that the calling-out behavior is maintained by the resulting teacher attention. Using DR procedures, the teacher would ignore the calling-out behavior and only call on the child when he or she raises his or her hand (an alternative behavior). Over time the DR procedures will result in higher rates of hand raising and lower rates of calling out. In the end, the child is trained to exhibit the desired behavior when he or she wants teacher attention. This brief was designed to provide a simple guide to DR procedures focusing on DR of incompatible or alternative behaviors (DRI and DRA, respectively). A DRA example involves providing reinforcement for an alternative behavior (hand raising in the above example). DRI is a version of DR that selects an incompatible behavior as the replacement behavior. For example, in-seat behavior is incompatible with out-of-seat behavior. Selecting an incompatible behavior as the replacement behavior minimizes the risk of inadvertently reinforcing the problematic behavior. For example, it is possible that the child may raise his or her hand while also calling out. Because hand raising is reinforced with teacher attention, the reinforcer is provided even though the problematic behavior also occurred and is similarly reinforced. If an incompatible behavior cannot be identified, then an alternative behavior will suffice (see 4a below).

What "Common Problems" Does This Address?

This intervention was designed to increase rates of appropriate behavior and decrease rates of problem behavior by selectively providing reinforcement only to the desired behavior. There have been many empirical demonstrations of the effectiveness of differential reinforcement (DR) interventions (Cooper, Heron, & Heward, 2007).

Procedure

1. Identify the consequence that is reinforcing the inappropriate behavior (e.g., verbal praise, escape).
2. Identify an incompatible or alternative behavior that can access the same consequence. Note that identification of an incompatible appropriate behavior is preferred.

(cont.)

3. Begin with a continuous fixed-ratio DR schedule. The goal of this step is to ensure that the child is reinforced for the alternative behavior in the initial stages of the DR intervention.
4. Once the DR schedule has been initiated, the teacher is instructed not to respond to the target problem behavior if it is presented.
   a. If using a DRA procedure and the child exhibits both the problem and alternative behaviors concurrently, the teacher is suggested to reinforce the child but note that the reinforcement is due to the alternative behavior.
5. If after a number of intervention days or sessions (for more severe cases) of applying the DR (e.g., 5 days or 20–25 sessions) shows a marked reduction in the problem behavior, start to fade in the reinforcement schedule. Note that after the intervention period is complete the desired behavior should continue to be reinforced at an appropriate level for the child and environment. If the desired behavior is not reinforced, the child will return to the problem behavior (or some new behavior) to access the desired reinforcement.

Critical Components That Must Be Implemented for the Intervention to Be Successful

- Successful identification of the reinforcer for the problematic behavior.
- Identification of an appropriate incompatible/alternative behavior that the child is capable of doing.
- An initial schedule of DR that ensures that the child will be reinforced when he or she exhibits the desired behavior. A continuous fixed-ratio schedule is preferred whereby the student receives reinforcement each time the alternative behavior occurs.
- The problem behavior should be ignored once the DR schedule is initiated.
- A fading process of the DR schedule that is gradual enough not to result in the child reengaging in the problem behavior. One way to accomplish this is to make the reinforcement intermittent (so every so many occurrences of the desired behavior are reinforced) and unpredictable or variable such that the child knows that the alternative behavior will be reinforced periodically but is not sure exactly which instance of the desirable behavior will occasion reinforcement.

Critical Considerations

DR interventions have a number of known limitations, as outlined by Vollmer, Iwata, Zarcone, Smith, and Mazaleki (1993):

- DR interventions are not considered the most effective approach for very severe behavior cases. Noncontingent reinforcement procedure should be considered for such cases.
- DR interventions can result in an extinction burst with associated issues.
- DR interventions can be cumbersome for teachers. Care should be taken when designing the intervention to consider feasibility issues.

References

Cooper, J. O., Heron, T. E., & Heward, W. L. (2007). *Applied behavior analysis* (2nd ed.). Columbus, OH: Prentice Hall.

Vollmer, T. R., Iwata, B. A., Zarcone, J. R., Smith, R. G., & Mazaleki, J. L. (1993). The role of attention in the treatment of attention-maintained self-injurious behavior: Noncontigent reinforcement and differential reinforcement of other behavior. *Journal of Applied Behavior Analysis, 26*, 9–21.

Noncontingent Reinforcement

Brief Description

Given that children will engage in problem behaviors if they are reinforced, one strategy to minimize the utility of the behavior is to saturate the environment with the reinforcer *prior* to the demonstration of the disruptive behavior. To understand why this intervention would be effective, think about a child who desires teacher attention and has found that calling out in class consistently results in the teacher focusing attention on him or her (albeit, not in a positive manner). An NCR intervention directs the teacher to provide him or her attention (in this case, a more positive version) prior to the child "asking" with the problem behavior. As such, the child has no need to be disruptive, and will hopefully, in time, prefer positive attention on a leaner schedule than negative attention on a more consistent schedule. This brief has been developed to present a fixed-time NCR delivery with extinction and schedule thinning, as this version of NCR was found to have a well-established evidence base by Carr and colleagues (2008).

What "Common Problems" Does This Address?

Noncontingent reinforcement (NCR) is a powerful method to reduce problematic behavior. NCR involves giving the student access to a reinforcer frequently enough that he or she is no longer motivated to exhibit disruptive behavior to obtain that same reinforcer. A classic example of NCR is a teacher placing a child on his or her lap during group instruction such that the child has no motivation to seek the teacher's attention while the teacher is conducting story time with the class. There have been many empirical demonstrations of the effectiveness of NCR interventions with a comprehensive demonstration of the evidence base by Carr, Severtson, and Lepper in 2008. In addition to being demonstrated effective in reducing problem behavior, NCR interventions have the distinct advantage of reducing problem behavior with less of a chance of an extinction burst period. Because the child is already receiving as much of the reinforcer as he or she could want, there is no brief increase in disruption that commonly follows treatments that involve withholding reinforcement from a child. There is a rich literature base on the use of NCR. Two cautions are worth noting. When thinning the NCR schedule (i.e., reducing the amount of reinforcement the student gets), disruptive behavior may reoccur and necessitate the use of extinction procedures. Second, reinforcer substitution may occur meaning the student may continue to exhibit disruptive behavior to obtain other reinforcers.

Procedure

1. Identify the reinforcer for the inappropriate behavior (e.g., verbal praise, escape).
2. Develop a fixed schedule to apply the NCR for the target child. The goal of this step is to develop an initial schedule that is likely to catch the child before he or she engages in the problem behavior, thereby making the disruptive behavior unnecessary.
   a. Adapt the schedule based on the age, developmental level, and severity of the behavior problem. For young children, or those with severe behavior problems, the initial NCR schedule will need to be very dense (e.g., once every 30 seconds). For higher-functioning children with more mainstream behavior difficulties the NCR schedule can be initially less ambitious

(cont.)

(e.g., once every 15 minutes). Implementers can easily determine how dense it should be by examining the frequency of disruptive behavior that is followed by reinforcement in the classroom at baseline and ensuring that their schedule is more frequent at first. So, for example, if talking out occurs once every 5 minutes on average in the classroom, then NCR should be delivered in less than 5-minute intervals.

3. When initially applying the NCR, do not refer to the problem behavior or note that the child is behaving appropriately.
4. Once the NCR schedule has been initiated, do not respond to the target problem behavior if and when it occurs.
5. If after a number of intervention days or sessions (for more severe cases) of applying the NCR (e.g., 5 days or 20–25 sessions), the child shows a marked reduction in the problem behavior, start to thin out the reinforcement schedule. Thinning the schedule means reducing the frequency with which the child is provided reinforcement when NCR is in effect. It is important to make gradual adjustments to the schedule to minimize the chances of a burst in disruptive behavior. When thinning the schedule, the problem behavior will likely reoccur. When it does, research suggests that withholding reinforcement (i.e., extinction) or delivering a mild consequence like response cost can effectively mitigate the reoccurrence. The value of NCR is that the extinction period is often less pronounced because the disruption has been reduced to zero levels.

Critical Components That Must Be Implemented for the Intervention to Be Successful

- Successful identification of the reinforcer for the problem behavior. This step is essential. NCR will not work if the function of disruption is unknown. This strategy is not the same as simply providing rewards on a very dense schedule.
- An initial schedule of NCR that minimizes the likelihood that the child will need to engage in the problem behavior to get the desired reinforcement.
- That problem behavior is ignored once the NCR schedule is initiated.
- A fading process that is gradual enough to minimize the degree to which the child reengages in the problem behavior.

Reference

Carr, J. E., Severtson, J. M., & Lepper, T. L. (2008). Noncontingent reinforcement is an empirically supported treatment for problem behavior exhibited by individuals with developmental disabilities. *Research in Developmental Disabilities, 30*, 44–57.

Mystery Motivator

Brief Description

Although many students will engage in appropriate academic and behavior task demands without systematic reinforcement plans, others will need additional behavioral supports. The mystery motivator intervention was designed to increased the proficiency of any academic or behavioral task demand by providing a "mystery" reinforcement using a random schedule (Jenson, Rhode, & Reavis, 1994). Assuming that the reinforcer pool has some reinforcing value, the lure of a mystery reinforcer should additionally motivate students to engage in the academic task, even when the task is difficult. It can be difficult for teachers to develop a deep enough pool of interventions that retain value for the entire school year. Adding a surprise component to the reinforcer pool helps keep the process fun and exciting. Mystery motivators can be used in a variety of content areas including reading, math, social studies, science, writing, and homework completion, as well as social behavior compliance. They can also be contingent on a variety of outcome-based criteria (e.g., high test averages, classroom participation, rule adherence). This intervention can be used to shape the behavior of an entire class or tailored to work for one individual.

What "Common Problems" Does This Address?

This intervention was developed to increase fluency through the application of positive reinforcement. There have been a number of empirical demonstrations of the effectiveness of the mystery motivator interventions (e.g., Madaus, Kehle Madaus, & Bray, 2003; Moore, Waguespack, Wickstrom, Witt, & Gaydos, 1994).

Procedure

1. Make reinforcement chart.
2. Construct a motivation chart for the entire class with all the student names and days of the week.
   a. Randomly place some letter on a few days of the week beside each student's name. For example, Jenson and colleagues (1994) suggest using an "M" to designate a mystery motivator day. Be sure to place more motivators on the calendar during the initial stages of the intervention so that children are more likely to earn a mystery motivator. Each child should have different placement of the mystery "M."
   b. Cover up all of the days using a note card.
   c. For each note card placed over the "M," place the name of the motivator on the back of the note card.
3. Define goal (e.g., 100% homework completion in all subject areas, 80% accuracy on test grades in math).
4. If the criterion is met, have the child remove the note card on that particular day. It is important to make this activity exciting. If the "M" is located on that day, the reinforcer should be given as soon as possible.
5. When there is not an "M" behind the note card, be sure to remind students that there will be other opportunities to earn the mystery motivator.

(cont.)

Critical Components That Must Be Implemented for the Intervention to be Successful

- Place many "M's" on the calendar during the teaching (initial) phase of the intervention.
- After the initial intervention phase of the intervention, place reinforcements randomly. A child should not be able to determine a pattern of when it is more likely that there will be an "M."
- All goals should be clearly noted in a manner that students fully understand. Students must know what they are expected to do to earn the chance to receive a mystery reinforcer for this intervention to be successful.
- Select a goal that is easy to attain during the initial stages of the intervention. This will increase the likelihood that the initial intervention implementation will be a success.
- Reinforcers should be given as soon as possible.

Critical Assumptions/Problem-Solving Questions to Be Asked

- It is important to know whether the students are performing their academic tasks at grade level and whether they are capable of performing the assigned tasks successfully. If not, a skill-based acquisition-level intervention should be selected to teach the academic/behavioral skill first.
- Students have to desire the mystery motivators; otherwise the intervention will be unsuccessful.
- Students in lower grades or with lower cognitive functioning may need more consistent reinforcement for them to understand the connection between the demonstration of an appropriate behavior and receipt of the mystery motivator. In such cases each day can have an "M" but with a different reinforcer on each day. In this case, the type of reinforcer is the surprise.
- Tangible motivators may be more enticing for younger students or students who are functioning at a lower cognitive level.

Materials

- Preferred reinforcing stimuli list.
- Reinforcers.
- Mystery motivator chart.
- Note cards.

References

Jenson, W. R., Rhode, G., & Reavis, H. K. (1994). *The tough kid tool box*. Longmont, CO: Sopris West.

Madaus, M. M. R., Kehle, T. J., Madaus, J., & Bray, M. A. (2003). Mystery motivator as an intervention to promote homework completion and accuracy. *School Psychology International, 24*, 369–377.

Moore, L. A., Waguespack, A. M., Wickstrom, K. F., Witt, J. C., & Gaydos G. R. (1994). Mystery motivator: An effective and time-efficient intervention. *School Psychology Review, 23*, 106–118.

Guided Notes

Brief Description

Guided notes provide premade notes that include blank spaces for writing down components from the lesson of the day. Using guided notes allows the student to have opportunities to demonstrate an ability to actively engage and increase the time-on task while a lesson is being taught. After the lesson has been completed, notes are reviewed by the teacher. In order to reinforce the student, the teacher should review the notes with excitement, praise, and other forms of positive reinforcement for each blank completed correctly. This intervention can be used with students in regular education settings (especially with those in grades 4 through 12) or with students receiving additional educational services. Guided notes provide a flexible intervention that can be adapted for any instructional level and altered for students with specific skill deficits. Guided notes are inexpensive, efficient, allow teachers to exhibit their own style, and are often preferred over "regular" notes by both teachers and students. In addition, the sheets provide prompts for students to actively listen and engage in the learning process.

What "Common Problems" Does This Address?

Guided notes are an evidence-based intervention strategy related to increasing academic performance (Konrad, Joseph, & Eveleigh, 2009). Guided notes can provide appropriate attending behavior prompts for students so that they may engage in on-task academic behavior and will allow for the student to be rewarded for listening to instruction (e.g., listening to the teacher instead of counting the number of tiles on the ceiling). Having the student engage in the appropriate attending behaviors will reduce the likelihood that he or she will engage in inappropriate behaviors (e.g., talking without permission, walking around the room). Guided notes, if implemented with integrity, will allow for students to receive positive reinforcement for their appropriate attending behavior.

Procedure

1. Make a lesson outline using a form of presentation software or overheads, concentrating on major concepts and facts to be learned.
2. Make a student handout from the lesson outline. Leave blank spaces for the student to fill in that corresponds to the most important concepts in the lesson plan. Blank spaces may be short (one to three words) or long (four to eight words) depending on the students' instructional level.
3. Lead a training activity to teach the student how to use guided notes while listening to instructions and looking at presentation materials (e.g., PowerPoints, transparencies).
   a. Explain to the student the way in which the notes work.
   b. Provide an example and model the way in which the student needs to fill in the notes.
   c. Hold a practice session with feedback so that the student will know whether he or she is filling them in correctly.
4. Teach the planned lesson utilizing the presentation software/overheads that go along with students' guided notes. Include prompts and/or questions while teaching the lesson if it seems necessary or it will aid in student learning.

(cont.)

5. Review the students' notes in order to provide positive reinforcement. This can be done by collecting, grading, and returning the notes to the student or, more preferably, by checking the notes in front of the student so that you can provide positive praise and specific feedback.
6. Supplemental strategies may be added to the guided notes intervention to further promote student success and responding (see below).

Supplemental Strategies

- Use guided notes as an intervention for the entire class.
- Combine guided notes with unison responding, a lottery incentive, or response cards.
- Quiz students on the material from the guided notes after a lesson.
- Offer extra credit to those who accurately fill in the guided notes.
- Use guided notes with an entire class, a small group of students, or an individual student.

Critical Components That Must Be Implemented for Intervention to be Successful

- The guided notes instruction and lesson plans/materials must match each student's instructional level.
- Students must have demonstrated that they are capable of completing guided notes.
- Training the students on how to use guided notes is necessary. Otherwise the intervention will likely fail.
- Guided notes should be reviewed by the teacher and/or turned in and handed back as soon as possible so that students may receive specific feedback about their performance along with positive reinforcement.
- Guided notes must contain enough blank spaces to give students an adequate amount of opportunities to respond.
- If guided notes are used as a classwide intervention, make sure that the criteria for earning a reinforcer is set at a level at which all students will be capable (intellectually, physically, etc.) of earning their reward.

Materials

- Guided notes (sample below).
- Presentation software/overheads.
- Response cards (if utilizing a supplemental strategy).
- Reinforcers valuable to students (if utilizing a lottery incentive).

Examples

Guided Notes—Second-Grade Social Studies
1. We elect a new president every _____ years.
2. Presidential candidates must be citizens of the _____.
3. Presidential candidates must be at least _____ years old.
4. They must have lived in the United States for at least _____ years.
5. Candidates campaign by traveling all over the United States and _____ as many people as they can.

(cont.)

Guided Notes—Fifth-Grade Writing

1. A _____ is a group of _____ that tell about one .
2. The _____ in a paragraph usually comes _____ and tells the main idea of the paragraph.
3. Sometimes, though, the topic sentence can come at the _____ or in the _____ of a paragraph.
4. When looking for a _____ sentence, try to find the one that tells the _____ of the paragraph.
5. _____ follow the topic sentence and provide details about the topic.

Guided Notes—Eighth-Grade Math

1. When two figures are _____, you can slide, flip, or _____ one so it fits exactly on the other one.
2. The _____ of the angles of any triangle is _____. The _____ of the angles of any quadrilateral is _____.
3. In the expression 6^3, six is the _____ and three is the _____. The problem would be solved by multiplying (_____) (_____) (_____) = _____.
4. To divide numbers or _____ with the same base, _____.
5. Whatever you do to one side of an equation, you must do to the other side of the equation in order to keep it _____ or _____.

Note. Example were produced with the Guided-Notes Maker on the Intervention Central website *rti2.org/rti2/guided_notes*.

Reference

Konrad, M., Joseph, L. M., & Eveleigh, E. (2009). A meta-analytic review of guided notes. *Education and Treatment of Children, 32,* 421–444.

Note. The lead student developer on this brief was Lindsey Long, a graduate of the MA/CAS School Psychology Program at East Carolina University.

Behavior Contracts

Brief Description

This intervention is intended to increase appropriate behavior and/or decrease inappropriate behavior. It may also be used as an intervention to increase teacher and student treatment integrity (by creating motivation for each party to follow through and be accountable). Behavior contracts are a formal method for a student and teacher to discuss and agree on the definitions of the incidences of behavior that need to be changed. In this process, they write a "contract" together that clearly states the definitions of the behaviors that are targeted for change along with the antecedents, behaviors, and consequences (reinforcers or punishers) both parties will be responsible for during the intervention. This intervention can also be used to create contracts for small groups, entire classrooms, or between peers.

What "Common Problems" Does This Address?

A short list of common behaviors addressed by this intervention includes decreasing the amount of time a student spends out of his or her seat, increasing a student's academic engagement, decreasing the number of times a student speaks out of turn, increasing prosocial behavior, decreasing frustration due to miscommunication, and almost any other behavior problem that occurs within an educational environment.

Procedure

1. Select two or less target behaviors for change.
2. Before starting the intervention tally the number of times the student is demonstrating each target behavior on a typical day in different settings.
3. Meet with the student and agree on a mutual definition (including examples and nonexamples) of the target behavior(s). Write the description of the target behavior into the contract. When trying to reduce instances of inappropriate behavior, try to focus on what you *want* the student to do instead of what you don't want him or her to do.
4. Meet with the student to discuss what reinforcers or punishers you and the student will expect when the target behaviors have been demonstrated.
5. Create a reinforcement schedule. Discuss the number of times (minutes, etc.) the student will have to demonstrate or refrain from the target behavior to earn his or her reward (there may be several opportunities for rewards throughout the day). Be sure to set the goal at an attainable level (do not expect an increase or decrease in behavior equal to more than 10% of the number of times collected in Step 2).
6. Include the reinforcer schedule in the contract as well as the criteria for earning/losing each reinforcer.
7. Have teacher, student, and parent (if possible) sign the contract. Make a copy of the contract for both the student and the teacher. Have it stored in an easy-to-reach place for both the student and the teacher.

(cont.)

8. Deliver the reward to the student *immediately* after he or she has earned it.
9. Five days into the intervention tally the number of times the child engages in the target behavior to determine whether to adjust the intervention (e.g., frequency of receiving reinforcement). Remember, do not increase or decrease goals by more than 10%.

Critical Components That Must Be Implemented for the Intervention to Be Successful

- Make sure that the student has the capability of producing the appropriate behavior in every setting where there are behavioral expectations outlined in the contract. Setting an impossible goal for a student to reach is the fastest way to sabotage the effectiveness of an intervention.
- It is also essential that you involve the student in the creation of the behavioral contract. Involving the student will create a collaborative relationship between both parties and empower the student to participate in a plan to change his or her own behavior.
- Be certain that the behavioral expectations are clear and concise. Clarify expectations vividly when writing them. Ask yourself: If a stranger read these expectations, would he or she be able to pick out the students who are doing what I expect in my class?
- Give the student multiple opportunities to be successful.

Critical Assumptions/Problem-Solving Questions to Be Asked

- Again, make sure the student is capable of demonstrating the desired behavior.
- Also, always evaluate the types of reinforcers being offered. It is typical and expected for students' desires to change over time. Always make sure that the reinforcers available for the student will also be motivating.

Examples

Sample Behavior Contract for a Fourth-Grade Student

I, **Alicia Wall**, agree to raise my hand and wait to be called upon before I talk. I agree to accept an answer to a question that I don't like rather than talk back. I agree to respect my teacher. That means that if I get mad I will let her know by writing "mad" on a piece of paper and I will hold it up for Ms. Winchester to read it. I know that she will come help me when she can. If I have to wait, I agree to ball up paper in order to release my anger and calm down while I'm waiting. I also agree to sit in my seat.

I, **Ms. Winchester**, agree to call on Alicia when she raises her hand before she talks at least two out of four times. I agree to allow Alicia to express her dislike with an answer/demand as long as she expresses it *one time* while using an appropriate voice. I understand that Alicia is entitled to her feelings, but that her feelings need to be expressed in an appropriate way. If she does not express herself using an appropriate voice or writing, I reserve the right to ignore her. I agree to respect Alicia and help her when I can. I care about Alicia and want what's best for her. I agree to address Alicia's need for help when she writes a note saying that she's angry. I agree to reward her points for appropriate behavior during class and follow the attached reinforcement schedule. I am available to listen to Alicia because I care about her.

Alicia Wall	Ms. Winchester
Date:	Date:

(cont.)

Sample Behavioral Intervention Reinforcement Schedule for a Fourth-Grade Student

1. Alicia will receive a daily points sheet each morning and afternoon. She will write her goal number of points for the day on the top of her points sheet. At the end of the day these sheets will be given back to Mr. Fridline.
2. Alicia will read through her expectations before the beginning of every class.
3. Alicia will keep her daily points sheet taped to her desk so that she and Ms. Winchester can see it and remind themselves of their agreement.
4. At the end of each activity, Alicia will earn 1 point from Mr. Fridline for each goals she completed according to the daily points sheet goals.
5. Once Alicia earns points those points cannot be removed by anyone.
6. If Alicia has an activity period during which she does not earn as many points as she would like, she will start a *new activity period* and try to earn all of her points for the next activity. If she becomes upset or refuses to do work during one activity period, allowing her to "start over" will improve her chances to engage in more appropriate behavior for the rest of the day.
7. If Alicia earns her goal points for each half of the day or her goal points for the entire day, Alicia will be able to choose from a list of rewards at the end of the day. If her reward is not available on the day that it is chosen, it will be carried over into the following day and be given to her as soon as Mr. Fridline deems it appropriate for her to have it (the sooner, the better!)
8. If Alicia does not earn her points, she and Mr. Fridline will say "It is ok, everyone has a bad day, we will start a new day tomorrow!"
9. Target number of points:

Dec 13–17	Jan 3–7	Jan 10–14	Jan 17–21	Jan 24–28
AM: 18	AM: 20	AM: 22	AM: 25	AM: 25
PM: 12	PM: 14	PM: 16	PM: 20	PM: 20
Daily: 25	Daily: 27	Daily: 30	Daily: 35	Daily: 35

I agree to abide by these instructions!

_____

Alicia Wall

Date: _____

_____

Ms. Winchester

Date: _____

Reference

Carns, A. W., & Carns, M. R. (1994). Making behavioral contracts successful. *School Counselor, 42,* 155–160.

Note. The lead student developer on this brief was Shannon Brooks, a psychology graduate student at East Carolina University.

CHAPTER 11

Maintenance and Generalization of Behavioral Interventions

OVERVIEW

The first goal of behavior intervention is to target and change a particular behavior (decrease problematic behavior, increase an alternative appropriate behavior) and thus far, this book has focused on this first goal. However, successful interventions are interventions that produce robust and enduring behavior change that can be used by the child to have a better quality of life in all of the contexts in which the child lives every day. If academic gains or improved social behavior that are learned during an intervention are not maintained and transferred into other settings, then the intervention has not been successful. For interventions to be truly effective, maintenance and generalization of the learned behavior must be realized. This chapter describes how to plan and program for behavior change that can be sustained and used in a variety of contexts.

SPECIFIC ISSUES WHEN PROGRAMMING FOR THE MAINTENANCE AND GENERALIZATION OF BEHAVIORAL GAINS

Generalization: What Is It and Why Does It Matter?

"Generalization" is a term that describes the occurrence of a trained behavior across time, setting, and target in the absence of the conditions that promoted its acquisition (Stokes & Baer, 1977). In other words, generalization refers to the occurrence of a behavior after the intervention has ended or in a place where the intervention has not yet occurred. For example, when a child uses social skills that are learned in a classroom social skills training group to interact with children on the playground the child has generalized his or her new skill (appropriate social behavior) to new settings (the playground). Similarly, if a child comes back from winter break and continues to exhibit the appropriate target behavior that was learned from an intervention that ended prior to winter break, then the intervention has generalized across time (sometimes called maintenance).

Programming for generalization involves altering the intervention in a manner that will make the occurrence of a target behavior more likely to occur in new settings with different stimuli and when the intervention conditions surrounding the new skill have been discontinued. Unfortunately, promoting initial behavior change and promoting generalization can be competing activities. Because the activities that promote rapid acquisition of a new skill are at odds with activities that promote robust and generalized skill development, interventionists must make choices about which strategies to emphasize during which stages of the intervention for optimal outcomes.

In the process of initial training, the general goal is to make the relationship between the antecedent stimuli, the target behavior, and planned consequences explicit and clear. From these planned instructional interactions, a child learns that if he or she behaves in a particular manner, in a specific situation, a consistent consequence will occur. Thus, consistency is important during initial training because any variation in the conditions above will slow the learning process. For example, use of posted classroom rules may serve as a powerful cue to the child that if certain behaviors occur in that setting, then predictable consequences will follow. When teachers monitor child behavior and respond with the expected consequences as specified by the classroom rules, the child gains confidence and skill in responding correctly. In this example, the posted rules are cues or prompts for behavior and a consistent reinforcement schedule will maximize the rate of acquisition.

> Promoting initial behavior change and promoting generalization can be competing activities. Because the activities that promote rapid acquisition of a new skill are at odds with activities that promote robust and generalized skill development, interventionists must make choices about which strategies to emphasize during which stages of the intervention.

Unfortunately, the very conditions that maximize how quickly a child learns something will weaken robust behavior change. For example, a student who has responded successfully to the above intervention may enter a new classroom and notice immediately that rules are not posted. In that circumstance, there is no signal or cue indicating to the child that certain behaviors are expected and will be reinforced or punished and hence, the student may be less likely to engage in the trained behaviors. Similarly, if the teacher simply stops reinforcing the behaviors consistently, the child will likely notice and may stop engaging in the trained behavior (the classroom rules no longer signify that reinforcement is consistently available for those behaviors). Generalization programming involves the use of strategies that are not the best methods for producing initial behavior change (e.g., making the cues or signals less salient or detectable to students, providing reinforcement less consistently or predictably, varying the training stimuli and settings).

In 1977, Stokes and Baer introduced the idea of generalization programming and argued that behavior change efforts that focused solely on rapid and accurate skill acquisition ultimately undermined the larger goals of intervention. According to Stokes and Baer, successful interventions required upfront thinking and planning to implement behavior change that could be useful to clients when the intervention ceased or the client returned to his or her everyday settings. Stokes and Baer outlined nine core methods of generalization programming. In 1989, Stokes and Osnes refined and revised Stokes and Baer's 1977 list of generalization programming techniques. The resulting list includes 12 methods that are categorized in three general categories of generalization. What follows is a review of the generalization programming methods presented in Stokes and Osnes's 1989 article along with one important model from Stokes and Baer's work in 1977.

Train and Hope (Stokes & Baer, 1977)

While not technically a "category" of generalization programming, the first approach presented in Stokes and Baer's classic 1977 article was called "train and hope," which is typical practice (Stokes & Baer, 1977, p. 351). In the train and hope approach, after a training program has changed the specific behavior, generalization of behavior is measured. Note that no actual steps are taken to increase generalization. Stokes and Baer wrote that while this approach is not truly a method to train generalization, it is important that generalization behaviors are assessed and analyzed. As such, this method does give some sort of indication of the extent to which generalization behavior is occurring. Unfortunately, in regard to educational intervention, the train and hope method as described above is somewhat fictional because assessment of generalization is often absent. The lack of data on generalization and maintenance rates concerns many education professionals.

Use What Is Already Working for the Student: Exploit Current Functional Contingencies (Stokes & Osnes, 1989)

The first category of generalization programming techniques is focused on using a system of contingencies that exists around the target behavior before the intervention is introduced. Stokes and Osnes (1989) divide consequences into two forms: natural and artificial. Natural consequences are those that exist prior to any sort of purposeful manipulation. For example, when a child naturally feels happy and pleased with his or her work completion, that feeling of being pleased and happy reinforces work completion for that student. For many children the natural consequence of successfully reading a passage has the effect of increasing the frequency and duration of reading. Pragmatically, these children were not taught to enjoy reading the material. Artificial rewards and punishers can be introduced to reinforce and or punish target behaviors. Artificial rewards and punishments are frequently used in schools and include things like small tangible rewards, loss of privileges or free time, and earning small privileges and preferred activities.

> **Natural consequences exist without constant manipulation, whereas artificial functional contingencies are typically dependent on the presence of an interventionist.**

Natural consequences have a number of advantages over artificial consequences, one of which is particularly relevant to generalization programming. Natural consequences

exist without constant manipulation, whereas artificial functional contingencies are typically dependent on the presence of an interventionist. As a result, when the interventionist
is no longer available, the artificial consequences are likely to disappear, whereas natural
consequences should remain. Specifically, Stokes and Osnes (1989) identified four ways to
exploit natural functional contingencies: (1) contact natural consequences, (2) recruit natural consequences, (3) modify maladaptive consequences, and (4) reinforce occurrences of
generalization.

Contact Natural Consequences

When target behaviors are selected based on whether they are likely to be naturally reinforced in the target setting, they are more likely to generalize. For example, if there are two
options for a student to request teacher assistance (raising hand or calling out) and we know
that one response is more likely to be reinforced (raising hand), then selecting that behavior
as the target behavior will increase the probability that the child will raise his or her hand
to gain adult assistance in new settings or when the intervention has ceased.

Recruit Natural Consequences

In some situations there are potential consequences in an environment that could act in a
manner that supports the acquisition of a target behavior but are not experienced by the
student for some reason. In a setting where a target behavior is reinforced, we may see that
reinforcement occurs only once a behavior reaches a certain rate or frequency or following
a certain interval of time. It could be that those demands are too high to establish the target
behavior. By analogy, if we water a plant every 2 weeks but the plant requires more water
than that to thrive, we would be wrong to conclude that watering the plant is not useful or
not needed. Instead, we would be wise to consider that perhaps the plant requires water
more frequently to grow successfully. If a target behavior occurs below the threshold needed
to contact the consequence, then the behavior will not be reinforced and established. For
example, if a teacher readily provides high levels of praise when a child is on task for 30 minutes, the student who works for only 15 minutes would not access that praise. Planning an
intervention that gets the teacher to provide the consequence at 15-minute intervals allows
the behavior to become established using a naturally occurring consequence that is more
likely to occur when the intervention has ceased or to occur in different settings (in contrast
with delivery of stickers for on-task behavior in 15-minute intervals).

   In a classic demonstration of this approach, Stokes, Fowler, and Baer (1978) trained
both regular-education and "disruptive" students to ask teachers, "How is my work?" after
periods of sustained effort to increase praise and attention. The results of the study indicated that children could actively recruit teacher praise through cuing, thus accessing a
naturally occurring reinforcer in the classroom environment. This trained reciprocal interaction logically provides both the needed prompt for the teacher to praise the student and
the necessary reinforcement for the student to continue the academic task demand. In other

situations it is possible that a child may not recognize the positive consequences that are available for certain behaviors. In such instances the child should be trained to recognize the consequences and/or the consequences should be made more explicit.

Modify Maladaptive Consequences

It would be ideal if all consequences in the natural environment reinforced the socially desirable behaviors. Realistically, however, there will be a number of conditions and occasions in which consequences reinforce maladaptive responses or punish desired responses. For example, when a student raises his or her hand and waits patiently to be called on, but the teacher ignores the raised hand or tells the student to put his or her hand down, hand raising has been punished and may be less likely to occur in the future. Similarly, when the child calls out (after raising his or her hand, waiting patiently, and being ignored or asked to put his or her hand down) and the teacher then responds to the child, then the teacher has inadvertently reinforced an undesired behavior and increased the likelihood that it will occur in the future.

> **It would be ideal if all consequences in the natural environment reinforced the socially desirable behaviors. Realistically, however, there will be conditions and occasions in which consequences reinforce maladaptive responses or punish desired responses.**

Reinforce Occurrences of Generalization

Similar to train and hope, this final subcategory involves noticing when desired generalization occurs and a reinforcing stimulus is applied to increase the likelihood of continued generalized behavior. For example, if a teacher notices that a student applies a behavioral strategy in one class that he or she learned in another, it is important to take the time to praise that generalization behavior. Providing praise (or other reinforcer) is critical, as the generalized behavior may not naturally be initially reinforced in the secondary setting. Using an academic example, while in time applying a study strategy in a new topic area (e.g., math and reading) may prove effective, it may initially not work due to differences in the topic. A teacher who reinforces the generalization of the strategy increases the likelihood that the student will keep trying it and thus increase the chances that the student will find success in the new application area.

Train Diversely (Stokes & Osnes, 1989)

As noted above, the strategies that facilitate generalization are often at odds with those strategies that facilitate acquisition. Training and instruction can be adjusted to maximize potential for generalization. Interventionists must balance strategies to ensure that the desired skills are established while making every effort to cultivate a robust skill set that can be adapted for use in a variety of contexts and persist across time. Stokes and Osnes (1989) describe four ways to alter training to facilitate generalization, which include (1) use sufficient stimulus exemplars, (2) use sufficient response exemplars, (3) make antecedents less discriminable, and (4) make consequences less discriminable.

Use Sufficient (or Different) Stimulus Exemplars

Any training program will naturally occur in a particular environment. This environment can be defined by the place, the time of day, the person who is doing the intervention, and the materials used during the intervention. The technical term for each aspect that defines the training environment is a "stimulus exemplar." In this category of training diversely, an attempt is made to use multiple stimulus exemplars. For example, if a social skills training group is conducted in the school psychologist's office, that location is considered the training environment or a stimulus exemplar. Stokes and Osnes (1989) note that this method is most effective when the stimulus exemplars match the goal of generalization. For example, a number of social skills training programs use a homework component so that the behaviors are practiced in two environments. A second example would be to have a peer who is in both the training setting and the target setting (e.g., playground).

Use Sufficient Response Exemplars

This tactic focuses on the specific behaviors used throughout the training of a desired behavior. Specific behaviors used to facilitate acquisition of a skill are called "response exemplars." Examples of response exemplars are modeling, feedback, and rehearsal. Research has shown that using multiple response exemplars in training increases generalization of the desired behavior (Plienis et al., 1987).

Make Antecedents Less Discriminable

Training programs typically rely on matching a specific stimulus with the desired behavior. While this method is highly effective in a training setting where the stimulus is likely to be presented, it is not effective in producing generalization. In the setting where generalization is desired, there is a high probability that the stimuli will not reliably occur. One tactic is to make the antecedents of the desired behavior less discriminable (in other words less detectable) in the training condition. Stokes and Osnes (1989) indicate that these programs have been called "loose training." The idea here is that if children only have a loose concept of when a behavior will work, once they start using the behavior they might try it out in a range of situations. While "loose training" is somewhat problematic for training, this tactic is aimed at producing a desired behavior that is not fully dependent on a specific stimulus.

Make Consequences Less Discriminable

Obviously, training programs also focus on the specific consequences of the desired behavior. Following the same logic used with making antecedents less discriminable, focusing on specific consequences has an enhanced affect on the acquisition of the desired behavior, but unfortunately limits the chance of generalization. For example, the more a child notices that only when a specific teacher is in the room will he or she be praised for behaving appropriately, the less likely the child is to behave in said appropriate manner when other teachers are around. This of course works the same way with punishment. As another example, it is understood that the presence of a police officer substantially increases the likelihood that a motorist who is driving well above the speed limit will get a ticket. As such, in the presence of a police officer motorists slow down, and then speed up when they don't see a police officer for a bit of time. In order to mitigate this effect, Stokes and Osnes (1989) suggest that three mechanisms exist to make consequences less discriminable. First, schedules of reinforcement have been used to present the consequence of a desired behavior in a manner that minimizes extinction. This same technology can be used with generalization. For example, if reinforcement is provided variably throughout training, then variable rates of reinforcement will be anticipated in other settings. Second, the use of delayed reinforcement has the potential to facilitate generalization. If reinforcement is delayed during acquisition, then the lack of immediate reinforcement will not preclude the continuation of desired behavior. Finally, the presence of the trainer who provides the consequence of the desired behavior can be varied. If the trainer is not always present during acquisition, then the trainee learns that the consequence is not always noticed and reinforcement is not always delivered.

Introduce a New Prompt or Consequence That Will Work in the Natural Environment: Incorporate Functional Mediators (Stokes & Osnes, 1989)

This final category is based on the idea of including mediators, or stimuli, in the training session that can then be transported into the setting where generalization is desired. These mediators should have some relevance in the training condition and they should not be chosen arbitrarily (e.g., based on availability). Conceptually, the mediator would then act to prompt the desired behavior in the setting where generalization is desired. Some mediators would also have embedded instructions to help the individual correctly do the behavior in that setting. Stokes and Osnes (1989) focus on four types of mediators that can be used to facilitate generalization, which include (1) incorporate common salient physical stimuli, (2) incorporate common salient social stimuli, (3) incorporate salient self-mediated physical stimuli, and (4) incorporate salient self-mediated oral and overt stimuli.

Incorporate Common Salient Physical Stimuli

Physical objects that can be incorporated in the training condition offer a noticeable stimulus that can be transported to other settings. Another option would be to use a physical object that happens to be present in both the training environment and the environment in which generalization is desired. Using this approach, the object would be incorporated in the training condition to either evoke the target behavior or as a part of a larger protocol. After this training condition has been completed, the object would be placed in the target environment. Conceptually, if the object functions as an antecedent stimulus for the desired behavior, then the likelihood of that behavior occurring increases. Examples include self-monitoring chart, response-cost lottery tickets, timers, green light/red light cues, and signal-discriminated time outs.

Incorporate Common Salient Social Stimuli

An overt social behavior could be used in both the training and generalization condition as a mediator. Such a mediator would be easily programmed in the natural environment, and ideally, a social stimulus that is naturally present in the generalization condition can be utilized in the training condition (e.g., having a teacher or peer in the natural environment use a social sign that is also used in the training condition to elicit the desired behavior).

Incorporate Salient Self-Mediated Physical Stimuli

Using the same logic that you would use when incorporating common physical stimuli, physical objects that can be carried by the child can also act as a mediator. For example, a child who brings a self-monitoring sheet from class is using a self-mediated physical stimulus. As with the previous categories, the self-mediated stimuli should be used as an integral part of training and then integrated into the target setting to facilitate generalization. For example, a first-grade student could be taught to rate his or her behavior toward two positively stated goals (e.g., I respond to teacher requests as soon as I hear them and I keep my hands to myself) every 15 minutes on a 3-point scale. The student could then be taught to use this rating as a self-monitoring tool and be given a plastic clipboard with the rating sheets attached.

Incorporate Salient Self-Mediated Oral and Overt Stimuli

Finally, a child can use an oral stimulus to work as a mediator. For example, self-instructions and oral goal setting can be used both in the training setting and by the child in another time and place. While physical mediators seem very easy to use, Stokes and Osnes (1989) note that oral mediators can be difficult to monitor.

SCHOOL-BASED BEHAVIORAL INTERVENTION APPLICATION OF PROGRAMMING FOR GENERALIZATION

Although it is difficult to ascertain to what extent generalization programming techniques are applied in school-based intervention practices, we can examine consultation models that are at the core of interventions in a secondary services model. Noell and Witt (1996) provided an overview of the extent to which school consultation models program for generalization and concluded that behavior consultation does not typically provide specific information on how to program for intervention generalization to other children with functionally similar problem behaviors. Consistent with much of the modern education, consultation typically relies on a train and hope approach to generalization that is more about monitoring strategy than a programming method.

Sheridan, Welch, and Orme (1996) noted that few studies regarding school consultation provided data on generalization and thus little is known about generalization of consultation-related behaviors. Although it would be ideal

> **Although it would be ideal to suggest that generalization programming is well developed in the consultative world, the reality is that popular school consultation models do not actively program for intervention generalization or other consultation-related behaviors.**

to suggest that generalization programming is well developed in the consultative world, the reality is that popular school consultation models do not actively program for intervention generalization or other consultation-related behaviors (Riley-Tillman & Eckert, 2001).

In order for school personnel to include steps to enhance generalizability of interventions, three issues must be considered. First, it is important for teachers to both maintain interventions over time, and for students to both maintain and generalize the positive outcomes of behavioral intervention. Second, there is an established generalization programming technology in the extant literature base. Finally, there has been a general lack of attention to the specific programming of generalization within the school-based intervention literature. Considering these three points, it is not surprising that it has been suggested that Stokes and Osnes's (1989) and Stokes and Baer's (1977) generalization programming tactics are a good framework on which to create a consultation generalization program (Kratochwill, Elliott, & Rotto, 1995; Lentz & Daly, 1996). Logical applications include train and hope tactics, exploit current functional contingencies, train diversely, and incorporate functional mediators.

Train and Hope (Stokes & Baer, 1977)

Though not actually a training model, the assessment aspect of "train and hope" is an important step in understanding treatment integrity. This process provides outcome data as to the rate of generalization behavior, which offers the opportunity for subsequent programming. For example, one can only reinforce generalization behaviors (a generalization programming tactic), if the presence or absence of such behaviors is noted. That being said, it is critical to again note that this is not a method of generalization programming. Rather, this is good general practice in assessing preferred outcome variables. In practice, if generalization is important, it should be actively monitored as part of the behavior change effort and a generalization programming method should be utilized.

Exploit Current Functional Contingencies (Stokes & Osnes, 1989)

As noted above, the first method of exploiting natural consequences is to select target behaviors that are likely to be reinforced in the desired settings (e.g., other classrooms or academic classes). This method requires that the educational professionals designing an intervention have a thorough understating of the contingencies that exist in the target environment. From there, appropriate behaviors that are most likely to come into contact with powerful consequences should be prioritized. In addition, although reinforcing stimuli often are present in a target setting, a child may not be attuned to such consequences. If there is a situation in which the child is not attending to the reinforcing stimuli, then you must teach the target child to attend to the natural consequences. This will increase the probably of generalizing the behavior. In other situations, where potentially reinforcing stimuli are not being provided, it will be important to recruit that stimuli. For example, a teacher may be providing potentially reinforcing praise to other children, but not the target child. By recruiting the teacher to provide the praise to the target child you will likely promote generalization of the child's appropriate behavior. Likewise, any punishing consequences that exist when the child exhibits the generalized behavior must be altered. If punishing consequences are allowed to exist in the desired setting, then the impact of reinforcing stimuli will be mitigated. Finally, even if other generalization programming methods are in place, it is critical that the child be reinforced when he or she exhibits occurrences of generalization of desired behaviors. This category directs the relevant educational professional to "catch" instances of generalization and use those opportunities to provide a reinforcing consequence. As noted above, this method is more likely if occurrences of generalization are actually being assessed.

Train Diversely (Stokes & Osnes, 1989)

Behavioral interventions can be very focused and tightly controlled. This is particularly the case with higher-stakes cases where it is essential to change the target behavior as fast as possible. Note that there is a tension here and the goals of the behavior change effort, the severity of the child's problem, and the capacities of the student have to be considered in determining what level of "looseness" can be tolerated and still work in the setting and for the student. As such, the educational professional and the child typically focus on one behavior in one setting. While this method should aid in effectively intervening with the target behavior in the training setting, it may also limit generalization. The following suggestions are in line with conducting behavioral interventions in a more diverse manner.

As behavioral interventions typically focus on one behavior in one situation, the use of two or more stimulus exemplars is a logical place to start. Conducting the intervention in multiple places and with a number of people should enhance generalization. For example, a study by Taylor and Harris (1995) focused on training the oral skill of asking "What's that?" for individuals with autism. Training concluded with a phase in which unexpected items were installed in different settings. Participants were given the opportunity to practice saying, "What's that?" and receive reinforcement when they encountered items that were out of place in particular contexts. This intervention resulted in generalization of the skill across target objects, adults, and places. In addition, allowing a range of acceptable behavioral responses allows the child to learn a range of alternative behavior, some of which may work more efficiently in other settings or times.

The final method in the category is making the antecedents and consequences less discriminable. While this may not be ideal in high-stakes cases, or in the initial stages of behavioral intervention, it can be used in latter stages after behavioral supports for the appropriate behavior have been established. Although training diversely can enhance generalization, they should be done with some caution. Logically, such methods will slow the progress of behavioral interventions, and consideration should be given as to the importance of immediacy of behavior change and generalization of behavior change. In cases where immediacy is critical, other generalization programming methods should be prioritized.

Incorporate Functional Mediators (Stokes & Osnes, 1989)

Considering the common use of physical or social stimuli in behavioral intervention, using functional mediators is the likely method of generalization programming. Either physical or social mediators that are also available in the desired generalization setting can also be incorporated in the training setting. In addition, mediators that the child can self-manage are commonly used. For example, self-monitoring sheets or daily behavior report cards can be used across a number of settings. The advantage of self-managed functional mediators is that they can work as a prompt for both the child and the educational professional in the secondary setting and align them to recruit natural occurrences. For example, in the case of a child who has a daily behavior report card that is filled out by each teacher, the card not only reminds the child what to do in each setting, but also should work as a prompt for the teacher to both provide appropriate feedback and a reinforcing stimulus.

CONCLUSION

While the bulk of intervention attention is focused on promoting the acquisition and proficiency of behaviors, it is also important to consider maintenance and generalization of behavior gains for the long-term success and viability of schoolwide problem-solving models. We offer evidence-based individual behavior maintenance and generalization interventions on pages 180–185 at the end of this chapter. Behaviors that are not maintained or generalized to other situations will result in the need for subsequent intervention. The long-term result of a lack of maintenance or generalization of intervention effects is the enviable overloading of the problem-solving model with neverending cases. Luckily, the technology for the promotion of generalization is fully available in the applied behavior analytic literature. This technology base should be embraced by educational professionals throughout the RTI framework to program for the long-term retention and expansion of intervention effects. Obviously, this issue is restricted to only behavioral interventions. The next chapter addresses the necessity and challenges in regard to programing for maintenance and generalization of academic interventions.

Generalization: Exploit Functional Contingencies

Brief Description

This generalization technique utilizes consequences found naturally in or artificially added to the environment in order to promote generalization of behavior. There are four ways to exploit natural functional contingencies: identify natural consequences, recruit natural consequences, modify maladaptive consequences, and reinforce occurrences of generalization. This generalization programming brief is based on Stokes and Osnes (1989).

What "Common Problems" Does This Address?

Student does not know how or when to exhibit the desired behavior in environments other than the one in which he or she was taught.

Procedure: Method 1. Contact Natural Consequences

Figure out which reinforcers are found naturally in the environment.

- Step 1. Identify the environment(s) in which you would like for the desired behavior to be exhibited. For example: Student will raise his or her hand to obtain teacher attention in the classroom and library.
- Step 2. Figure out why the student is responding inappropriately within those environments. For example: Student calls out the answer and the teacher sporadically acknowledges him or her by a nod of the head. After looking at the antecedents and consequences of calling out, you figure out that he or she wants the teacher's attention.
- Step 3. When implementing an intervention, try to find reinforcers that exist naturally within the environments. For example: We know that most teachers will acknowledge a student who raises his or her hand appropriately so acknowledgment (attention) will be the natural consequence that we try. When a student raises his or her hand quietly, the teacher looks at the student, listens to his or her answer, and nods. This should increase the frequency at which the student raises his or her hand in class.

Procedure: Method 2. Recruit Natural Consequences

Employ natural reinforcers at a higher frequency when the student is learning a new behavior.

- Step 1. Identify the student's natural reinforcers. For example: The student likes to acquire the teacher's attention.
- Step 2. Deliver the identified frequency at a high rate when the student is first starting to learn an appropriate response. For example: Step 1 of student's intervention—the teacher calls on the student every time he or she raises his or her hand with a quiet voice. Step 2—Once student has learned the appropriate behavior, the teacher calls on the student every two times the student raises his or her hand appropriately.
- Step 3. If the student is still exhibiting target behavior at a high frequency, the teacher will call on the student at the same rate as the other students.

(cont.)

Procedure: Method 3. Modify Maladaptive Consequences

Make sure that the desired behavior is not accidentally being punished.

- Step 1. When the frequency of the desired behavior decreases, analyze the antecedents and consequences of the behavior in order to determine the connections that exist between the desired behavior and the environment. For example: Student raises hand quietly but teacher does not acknowledge him or her.
- Step 2. After paying attention to antecedents and consequences, determine whether consequence is the reason why behavior is decreasing. For example: Student raises hand less and calls out more if teacher does not acknowledge his or her raised hand.
- Step 3. When punishment is figured out, replace punishment with a consequence that is reinforcing to the child. For example: Student raises hand quietly and teacher calls on him or her. Student raises his or her hand three more times.

Procedure: Method 4. Reinforce Occurrences of Generalization

Notice when generalization occurs and provide reinforcement.

- Step 1. Observe student in new environment.
- Step 2. Immediately reinforce the student when he or she engages in desired behavior.

Critical Components That Must Be Implemented for the Intervention to Be Successful

- Must accurately identify the antecedent, behavior, and consequence.
- Must know the function of the behavior. (Why does the child engage or not engage in the behavior? Hint: Study the antecedents and consequences of the target behavior.)
- Must alter contingencies so that target behavior is being reinforced.
- Must strictly follow set schedule of reinforcement.
- Must heavily reinforce first few occurrences of generalization.

References

Stokes, T. F., & Baer, D. M. (1977). An implicit technology of generalization. *Journal of Applied Behavior Analysis, 10*, 349–367.
Stokes, T. F., & Osnes, P. G. (1989). An operant pursuit of generalization. *Behavior Therapy, 20*, 337–355.

Note. The lead student developer on this brief was Shannon Brooks, a psychology graduate student at East Carolina University.

Generalization: Incorporate Functional Mediators

Brief Description

This method incorporates teaching with artificial cues (cues that are not naturally used in generalizing environment) that include using physical object cues, social cues, self-regulated physical object cues, and self-regulated verbal cues. This generalization programming brief is based on Stokes & Osnes (1989).

What "Common Problems" Does This Address?

The student will not perform target behavior in another environment.

Procedure: Method 1. Incorporate Common Salient Physical Stimuli in Both the Training and the Natural Environment (the Environment in Which You Would Like the Target Behavior to Generalize)

- Step 1: Choose a significant (salient) physical stimulus that can be found in both the training environment and the natural environment. For example: Clearly written rules written in the cafeteria and in the library. The target behavior is using quiet voices that are included in both places' rules.
- Step 2: Use the significant physical stimuli (objects) when teaching the target behavior in the training environment. For example: Have the student look at rules every time he or she comes into the cafeteria. You may have to reinforce him or her for both attending to the new physical stimuli *and* being quiet if you have verbally reminded him or her of the rules in the past.
- Step 3: Introduce the student to the new environment and reinforce the student *immediately* if he or she engages in the target behavior. For example: When the student walked into the library he or she immediately looked at the rules and sat down quietly. The student received 2 extra minutes of free time.

Procedure: Method 2. Incorporate Common Salient Social Stimuli

Train an outstanding mediator as a stimuli in both the training environment and in the natural environment.

- Step 1: Choose a mediator that will exist in both the training environment and the natural environment (the environment in which you would like to generalize). For example: Choose a peer who shares the same schedule as the target student.
- Step 2: Train the mediator to model appropriate behavior for the target student and prompt the target student's behavior change if the student is behaving inappropriately. For example: Train a peer to sit beside the target student in all classes and elbow the target student when the student needs to lower his or her voice.
- Step 3: Reinforce the target student and the peer if the target behavior occurs in the natural (not training) environment.

(cont.)

Procedure: Method 3. Incorporate Salient Self-Mediated Physical Stimuli

Use self-mediated stimuli such as a token board, a rule sheet, or a self-monitoring sheet that the student can carry around with him or her from setting to setting (e.g., from class to cafeteria).

- Step 1: Choose a stimuli (such as a clipboard or index card) that is transportable and write down the rules for proper behavior.
- Step 2: Model and discuss the rules for appropriate behavior with the target student.
- Step 3: Teach the target student how to check off the behavior that he or she is exhibiting. For example: Put a check beside quiet voice if your voice is quiet.
- Step 4: Make sure that all of the teachers know why the student is carrying around stimuli.
- Step 5: Reinforce the student *immediately* when he or she engages in a target behavior when that is generalized to a new environment.

Procedure: Method 4. Incorporate Salient Self-Mediated Verbal Stimuli

Use verbal communication (can be the student talking to him- or herself or the teacher verbally talking to the student) to set goals and remind the student of how and when to engage in appropriate behavior.

- Step 1: Decide what the goal and verbal prompts are that go with target behavior (e.g., "When I walk into music class I will sit quietly and put my hands in my lap. If I talk I will lose a card.").
- Step 2: Teach the child to use the verbal prompt in order to engage in target behavior.
- Step 3: Reinforce the child when he or she engages in generalized target behavior.

Critical Components That Must Be Implemented for the Intervention to Be Successful

All stimuli must be transportable so that they can be easily located an taken and used in every environment in which you want the behavior to generalize.

- Choose a reward that will be reinforcing to target student.
- Reward student *immediately* when he or she generalizes a new behavior.
- Also, be meticulous when choosing a transportable stimulus to make sure that it is relevant to the target behavior occurring in the new environment.

Critical Assumptions/Problem-Solving Questions to Be Asked

- The child will be able to recognize the transportable stimuli in the new environments.
- The portable stimuli are relevant enough to be related to target behavior.
- The trainer will be near enough to the target child to catch the first generalization of the behavior and reinforce it immediately.
- The mediator will be capable of prompting and modeling appropriate behavior.

References

Stokes, T. F., & Baer, D. M. (1977). An implicit technology of generalization. *Journal of Applied Behavior Analysis, 10*, 349–367.

Stokes, T. F., & Osnes, P. G. (1989). An operant pursuit of generalization. *Behavior Therapy, 20*, 337–355.

Note. The lead student developer on this brief was Shannon Brooks, a psychology graduate student at East Carolina University.

Generalization: Train Diversely

Brief Description

Training and instruction can be adjusted to maximize potential for generalization. Trainers need to cautiously keep the balance between behavior acquisition (learning the behavior) and behavior robustness (how many environments the trained behavior can be used in). Four ways to alter training to facilitate generalization are: use sufficient stimulus exemplars, use sufficient response exemplars, make antecedents less discriminable, and make consequences less discriminable. This generalization programming brief is based on Stokes & Osnes (1989).

What "Common Problems" Does This address?

Student in new environment does not engage in target behavior.

Procedure: Method 1. Use Sufficient Stimulus Exemplars

Change components of the teaching environment to increase likelihood that target behavior will generalize.

- Step 1. Identify the setting in which the target behavior is being taught.
- Step 2. Alter aspects of the environment while teaching the behavior (could include moving to a different place in the room, using different paper, performing behavior in another classroom or outside, etc.)

Procedure: Method 2. Use Sufficient Response Exemplars

Respond and teach in varied ways to promote generalization.

- Step 1. Identify current teaching and response methods.
- Step 2. Change components of teaching (modeling, prompting: visual, verbal, auditory) and/ or components of responding (verbal praise, high fives, applause, etc.) when teaching the target behavior. Choose teaching methods and responses that will easily be applicable to or naturally occur in other environments.

Procedure: Method 3. Make Antecedents Less Discriminable

Make antecedents blend into the natural environment.

- Step 1. Identify the target behavior's antecedent.
- Step 2. When teaching the target behavior, choose an antecedent that blends in with the natural environment as much as possible. For example: Rather then teaching a child to put away his or her books when seeing a cue card, teach the target student to put the books away when he or she sees that other students have closed their books and begun to put them away.
- Step 3. Reinforce target behavior. For example: Verbally recognize the student's behavior: "I see that you put your books away like everyone else! I'm so proud of you!"

(cont.)

Procedure: Method 4. Make Consequences Less Discriminable

- Step 1. Identify the consequence of the target behavior.
- Step 2. When developing a new consequence to promote behavior change, teach the new behavior using a consequence that will most likely be found in the natural environment.
- Step 3. Reinforce target behavior For example: Verbally recognize the student's behavior: "I see that you put your books away like everyone else! I'm so proud of you!" Remember—in order to decide whether your consequence is reinforcing you must observe the behavior to see whether it increases (not decreases).

Critical Components That Must Be Implemented for the Intervention to Be Successful

- Reinforce the target behavior as soon as it occurs in the natural setting.
- Figure out which naturally occurring antecedents and consequences reinforce (increase) or punish (decrease) the desired behavior.
- Use the natural antecedents and consequences first before introducing consequences that do not occur naturally within the environment.
- Reinforcers and punishers must be embedded within the natural environment.

Critical Assumptions/Problem-Solving Questions to Be Asked

- This intervention assumes that naturally occurring antecedents and consequences can be found in the teaching environment.
- It also assumes that both the naturally occurring antecedent and the naturally occurring consequence will serve as a reminder and reward/punisher that will be effective for the child.
- In addition, this procedure assumes that the child can fluently and accurately perform the target behavior for which generalization is programmed.

References

Stokes, T. F., & Baer, D. M. (1977). An implicit technology of generalization. *Journal of Applied Behavior Analysis, 10*, 349–367.

Stokes, T. F., & Osnes, P. G. (1989). An operant pursuit of generalization. *Behavior Therapy, 20*, 337–355.

Note. The lead student developer on this brief was Shannon Brooks, a psychology graduate student at East Carolina University.

CHAPTER 12

Maintenance and Generalization of Academic Interventions

OVERVIEW

Acquisition and development of proficiency of a skill are obviously important, but children with academic difficulties often struggle to retain and actually use the newly learned information for math (Geary et al., 2006) and reading (Swanson, 2003; Swanson & Jerman, 2007). As stated in the previous chapter, successful interventions produce robust and enduring behavior change across time, target, and setting, and if academic gains are not maintained and transferred into other settings, then the interventions have not been successful.

MAINTENANCE AND GENERALIZATION AS PART OF THE LEARNING PROCESS

The primary objective for initial interventions is to enhance the accuracy with which academic skills are completed and the focus then shifts to proficiency in which accurate rehearsal is used (Haring & Eaton, 1978). Maintenance is the phase in which the child can accurately and fluently complete the task, following a delay after the initial acquisition and proficiency, without reteaching the skill (Alberto & Troutman, 2006). As noted in the previous chapter, generalization occurs when a trained behavior continues to occur across time, target, and setting in the absence of the conditions that promoted its acquisition (Stokes & Baer, 1977). From a more academic perspective, generalization involves demonstration of a newly learned skill in different conditions than those in which the skill was learned (Alberto & Troutman, 2006). For example, if a child is taught the sound for the letter *t* and then the child correctly reads the letter in the word *hat*, then he or she is demonstrating basic transfer and generalization. Applying math facts to solve word problems also requires generalization. In fact, just about all reading, writing, and spelling skills that are taught, and may be taught in isolation within an intervention, are actually used within a different context.

Maintenance of learned information is critical because it directly precedes generalization and is necessary for global gains in the skill (Ardoin, 2006), but research with academic interventions tends to focus on acquisition (e.g., Cates et al., 2003; Skinner, Belfiore, Mace, Williams-Wilson, & Johns, 1997) and has frequently neglected maintenance and generalization (Burns, 2004). Previous research found that some interventions were more effective than others when acquisition of the skill was examined, but then the more effective intervention was the inferior option when maintenance and generalization were considered (Burns & Sterling-Turner, 2010). In other words, some interventions are more appropriate for initially teaching a skill, but others are more effective for retaining and generalization of the skill.

> **Some interventions were more effective than others when acquisition of the skill was examined, but then the more effective intervention was the inferior option when maintenance and generalization were considered.**

For example, Nist and Joseph (2008) compared different flash-card approaches to teaching word recognition to six first-grade students identified as struggling learners. The two conditions were traditional drill (TD; 100% unknown words rehearsed on flash cards) and incremental rehearsal (IR; Tucker, 1989; 10% unknown and 90% known words rehearsed in an incremental method in which one additional known word was added each time the unknown word was presented). The results indicated that the students learned more words with IR, but that TD was more efficient because it resulted in more words acquired per instructional minute. However, Nist and Joseph examined generalization by having students read the newly learned words in sentences and found that all of the participants generalized over 90% of the newly learned words when they were taught with IR (range 91 to 98%, median = 94%), but only one student generalized 90% of the words for the TD model, three generalized between 80 and 89%, and two generalized approximately 75% of the words (median = 81%). Moreover, a comparison of the efficiency of IR and TD found that the latter was more efficient when considering acquisition, but the former was as efficient when considering retention rather than acquisition (Burns & Sterling-Turner, 2010).

SCHOOL-BASED BEHAVIORAL INTERVENTION APPLICATION OF PROGRAMMING FOR GENERALIZATION

The concept of generalization has its roots in behavioral interventions (Stokes & Baer, 1977) and was explained in greater detail in Chapter 11. Moreover, the three issues outlined for behavior interventions are also true for academic interventions in that (1) it is important that students both maintain and generalize the positive outcomes of academic interventions, and (2) there has been a general lack of attention to the specific programming of generalization within the school-based academic intervention literature. However, the third consideration for generalization of behavior intervention (i.e., there is an established generalization programming technology in the extant literature base) is much less true for academic interventions. Moreover, unlike other phases of learning addressed in this book, there are very few "generalization" interventions. Instead, interventionists use various strategies to make modifications to interventions to better ensure generalization.

Research has consistently examined the generalization strategies recommended by Stokes and colleagues (Stokes & Baer, 1977; Stokes & Osnes, 1989), but those generalization programming tactics have been much less frequently applied to academic concerns (Burns, 2004). Below are descriptions of the applications of Stokes and colleagues' generalization frameworks described in Chapter 11 and how they could be applied to interventions that focus on reading, math, and writing.

Train and Hope (Stokes & Baer, 1977)

As stated in the previous chapter, "train and hope" is not a category of generalization programming but instead involves measuring generalization after a training program has changed the specific behavior, without actually taking steps to increase generalization. Train and hope does not necessarily lead to generalization, but examining outcome data regarding generalization is an important first step to actually increasing generalization.

Assessing maintenance is fairly straightforward because it involves determining whether the child retained the skill after a period of time. Teachers who conduct weekly or monthly review tests of previously mastered material are conducting maintenance assessments. As stated earlier, it is important to assess maintenance because some interventions may increase the rate at which skills are acquired but do not effectively lead to longer-term retention; other interventions might enhance maintenance more effectively. Moreover, it is possible that there are children who learn the new material well but who significantly struggle to recall it at a later time (Geary et al., 2007; Swanson, 2003).

How much retention is enough? Many practitioners use 80% as a criterion for meeting goals, but 80% retention for some skills is clearly too low, a point well demonstrated by the commonly used facetious example of setting a criterion of 80% successfully crossing the street. Although it is difficult to establish a criterion for all academic tasks, 90% has been shown to represent an appropriate level of challenge for most academic tasks (e.g., spelling, math facts, sight words, letter sounds; Burns, 2004) and could suggest a potential criterion. However, the appropriate level of challenge for contextual reading is slightly higher at 93 to 97% (Gickling & Armstrong, 1978; Treptow et al., 2007), and maintenance precedes generalization, which suggests that the higher criterion is needed when the skill is to be applied to reading in context.

Generalization can be assessed by having the student use the newly learned information in a new context. For example, Nist and Joseph (2008) asked students to read newly learned words in the context of a simple sentence, and if the student read the word correctly in the sentence, it was considered generalized. However, in order to test generalization of the newly learned words, all of the other words within the sentences should be ones that the student knows without intervention. Of course, the easiest and most authentic way to assess generalization of word reading is to have the student read connected text from his or her curriculum and to note how frequently taught words are read correctly. Assessment of generalization of decoding skills can be accomplished by having the student spell words that contain the target sound, especially among more complex graphophonemic patterns (Robbins, Hosp, Hosp, & Flynn, 2010), and math facts by having the student complete written worksheets that contain the target problems among others or by having him or her complete word problems with the facts embedded in them (again being sure that the student can read the words and understands the operation).

Generalization is more difficult to assess for comprehension because it involves so many processes, most of which are not observable. Comprehension is most heavily influenced by background knowledge and vocabulary, and less so by inferences, word reading, and strategy use (Cromley & Azevedo, 2007), but we often focus our interventions on strategy use. Interventionists can assess how well vocabulary is generalized by simply asking the student to use the newly taught word in a sentence (Afflerbach, 2011). Assessing whether or not a taught strategy is used in context depends on the strategy being taught. For example, prediction could be assessed by providing the student a title and asking him or her to predict what the story will be about, and clarification could be assessed by having the student circle words that needed clarifying as he or she reads (Sporer, Brunstein, & Kieschke, 2009). More metacognitive approaches are probably only assessable through self-report and self-monitoring (Aaron & Joshi, 1992).

> **The most authentic way to assess generalization of word reading is to have the student read connected text from his or her curriculum and to note how frequently taught words are read correctly.**

Exploit Current Functional Contingencies (Stokes & Osnes, 1989)

The first strategy in generalization training is to select target behaviors that are likely to be reinforced in the desired settings (e.g., other classrooms or academic classes), and to prioritize behaviors that are most likely to come into contact with powerful reinforcement. An academic application of this approach would be to contextualize the newly learned items within easily accomplished tasks and to focus on skills that are frequently used in naturally occurring environments. Research has consistently demonstrated that having students practice target math facts with easily completed facts led to more target problems being completed (Wildmon, Skinner, Watson, & Garrett, 2004), and children demonstrated better reading comprehension when they could read at least 93% of the words correctly (Gickling & Armstrong, 1978; Treptow et al., 2007). Moreover, incremental rehearsal has consistently led to high levels of generalization for reading (Burns, 2002, 2007) and math (Codding et al., 2010), and led to greater generalization than traditional flash-card methods (Nist & Joseph, 2008). Thus, it seems that rehearsing skills within a large proportion of easier items increases generalization of the newly learned items. It also makes intuitive sense to have students practice newly learned skills in applied items so that the practice closely approximates the natural setting.

The second aspect of exploiting current functional contingencies, to teach skills that occur frequently in naturally settings, is somewhat self-evident. Given that time is such a precious commodity in K–12 schools, teachers have to focus on the skill that is the highest priority. Moreover, generalization will be more likely to occur if students are taught the aspect of a skill that will occur most frequently. For example, teaching vowel combinations would lead to better generalization than teaching words that contain the combination. Overlearning (i.e., continuing to practice once the student reaches a learning criterion) with newly learned skills also leads to increased retention and generalization (Driskell, Willis, & Copper, 1992), which suggests that using more frequently occurring stimuli would lead to more naturally occurring repetition and resulting generalization.

Train Diversely (Stokes & Osnes, 1989)

Training diversely for behavioral interventions can be accomplished by using a high number of different exemplars during training or by conducting the intervention in multiple places. Of the generalization strategies, this is likely the one that is most transferable to academic skills. For example, a student learning the *ing* suffix could rehearse it with several different base words, practice reading various phonemes in different words, read words in different contexts, and practice multiplication facts through various games. These approaches likely accomplish both aspects of training diversely. Behavioral interventions should also be implemented in multiple contexts, which usually means locations, but learning academic skills in different rooms would likely do little to enhance generalization. Instead, academic skills are rehearsed in different contexts and by applying them in diverse ways.

Incorporate Functional Mediators (Stokes & Osnes, 1989)

Physical or social mediators that are also available in the desired generalization setting can also be used in the training setting to enhance generalization and are especially useful when they can be self-managed by the student. Mediators can also be effective to enhance the generalization of academic skills because they can help recall previous information or can be prompts to utilize different approaches.

Mnemonic strategies have been shown to substantially increase the rate at which students with academic difficulties recall previously learned information (Kavale & Forness, 2000), and simply cuing a student response could increase the likelihood that it will accurately occur (Rogevich & Perin, 2008). Moreover, metacognitive strategies, which involve teaching students to monitor their own learning and to implement appropriate strategies based on the task demand, has led to increased reading comprehension (Malone & Mastropieri, 1992). Finally, generalization for word recognition was directly enhanced by having the students state a definition of the word as they rehearsed it (Peter-

> Mnemonic strategies, cuing, metacognition, and linking to a definition all involve prompting a student response and could lead to enhanced generalization, which essentially mediates the relationship between the stimulus (e.g., the printed word) and the correct responding (e.g., reading the word).

son-Brown & Burns, 2011). It seems that these four approaches (mnemonic strategies, cuing, metacognition, and linking to a definition) all involve prompting a student response, which essentially mediates the relationship between the stimulus (e.g., the printed word) and the correct responding (e.g., reading the word) and could lead to enhanced generalization.

CONCLUSION

Generalization is an important but often overlooked component of academic intervention research. There are few interventions specifically designed for maintenance and generalization, but there are techniques that can be applied during initial learning and practice to enhance both. We offer evidence-based individual academic maintenance and generalization interventions on pages 192–199 at the end of this chapter. We can learn a great deal from existing research with behavior interventions and the principles learned can guide our efforts. However, there is a developed theory for designing academic generalization interventions, which should be given additional research attention.

Maintenance: Incremental Rehearsal

Brief Description

Incremental rehearsal (IR; Tucker, 1989) can be used for students with varying difficulties, for different age groups, and for various skills. Research has consistently shown that IR increased retention (MacQuarrie-Klender, Tucker, Burns, & Hartman, 2002; Burns & Sterling-Turner, 2010) and generalization (Burns, 2007; Codding, Archer, & Connell, 2010; Nist & Joseph, 2008) for word recognition, math facts, vocabulary, letter sounds, and many other skills.

What "Common Problems" Does This Address?

IR is an intensive intervention and should only be used for students who really struggle with retaining and using newly learned information. It is generally used after a skill or stimulus has been initially taught. For example, IR could be used for math facts after the student understands the concept of the operation or for letter sounds after he or she has been taught what sound the letter makes in context. The intervention will be described here for use with word recognition, math facts, and spelling words, but IR could be used for almost any material that requires rote memorization.

Word-Recognition Procedure

1. As with any intervention of explicit items, begin with an assessment of what the student knows and only teach what he or she does not know, but use what he or she has already learned to support the process.
2. Individually present each word to the student in random order to assess whether they are known or unknown. Words correctly identified by the student (e.g., orally read) within 2 seconds are considered known, and those not correctly read within 2 seconds are unknown. The time limit of 2 seconds is oftentimes used to assess known words, but 3 seconds could be used for English-language learners to accommodate for dialectical and pronunciation issues.
3. Write each unknown word horizontally on a 3″ × 5″ index card. Also write down 8 to 10 words on an index card that the student can read within 1 second of presentation. The latter words will be used as known words.
4. Present the first unknown word to the student while orally providing the correct pronunciation. Next, ask the student to orally restate the word.
5. Ask the student to use the word in a sentence. If the word is used grammatically and semantically correctly, even if the sentence is simplistic, then reinforce the child and move to Step 5. If the word is not correctly used, then provide a short definition or synonym, and use the word in a sentence. Next, ask the child to make up a different sentence with the word in it and move to the next step if he or she does so correctly. Words not used correctly at this point should be removed and instructed in more depth.
6. Rehearse the unknown word with the following sequence and ask the student to state the word every time it is presented:
   a. Present the first unknown word and the first known word.
   b. Present the first unknown word, the first known word, and the second known word.

(cont.)

---

   c. Present the first unknown word, the first known word, the second known word, and the third known word.

   d. Present the first unknown word, the first known word, the second known word, the third known word, and the fourth known word.

   e. Present the first unknown word, the first known word, the second known word, the third known word, the fourth known word, and the fifth known word.

   f. Present the first unknown word, the first known word, the second known word, the third known word, the fourth known word, the fifth known word, and the sixth known word.

   g. Present the first unknown word, the first known word, the second known word, the third known word, the fourth known word, the fifth known word, the sixth known word, and the seventh known word.

   h. Present the first unknown word, the first known word, the second known word, the third known word, the fourth known word, the fifth known word, the sixth known word, the seventh known word, and the eighth known word.

7. After completing the rehearsal sequence with the first word, that first unknown word is then treated as the first known word, the previous eighth known word is removed, and a new unknown word is introduced. Thus, the number of cards always remains nine.

8. Continue individually rehearsing unknown words until three errors occur while rehearsing one word. Errors need not only occur on the word currently being rehearsed. Any inability to state a word correctly within 3 seconds counts as an error, even if that error occurs on a previously rehearsed word or a word that was known before the sequence began.

Math Facts Procedure

1. As with any intervention of explicit items, begin with an assessment of what the student knows and only teach what he or she does not know, but use what he or she has already learned to support the process.

2. Individually present each fact (e.g., $4 \times 3 = ??$) to the student in random order to assess whether they are known or unknown. Facts correctly answered by the student within 2 seconds are considered known, and those not correctly read within 2 seconds are unknown.

3. Write each unknown fact horizontally on a $3'' \times 5''$ index card. Also write down 8 to 10 math facts that the student can answer within 1 second. The latter facts will serve as known items.

4. Present the first unknown fact to the student while orally providing the correct pronunciation. Next, ask the student to orally restate the fact. For example, say, "Four times three is twelve. What is four times three?" If the child responds "twelve," then say, "Good, four times three is twelve. Please say the correct answer when you see this problem."

5. Rehearse the unknown fact with the following sequence and ask the student to state the fact every time it is presented:

   a. Present the first unknown fact and the first known fact.

   b. Present the first unknown fact, the first known fact, and the second known fact.

   c. Present the first unknown fact, the first known fact, the second known fact, and the third known fact.

   d. Present the first unknown fact, the first known fact, the second known fact, the third known fact, and the fourth known fact.

   e. Present the first unknown fact, the first known fact, the second known fact, the third known fact, the fourth known fact, and the fifth known fact.

   f. Present the first unknown fact, the first known fact, the second known fact, the third known fact, the fourth known fact, the fifth known fact, and the sixth known fact.

(cont.)

g. Present the first unknown fact, the first known fact, the second known fact, the third known fact, the fourth known fact, the fifth known fact, the sixth known fact, and the seventh known fact.

h. Present the first unknown fact, the first known fact, the second known fact, the third known fact, the fourth known fact, the fifth known fact, the sixth known fact, the seventh known fact, and the eighth known fact.

6. After completing the rehearsal sequence with the first fact, that first unknown fact is then treated as the first known fact, the previous eighth known fact is removed, and a new unknown fact is introduced. Thus, the number of cards always remains nine.

7. Continue individually rehearsing unknown facts until three errors occur while rehearsing one fact. Errors need not only occur on the fact currently being rehearsed. Any inability to state a fact correctly within 3 seconds counts as an error, even if that error occurs on a previously rehearsed fact or a fact that was known before the sequence began.

Spelling Procedure

1. As with any intervention of explicit items, begin with an assessment of what the student knows and only teach what he or she does not know, but use what he or she has already learned to support the process.

2. Individually present each spelling word to the student in random order to assess whether they are known or unknown. As the student to spell each word on a small portable whiteboard after you orally state the word. Words correctly spelled within a reasonable time are considered known. Unlike other stimuli (e.g., word recognition and math facts) there is not an acceptable time limit to assume automaticity. A student who takes 5 seconds to correctly write the spelling of a word may have the same level of automaticity for spelling that word as a student who takes only 2 seconds to spell it. Because the response is written, it is difficult to judge if a slow or fast response accurately represents automaticity. However, a student who correctly spells the word in say, 20 seconds, likely cannot spell the word effortlessly enough to use it in context.

3. Record the words that the student correctly spelled in a reasonable time (knowns) and those that were incorrectly spelled or required an excessive length of time (unknowns).

4. Write down the first unknown word on the whiteboard and orally read it to the student while pointing at the individual letters.

5. Ask the student to use the word in a sentence. If the word is used grammatically and semantically correctly, even if the sentence is simplistic, then reinforce the child and move to Step 5. If the word is not correctly used, then provide a short definition or synonym, and use the word in a sentence. Next, ask the child to make up a different sentence with the word in it and move to the next step if he or she does so correctly. Words not used correctly at this point should be removed and instructed in more depth.

6. Have the student copy the word by tracing it while saying the letters orally.

7. Cover the word with your hand and ask the student to spell the word from memory.

8. Remove your hand and have the student compare his or her spelling to the model. If it is correct, then say, "Good job" and proceed to the next step. If the word is not correct, then repeat Steps 6 and 7 until it is spelled correctly.

9. Erase the model and what the student wrote. Rehearse the unknown word with the following sequence and ask the student to state the word every time it is presented:

   a. Orally state the first unknown word and ask him or her to spell it and then spell the first known word. Erase the writing.

   b. Orally state the first unknown word and ask him or her to spell it, spell the first known word, and spell the second known word. Erase the writing.

(cont.)

    c. Orally state the first unknown word and ask him or her to spell it, spell the first known word, spell the second known word, and spell the third known word. Erase the writing.

    d. Orally state the first unknown word and ask him or her to spell it, spell the first known word, spell the second known word, spell the third known word, and spell the fourth known word. Erase the writing.

    e. Orally state the first unknown word and ask him or her to spell it, spell the first known word, spell the second known word, spell the third known word, spell the fourth known word, and spell the fifth known word. Erase the writing.

10. After completing the rehearsal sequence with the first word, that first unknown word is then treated as the first known word, the previous fifth known word is removed, and a new unknown word is introduced. Thus, the number of words always remains six.

11. Continue individually rehearsing unknown words until three errors occur while rehearsing one word. Errors need not only occur on the word currently being rehearsed.

Critical Components That Must Be Implemented for the Intervention to Be Successful

The critical component of IR is the high repetition (Szadokierski & Burns, 2008), but the high percentage of known items also allows the student to be successful during the intervention. However, not every student needs eight knowns. The rule of thumb is to start with eight knowns. If the student seems bored, then take out the knowns but generally do not go below five. If the student has difficulty retaining the information, then add knowns in but do not go above nine. Spelling is an obvious exception in which five seems sufficient, and the short attention span of young children might also suggest a need for fewer knowns (e.g., five).

Materials

- 3″ × 5″ index cards or a dry-erase whiteboard, erasable marker, and eraser.
- A list of known and unknown items.
- Reinforcers as needed.

References

Bunn, R., Burns, M. K., Hoffman, H. H., & Newman, C. L. (2005). Using incremental rehearsal to teach letter identification with a preschool-aged child. *Journal of Evidence Based Practice for Schools, 6*, 124–134.

Burns, M. K., Dean, V. J., & Foley, S. (2004). Preteaching unknown key words with incremental rehearsal to improve reading fluency and comprehension with children identified as reading disabled. *Journal of School Psychology, 42*, 303–314.

Burns, M. K., & Kimosh, A. (2005). Using incremental rehearsal to teach sight-words to adult students with moderate mental retardation. *Journal of Evidence Based Practices for Schools, 6*, 135–148.

Burns, M. K., & Sterling-Turner, H. (2010). Comparison of efficiency measures for academic interventions based on acquisition and maintenance of the skill. *Psychology in the Schools, 47*, 126–134.

Codding, R. S., Archer, J., & Connell, J. (2010). A systematic replication and extension of using incremental rehearsal to improve multiplication skills: An investigation of generalization. *Journal of Behavioral Education, 19*, 93–105.

MacQuarrie-Klender, L. L, Tucker, J. A., Burns, M. K., & Hartman, B. (2002). Comparison of retention rates using traditional drill sandwich, and incremental rehearsal flash card methods. *School Psychology Review, 31*, 584–595.

Nist, L. & Joseph, L. M. (2008). Effectiveness and efficiency of flashcard drill instructional methods on urban first-graders' word recognition, acquisition, maintenance, and generalization. *School Psychology Review, 37*, 294–308.

Tucker, J. A. (1989). *Basic flashcard technique when vocabulary is the goal*. Unpublished teaching materials, School of Education, University of Chattanooga, TN.

Generalization: Cue Cards

Brief Description

Cue cards are a method to prompt students about using previously learned skills. They involve writing steps (presented in writing or pictorially), mnemonic statements, or descriptions of strategies, and the student refers back to them as he or she completes an assignment. For example, a student is more likely to follow the steps of a comprehension strategy if he or she is also looking at a card that lists the steps within the strategy.

What "Common Problems" Does This Address?

Cue cards are ideal for reminding students to actually use the information that they learned. This approach facilitates generalization and can be applied to a variety of settings and skills.

Procedure

1. After teaching a student the strategy that needs to be generalized, make sure he or she understands all of the steps within it.
2. Select a 3" × 5" index card for portability or use a larger piece of paper for more involved strategies.
3. Select a title for the card that contains only three to five words and adequately describes what the cue card will convey. Write the title in print that is larger than the rest of the writing on the card.
4. Write the information in steps, in columns (e.g., include a column with Yes or No at the top so that the student could select whether he or she did the item), or in a sequence of pictures.
5. Teach the student when it would be appropriate to use the card.
6. Determine the best way for the student to carry around the cue card. There are several options including in a notebook or in a small spiral-bound binder for 3" × 5" cards with three holes punched in them.
7. Model how to best use the cue card with the student and provide some guided practice with it.
8. Reinforce the student for using the cue card while completing independent work.
9. Wean the student off of use of the cue card once he or she demonstrates that he or she can accurately complete the steps on the card without referring to it. This can be done through a variety of methods including erasing the first or last step and gradually erasing additional steps, by removing half of the information on the card, or by asking him or her to take out the card but to turn it over without looking at it first.

Critical Components That Must Be Implemented for the Intervention to Be Successful

In order for this intervention to work, the steps must be clearly articulated and the strategy or process described but represent the appropriate intervention for that given student. The student must also understand the skill being taught but just struggles with generalizing it. Moreover, the student must be taught how to appropriately use the cue card.

(cont.)

Materials

- 3″ × 5″ index cards or larger stock paper.
- A binder or some other mechanism to carry the cue cards.
- Reinforcers as needed.

References

Conderman, G., & Hedin, L. (2011). Cue cards: A self-regulatory strategy for students with learning disabilities. *Intervention in School and Clinic, 46*, 165–173.

Rogevich, M. E., & Perin, D. (2008). Effects on science summarization of a reading comprehension intervention for adolescents with behavior and attention disorders. *Exceptional Children, 74*, 135–154.

Sporer, N., Brunstein, J. C., & Kieschke, U. (2009). Improving students' reading comprehension skills: Effects of strategy instruction and reciprocal teaching. *Learning and Instruction, 19*, 272–286.

Generalization: Cognitive Routine for Math Problem Solving

Brief Description

This problem-solving strategy was developed by Montague and Bos (1986) to address self-regulation within cognitive strategy instruction for math problem solving. It is a seven-phase model for which there is a solid research base.

What "Common Problems" Does This Address?

Students with learning difficulties tend to struggle with recall and do not use consistent strategies to solve problems. Thus, the cognitive routine strategy described below provides explicit instruction in selecting the appropriate strategy and includes procedures for generalizing the skill to different settings and problems. This intervention is appropriate for students who understand the computation and concepts involved in each problem but just struggle in determining how to apply them.

Procedure

1. Provide the student with a math application/problem-solving item to model the process. As is the case with just about any intervention, the strategy must be modeled first. This is especially important for a metacognitive strategy.
2. Start by saying that you are going to *read* the problem first to see whether you understand it. Then read the problem orally and say, "Now I will think to myself—do I understand the problem? If not, then I will read it again."
3. Next, *paraphrase* the problem by saying, "After I'm sure that I understand the problem, I will say it to myself using my own words while I underline the important information. Does the information that I've underlined go with the problem? What question am I trying to answer?"
4. *Visualize* by drawing a picture or diagram to go with the problem and that clearly demonstrates the relationship among the parts of the problem. After you have done that ask, "Does the picture fit the problem? Did I show all of the relationships?"
5. *Hypothesize* by deciding what steps and operations are needed to complete the problem and write out the operation symbols.
6. *Estimate* by rounding the numbers and completing the problem in your head. Be sure to explain what you are doing.
7. *Compute* the problem and compare your answer to the estimate that you completed. Say out loud, "Does my answer make sense? Is it close to my estimate? Do I have all of the decimal points and signs (e.g., money signs) correct?
8. *Check* your work to make sure that both the plan and computation are correct. Ask yourself orally, "Have I checked every step? Is my answer right?"
9. After modeling the process, work through a second problem by stating every step in the sequence as it is needed, but have the student complete the step as you give feedback.

(cont.)

10. Work with the student to practice the sequence until he or she can do it independently. The previous research required the student to memorize the strategy, but perhaps the following could be put on a cue card:

     READ for understanding.
     PARAPHRASE—put it in your own words.
     VISUALIZE—draw a picture or diagram.
     HYPOTHESIZE—develop a plan to solve the problem.
     ESTIMATE—round and predict your answer.
     COMPUTE—do the computations.
     CHECK—make sure everything is right.

Critical Components That Must Be Implemented for the Intervention to Be Successful

In order for this intervention to work, the student must understand each step and be able to implement each independently. Because this is a cognitive strategy, the interventionist needs to "think aloud" as he or she models the strategy and encourages the student to also do so during guided practice.

Materials

- Problems that apply concepts and computations that the student understands.
- Written steps that can be refered to during initial modeling or a cue card as needed.
- Reinforcers as needed.

References

Montague, M. (2008). Self-regulation strategies to improve mathematical problem-solving for students with learning disabilities. *Learning Disability Quarterly, 31*, 37–44.

Montague, M., & Bos, C. S. (1986). The effect of cognitive strategy training on verbal math problem solving performance of learning disabled adolescents. *Journal of Learning Disabilities, 19*, 26–33.

CHAPTER 13

Putting It All Together

OVERVIEW

The potential difficulty with discussing aspects of an RTI framework within individual chapters is that it appears to be a disconnected process. Classwide interventions are important for Tier 1, small-group interventions for Tier 2, and individual interventions for Tier 3, but the distinction between them should be more blurred than stark. Thus, in the current chapter we discuss how the three tiers work together by providing an example but first discuss the potentially missing link to successful implementation by starting with an overview of assessing implementation integrity.

FIRST THINGS FIRST: IMPLEMENTATION INTEGRITY

The two most common reasons why interventions fail are that the intervention did not adequately address the correct problem, or it was not implemented with fidelity. The first reason was thoroughly discussed in Chapter 2 and is the main focus of this book. However, even the best intervention will not work if it is not correctly implemented. Research suggests that as intervention implementation deteriorates, treatments become increasingly likely to lose effectiveness or fail entirely (Gansle & McMahon, 1997; Noell, Duhon, Gatti, & Connell, 2002; Vollmer, Roane, Ringdahl, & Marcus, 1999). Some omissions in treatment implementation appear to be less critical and some are likely to have little practical consequence (Noell & Gansle, 2006). However, occasionally only seemingly minor variations from proposed treatment plans result in failure.

> **Even the best intervention will not work if it is not correctly implemented.**

Intervention fidelity is a multidimensional construct that involves the extent to which essential intervention components are delivered in a consistent and comprehension manner by a trained interventionist (Hagermoser Sanetti, & Kratochwill, 2009). Thus, data should be gathered within an RTI model that examines the most important aspects of interventions, the integrity with which systems (e.g., reading curriculum, problem-solving team process) are implemented, and the training that each interventionist receives.

Although most would agree that intervention integrity is a multidimensional concept, there is less consensus as to what makes up those dimensions. To fully discuss assessing integrity goes beyond the scope of this chapter and will be addressed in more detail in the next volume of this book series. However, we recommend that practitioners assess intervention integrity with multiple measures that rely on direct observation, self-report, and examining permanent products.

Perhaps the gold standard for brief assessments of implementation integrity is direct observation. Standard practice is to observe 25 to 33% of the intervention sessions with an observation checklist. The steps included in the evidence-based intervention sections of the individual chapters could serve as observation checklists. Practitioners could observe the intervention while following along on the checklist and record the steps that are observed. The total number observed divided by the total number of items is the percentage of implementation integrity and provides a reliable estimate of how well the intervention was implemented. However, it is unclear as to how much integrity is enough. Many would suggest that 80 or 90% would be sufficient, but what if the intervention was a behavior modification plan based on positive reinforcement and the interventionists correctly implemented 9 out of the 10 steps, but providing the positive reinforcement was the only item not implemented? Clearly the intervention would not be effective. Thus, consistent with a partnership model of treatment integrity (Power et al., 2005; Kelleher, Riley-Tillman, & Power 2008) we suggest identifying the one or two critical components of the intervention on the checklist that are most essential to intervention effectiveness and measuring both overall implementation and integrity of the critical items. Moreover, the integrity assessment should not end with data collection. The interventionist should receive the observation data as feedback so that he or she will better understand the intervention and how it can be best implemented. This feedback should be presented with other progress monitoring data so that the need to alter intervention delivery is couched within an analysis of the effectiveness.

> **We suggest identifying the one or two critical components of the intervention on the checklist that are most essential to intervention effectiveness and measuring overall implementation and integrity of the critical items.**

Assessing implementation integrity should involve observing the intervention being implemented, but doing so presents some problems. First, who has time in a typical school day to conduct the observations? School psychologists often have flexible schedules and appropriate training and may be good candidates to conduct the observation. However, teachers and interventionists may see these observations as evaluations, which can create potential bargaining unit difficulties if the observer and implementer have lateral positions (e.g., teacher and school psychologist). Third, observing the intervention often increases the integrity within that session, but the integrity within other sessions may be lower (Brackett, Reid, & Green, 2007). Finally, if 25% of the intervention sessions are observed, then how do we know that intervention occurred the other 75% of the time? Thus, we recommend that self-report be included in the integrity assessment. Self-report measures tend to overestimate the integrity and assessments should not be solely based on this approach. However, there are many objective aspects of an intervention that can be recorded (e.g., length of session, date of session, pages covered in an intervention manual, or intervention materials) to support the assessment process. Moreover, the interventionist could rate how well he or she implements each item on the intervention checklist on a daily basis.

The third aspect of a comprehensive approach to assessing implementation integrity is to examine permanent products (Mortenson & Witt, 1998). Essentially any intervention involves creating something (e.g., flash cards, graphs, writing samples), and an efficient way to assess implementation integrity is to simply examine the resulting permanent product. Certainly the permanent products can be created without the intervention actually occurring (Noell et al., 2002), but permanent products may serve as a part of a comprehensive integrity assessment.

Grade-level and problem-solving teams should explicitly discuss and document how implementation integrity assessments will occur. Teams should also follow two simple rules. First, if the students are doing well, then implementation integrity usually does not matter. The only exception to the first rule is if additional resources are dedicated to the intervention in order to maintain the success, then practitioners should be confident that the positive change in behavior was due to the intervention and not something else. Second, the higher the consequence and the more analysis that went into designing the intervention, the more important integrity data are. For example, a low-level assessment of integrity is needed within Tier 1, but a multicomponent approach is needed for just about any intervention delivered in Tier 3. We suggest that problem-solving teams end each meeting by identifying (1) who will observe the intervention, how often, and with what checklist; (2) what the teacher will record each time; and (3) what permanent products will be created. All three components and the resulting data should be documented on the problem-solving team summary form.

PUTTING ALL OF THE PIECES IN PLACE

The three authors of this book have used this intervention framework numerous times for research and consultation. We have seen firsthand how effective it is to identify classwide problems, to implement small-group interventions, and to use the instructional hierarchy to target interventions. Simply put, a multi-tier intervention approach focused on solving the most likely reason for the child's academic or behavior difficulties is the most efficient and effective manner in which to conduct schoolwide intervention services. In addition, treating each case as solvable in the school setting, in contrast to focusing on difficult to influence variables such as home issues or suggested psychopathology, allows more extensive service to be provided to the true low-incidence population. Below we provide an example taken from one school that focuses on reading, but it represents our experience with numerous schools and a variety of academic and behavior cases.

Williams Elementary was located in a rural but impoverished area and served approximately 350 students in grades K–5. There were three classrooms per grade in kindergarten through second grade and two per grade for third through fifth (total of 15 classroom teachers). The students who attended this school were mostly white, and approximately 51% of them were from low-income backgrounds so that they received a free or reduced-price lunch. A total of 58.2% of the students scored within the proficient range on the state accountability test for reading. When Mr. Shafer, Williams Elementary's school principal, contacted us, he was concerned because his school was not making adequate yearly progress and was in danger of being reorganized in the near future.

Classwide Interventions

The first step in an RTI model is to examine whether any classwide problems exit. Thus, we followed the procedures outlined in Chapter 3 but used different measures for each grade (e.g., phoneme segmentation fluency in kindergarten, nonsense word fluency for first grade, and oral reading fluency for second through fifth grade). We discovered that there were classwide problems in *every* classroom (i.e., median score fell below the criterion). This might sound like an extreme example, but it is not unusual. Thus, we started a three-part intervention. First, we worked with the teachers and principal to ensure that all students received 120 minutes each day of reading instruction. Second, we had the grade-level teachers start meeting each week as a grade-level team to examine student data and discuss instruction. We also had the teachers read Shanahan (2006), which is available for free at *www.learningpt.org/pdfs/literacy/nationalreading.pdf*, and discussed the components of effective reading instruction. Finally, we had them engage in the peer practice fluency activity (see Form 3.1 at the end of Chapter 3). Students in upper grades rehearsed reading fluency, and younger students rehearsed more fundamental skills such as letter names, letter sounds, and phoneme sounds.

After classwide problems were identified and interventions started, we also monitored progress for every student on a weekly basis. It did not take long to reduce the frequency of classwide problems, and all of the class medians were above criterion in about 4 to 6 weeks. At that point, the number of students who required intervention (i.e., scored below the 25th percentile on a national norm) fell to approximately 25%. It was at this point that the group of students who needed intervention became manageable, we were confident that students were benefiting from core reading instruction, and we began small-group (Tier 2) interventions.

Small-Group Interventions

Once the number of students reached a workable level, we started small-group interventions as the Tier 2 of our RTI model. We assessed reading skills to identify the category of the problem based on the National Reading Panel (2000) areas as discussed in Chapter 5 and implemented standard protocol interventions. Kindergarteners and some older students who struggled with phonemic awareness received *Road to the Code* (Blachman, Ball, Black, & Tangel, 2000) in small groups of two to three students, but the groups were somewhat larger for older students (e.g., four or five for first, second, and third graders, but five or six for fourth and fifth graders). Students who struggled with decoding but who had adequate phonemic awareness received a decoding intervention, and those for whom fluency was the appropriate intervention participated in the small-group repeated reading with error correction intervention (see pages 56–57 at the end of Chapter 5) or some other fluency-based intervention (e.g., *Six-Minute Solution*; Adams & Brown, 2006).

The targeted interventions occurred in this school four times each week and were delivered by classroom teachers using a power-hour (Burns & Gibbons, 2008) approach. It would go beyond the scope of this book to describe the schedule and so on with which the interventions were delivered, but it essentially involved flexible and dynamic groups. For example, if there were 50 students in third grade, and 25% required an intervention, then approximately 12 students participated in the intervention. The 12 students were divided into two groups based on need (e.g., one group focused on fluency and one on decoding) and simultaneously received an intervention during a 30-minute grade-level daily intervention time. The interventions were delivered by one classroom teacher and one paraprofessional. The remaining 38 students engaged in independent reading during intervention time, from books that they self-selected that were at their individual instructional levels, and from which they looked for answers to five preassigned basic comprehension questions.

After addressing classwide problems, approximately 85 students (25%) continued to require intervention. We implemented the small-group interventions and monitored progress on a weekly basis, the result of which was that approximately 70 (80% of the students getting an intervention) made sufficient progress, and only approximately 15 (5%) required an individualized intervention within Tier 3.

Individual Interventions

As stated above, only approximately 15 of the students required an individualized intervention. This is quite impressive given that just 1 year earlier Williams Elementary's problem-solving team discussed individualized interventions for approximately 100 students. It is obvious to see that the likelihood of success is much greater with 15 students than it is for 100. It would be difficult to discuss the interventions for all 15 students, so we expand on two examples below. The data presented here are based on the actual student data but are modified to protect the students' anonymity.

The first student, pseudonymously named Tom, was a third-grade Caucasian male who participated in the Read Naturally (2004) program during the entire second grade (before we consulted with the school) and the beginning of the third grade. His reading level, according to Read Naturally assessments, was 1.0 at the beginning of second grade and remained at that level through the beginning of the current school year. He scored below the fifth percentile on the most recent state accountability group-administered reading test.

Through assessment and use of the model described in Chapter 2, we identified the student's specific reading deficit and targeted the interventions appropriately. Tom's oral reading fluency from grade-level text resulted in approximately 35 WCPM, but he only correctly read between 68 and 72% of the words correctly, which fell below the accuracy criterion of 93% correct and suggested that he was functioning within the acquisition phase of learning. We also screened Tom's phonetic skills with a nonsense word fluency assessment that resulted in a rate of 65 sounds read correctly per minute with 94% correct. These data were above criteria for speed and accuracy and suggested that fluency was the appropriate target. We further judged that Tom required an acquisition intervention based on the low accuracy. Thus, Tom participated in the supported cloze procedure outlined on pages 91–92 at the end of Chapter 7 four times each week. We also simultaneously taught unknown high-frequency words with a whole-word approach called incremental rehearsal (see pages 130–131 and pages 192–195 at the end of Chapters 9 and 12, respectively).

Tom's progress was monitored each week using grade-level text taken from the Oral Reading Fluency probes of the AIMSweb (Pearson, 2008) program and are displayed in Figure 13.1. We started by monitoring the percentage of words read correctly in each passage. Tom correctly read approximately 79% of the words in the baseline probes and we started the intervention after 5 weeks of baseline. We saw an immediate change in level. Our target, as mentioned in Chapter 2, was for Tom to correctly read 93% of the words, which he immediately did after implementing the intervention. After he correctly read 93% of the words three consecutive times (eighth week of intervention), we stopped the intervention and switched to repeated reading, but continued to collect accuracy data. In baseline for reading fluency, Tom read approximately 25 WCPM, which fell below the tenth percentile on national norms. Although his ending fluency data were still below the 25th percentile, he increased by almost six WCPM each week.

The second student was named Jim (pseudonym), a second grader who also participated in the Read Naturally (2004) program with little reported success. Jim was a Hispanic male who spoke English as his first language. He consistently scored below the fifth percentile on the state accountability reading test, and his reading level fell below the first grade according to Read Naturally assessments.

Jim's reading fluency assessments resulted in a score of 13 WCPM with 60% known, both of which were well below expectations (i.e., the 25th percentile for fluency and 93% correct for accuracy). We continued the assessment by screening phonetic skills with nonsense word fluency. He correctly identified 24 sounds/minute with 67% correct and appeared to demonstrate phonetic skills that functioned in the acquisition stage. However, in order to target the appropriate skill for intervention, we also evaluated his phonemic awareness, which fell within the acceptable range. Thus, the intervention focused on teaching letter sounds with incremental rehearsal three times each week.

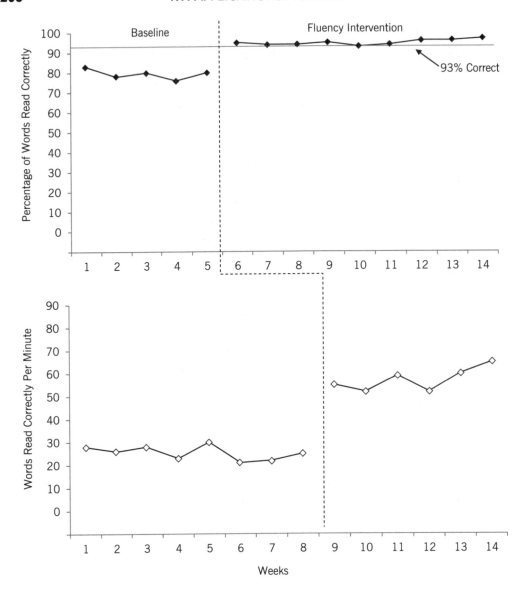

FIGURE 13.1. Reading intervention data for Tom.

Jim's phonetic skills were monitored with weekly letter-sound correspondence assessments and are displayed in Figure 13.2. As was also the case with Tom, we started by assessing Jim's accuracy. He correctly identified the sounds for approximately 70% of the letters and letter combinations that we presented to him. We implemented the intervention after 4 weeks and again saw an immediate increase in his accuracy. Our target this time was 90% of the sounds correctly identified, which he accomplished after 4 weeks of inter-

Only two students in the entire building fell below the 25th percentile on grade-appropriate measures of reading.

vention. Thus, after 8 total weeks we stopped the intervention and switched to a word sort (see pages 134–136 at the end of Chapter 9) for him to practice using the sounds to make

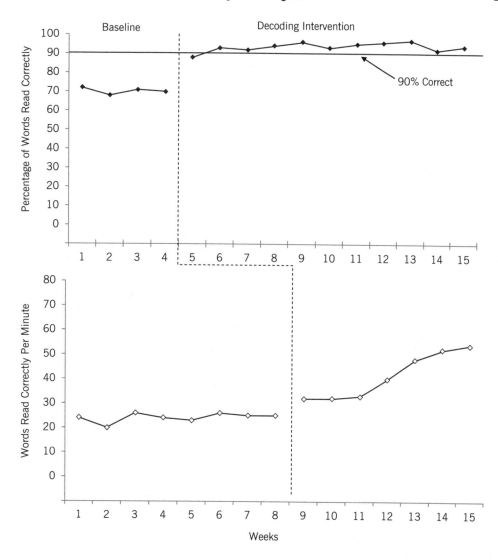

FIGURE 13.2. Reading intervention data for Jim.

words. Jim's scores increased from approximately 24 sounds per minute to over 50 sounds per minute by the end of the intervention.

The data presented here suggested that the classwide, small-group, and individual interventions were effective. When we started working with the school, only approximately 58% of the students scored within the proficient range on the state test and we noted classwide problems in every room. Our work in Williams Elementary began in the fall of 2008 but was reduced to infrequent consultation during the 2009–2010 school year. Mr. Shafer called us in the fall of 2010 with an unusual question. He reminded us about the process that we developed with them to look for classwide problems and identify students who need small-group interventions, and then indicated that only two students in the entire building fell below the 25th percentile on grade-appropriate measures of reading. His exact words were, "So now what do we do?" Our answer—"Congratulate your teachers and staff!"

CONCLUSION

This book was developed to provide a multi-tier presentation of both academic and behavioral interventions for use in an RTI framework. In this presentation, this book made several contributions to the literature including using the instructional hierarchy as the framework for selecting interventions within an RTI framework, applying the instructional hierarchy to learning behavior competence, framing academic interventions within a generalization framework, discussing the identification of classwide behavior problems, and examining the role of classwide interventions within an RTI framework. It was the authors' goal to show that interventions do not need to be complicated to be effective, but they do need to be correctly identified and implemented. While we fully support the evidence-based intervention movement, it is critical that the concept is fully understood. Evidence-based interventions must be both selected and implemented correctly to be considered "evidence based." A hammer is clearly an effective and appropriate tool, but only for trying to drive a nail into wood. A hammer is not only ineffective but can be damaging in the case of inserting a screw. In addition, the true professional knows how to use the hammer with few efficient and accurate strikes. In parallel, the true educational professional understands how to breathe life into a functionally relevant evidence-based intervention.

Finally, while selecting and implementing interventions in a logical manner is necessary for an effective schoolwide problem-solving model, it is not sufficient. Even a correctly matched and implemented intervention may not be effective for every student, and we do not truly understand why. Effective intervention selection should be thought of as the first step in an intervention case rather than the conclusion. Selecting the intervention in education is akin to a scientist developing a hypothesis (Riley-Tillman & Burns, 2009). While a great deal of time and work may go into that development process, it is only after experimentation and analysis that the hypothesis is supported or refuted. In education, experimentation is the act of conducting the intervention as designed, and analysis is the consideration of the outcome data (e.g., reading fluency or academic engagement data) in reference to the planned effect of the intervention. Implementing the subsequent steps of assessment, analysis, and decision making complete the full process necessary for the effective RTI framework. As such, it is critically important for school personnel to closely monitor the effectiveness of interventions and to make modifications as needed, which we discuss in considerable detail in the next volume of this book. Although not a perfect science, the likelihood of success can be enhanced when practitioners use data to identify the correct intervention target and then use the instructional hierarchy to focus their intervention efforts. It is with such an approach that practitioners are most likely to hit the intervention bull's-eye and benefit the students in need.

> The likelihood of success can be enhanced when practitioners use data to identify the correct intervention target and then use the instructional hierarchy to focus their intervention efforts.

References

Aaron, P. G., & Joshi, R. M. (1992). *Reading problems: Consultation atnd remediation*. New York: Guilford Press.

Adams, G., & Brown, S. (2006). *Six-minute solution: A reading fluency program*. Longmont, CO: Sopris West.

Adams, M. J., Foorman, B. R., Lundberg, I., & Beeler, T. (1998). *Phonemic awareness in young children: A classroom curriculum*. Baltimore, MD: Brookes.

Afflerbach, P. (2011). Assessing reading. In T. V. Rasinski (Ed.), *Rebuilding the foundation: Effective reading instruction for 21st century literacy* (pp. 293–314). Bloomington, IN: Solution Tree.

Albers, C. A., Glover, T. A., & Kratochwill, T. R. (2006). Introduction to the special series: How can universal screening enhance educational and mental health outcomes? *Journal of School Psychology, 45*, 113–116.

Alberto, P., & Troutman, A. C. (2006). *Applied behavior analysis for teachers* (6th ed.). Upper Saddle River, NJ: Merrill Prentice Hall.

American Psychological Association Presidential Task Force on Evidence-Based Practice. (2006). Evidence-based practice in psychology. *American Psychologist, 61*, 271–285.

American Psychological Association Task Force on Evidence-Based Practice for Children and Adolescents. (2008). *Disseminating evidence-based practice for children and adolescents: A systems approach to enhancing care*. Washington, DC: American Psychological Association.

Angello, L. M., Volpe, R. J., Diperna, J. C., Gureasko-Moore, S. P., Gureasko-Moore, D. P., Nebrig, M. R., et al. (2003). Assessment of attention-deficit/hyperactivity disorder: An evaluation of six published rating scales. *School Psychology Review, 32*, 241–262.

Ardoin, S. P. (2006). The response in response to intervention: Evaluating the utility of assessing maintenance of intervention effects. *Psychology in the Schools, 43*, 713–725.

Ardoin, S. P., & Daly, E. J., III. (2007). Introduction to the special series: Close encounters of the instructional kind—How the instructional hierarchy is shaping instructional research 30 years later. *Journal of Behavioral Education, 16*, 1–6.

Ardoin, S. P., Williams, J. C., Klubnik, C., & McCall, M. (2009). Three versus six rereadings of practice passages. *Journal of Applied Behavior Analysis, 42,* 375–380.

Axelrod, S. (1973). Comparison of individual and group contingencies in two special classes. *Behavior Therapy, 4,* 83–90.

Baer, R. A., Williams, J. A., Onses, P. G., & Stokes, T. F. (1985). Generalized verbal control and correspondence training. *Behavior Modification, 9,* 477–489.

Baker, S., Gersten, R., & Lee, D. S., (2002). A synthesis of empirical research on teaching mathematics to low-achieving students. *Elementary School Journal, 103,* 51–73.

Barrish, H. H., Saunders, M., & Wolf, M. M. (1969). Good behavior game: Effects of individual contingencies for group consequences on disruptive behavior in a classroom. *Journal of Applied Behavior Analysis, 2,* 119–124.

Bear, D. R., Invernizzi, M., Templeton, S. R., & Johnston, F. (2003). *Words their way: Word study for phonics, vocabulary, and spelling instruction.* Upper Saddle River, NJ: Prentice Hall.

Beck, M., Burns, M. K., & Lau, M. (2009). Preteaching unknown items as a behavioral intervention for children with behavioral disorders. *Behavior Disorders, 34,* 91–99.

Beck, I. (1989). *Reading today and tomorrow: Teacher's editions for grades 1 and 2.* Austin, TX: Holt.

Beck, I., & Hamilton, R. (2000). *Beginning reading module.* Washington DC: American Federation of Teachers.

Bergan, J. R. (1977). *Behavioral consultation.* Columbus, OH: Merrill.

Bergan, J. R., & Kratochwill, T. R. (1990). *Behavioral consultation and therapy.* New York: Plenum.

Berninger, V. W., Abbott, R. D., Vermeulen, K., & Fulton, C. M. (2006). Paths to reading comprehension in at-risk second-grade readers. *Journal of Learning Disabilities, 39,* 334–351.

Betts, E. A. (1946). *Foundations of reading instruction.* New York: American Book.

Billingsley, B. S., & Wildman, T. M. (1990). Facilitating reading comprehension in learning disabled students: Metacognitive goals and instructional strategies. *Remedial and Special Education, 11,* 18–31.

Binder, C. (1996). Behavioral fluency: Evolution of a new paradigm. *Behavior Analyst, 19,* 163–197.

Blackman, B. Ball, E., Black, S. & Tangel, D. (2001). *Road to the code.* Baltimore, MD: Brookes.

Brackett, L., Reid, D. H., & Green, C. W. (2007). Effects of reactivity to observations on staff performance. *Journal of Applied Behavior Analysis, 40,* 191–195.

Bradshaw, C., Reinke, W., Brown, L., Bevans, K., & Leaf, P. (2008). Implementation of school-wide positive behavioral interventions and supports (PBIS) in elementary schools: Observations from a randomized trial. *Education and Treatment of Children, 31,* 1–26.

Briesch, A. M., Chafouleas, S. M., & Riley-Tillman, T. C. (2010). Generalizability and dependability of behavior assessment methods to estimate academic engagement: A comparison of systematic direct observation and Direct Behavior Rating. *School Psychology Review, 39,* 408–421.

Broughton, S. F., & Hester, J. R. (1993). Effects of administrative and community support on teacher acceptance of classroom interventions. *Journal of Educational and Psychological Consultation, 4,* 169–177.

Bunn, R., Burns, M. K., Hoffman, H. H., & Newman, C. L. (2005). Using incremental rehearsal to teach letter identification with a preschool-aged child. *Journal of Evidence-Based Practices for Schools, 6,* 124–134.

Burns, M. K. (2002). Comprehensive system of assessment to intervention using curriculum-based assessments. *Intervention in School and Clinic, 38,* 8–13.

Burns, M. K. (2004). Empirical analysis of drill ratio research: Refining the instructional level for drill tasks. *Remedial and Special Education, 25,* 167–175.

Burns, M. K. (2005). Using incremental rehearsal to increase fluency of single-digit multiplication facts with children identified as learning disabled in mathematics computation. *Education and Treatment of Children, 28,* 238–249.

Burns, M. K. (2007). Reading at the instructional level with children identified as learning disabled: Potential implications for response-to-intervention. *School Psychology Quarterly, 22,* 297–313.

Burns, M. K. (2011). Matching conceptual and procedural math interventions to student deficits. *Assessment for Effective Intervention, 36,* 210–218.

Burns, M. K., Appleton, J. J., & Stehouwer, J. D. (2005). Meta-analysis of response-to-intervention research: Examining field-based and research-implemented models. *Journal of Psychoeducational Assessment, 23,* 381–394.

Burns, M. K., & Dean, V. J. (2005). Effect of drill ratios on recall and on-task behavior for children with learning and attention difficulties. *Journal of Instructional Psychology, 32,* 118–126.

Burns, M. K., Dean, V. J., & Foley, S. (2004). Pre-teaching unknown key words with incremental rehearsal to improve reading fluency and comprehension with children identified as reading disabled. *Journal of School Psychology, 42,* 303–314.

Burns, M. K., Ganuza, Z., & London, R. (2009). Brief experimental analysis of written letter formation: A case demonstration. *Journal of Behavioral Education, 18,* 20–34.

Burns, M. K., & Gibbons, K. (2008). *Response to intervention implementation in elementary and secondary schools: Procedures to assure scientific-based practices.* New York: Routledge.

Burns, M. K., Hall-Lande, J., Lyman, W., Rogers, C., & Tan, C. S. (2006). Tier II interventions within response-to-intervention: Components of an effective approach. *Communiqué, 35*(4), 38–40.

Burns, M. K., Kanive, R., & DeGrande, M. (in press). Effect of a computer-delivered math fact intervention as a supplemental intervention for math in third and fourth grades. *Remedial and Special Education.*

Burns, M. K., & Kimosh, A. (2005). Using incremental rehearsal to teach sight-words to adult students with moderate mental retardation. *Journal of Evidence-Based Practices for Schools, 6,* 135–148.

Burns, M. K. & Kwoka, H., Lim, B., Crone, M., Haegele, K., Parker, D. C., Petersen, S. & Scholin, S. E. (2011). Minimum reading fluency necessary for comprehension among second-grade students. *Psychology in the Schools, 48,* 124–132.

Burns, M. K., Senesac, B. V., & Symington, T. (2004). The effectiveness of the HOSTS pro-gram in improving the reading achievement of children at-risk for reading failure. *Reading Research and Instruction, 43,* 87–104.

Burns, M. K., & Sterling-Turner, H. (2010). Comparison of efficiency measures for academic interventions based on acquisition and maintenance of the skill. *Psychology in the Schools, 47,* 126–134.

Burns, M. K., Tucker, J. A., Hauser, A., Thelen, R., Holmes, K., & White, K. (2002). Minimum reading fluency rate necessary for compre-hension: A potential criterion for curriculum-based assessments. *Assessment for Effective Intervention, 28,* 1–7.

Burns, M. K., VanDerHeyden, A. M., & Boice, C. H. (2008). Best practices in delivery intensive academic interventions. In A. Thomas & J. Grimes (Eds.), *Best practices in school psy-chology* (5th ed., pp. 1151–1162). Bethesda, MD: National Association of School Psycholo-gists.

Burns, M. K., VanDerHeyden, A. M., & Jiban, C. (2006). Assessing the instructional level for mathematics: A comparison of methods. *School Psychology Review, 35,* 401–418.

Burns, M. K., & Wagner, D. (2008). Determin-ing an effective intervention within a brief experimental analysis for reading: A meta-analytic review. *School Psychology Review, 37,* 126–136.

Buschman, L., & the National Council of Teachers of Mathematics. (2003). *Share and compare.* Reston, VA: National Council of Teachers of Mathematics.

Canobi, K., Reeve, R., & Pattison, P. E. (2003). Pat-terns of knowledge in children's addition. *De-velopmental Psychology, 39,* 521–534.

Canobi, K. C., Reeve, R. A., & Pattison, P. E. (2002). Young children's understanding of ad-dition concepts. *Educational Psychology, 22,* 513–532.

Carnine, D.W., Silbert, J., Kame'enui, E.J., & Tarver, S. G. (2004). *Direct instruction read-ing* (4th ed.). Upper Saddle River, NJ: Merrill Prentice-Hall.

Carns, A. W., & Carns, M. R. (1994). Making be-havioral contracts successful. *School Coun-selor, 42,* 155–160.

Carr, J. E., Severtson, J. M., & Lepper, T. L. (2008). Noncontingent reinforcement is an empirically supported treatment for problem behavior exhibited by individuals with developmental disabilities. *Research in Developmental Disabilities, 30,* 44–57.

Case, L. P., Harris, K. R., & Graham, S. (1992). Improving the mathematical problem-solving skills of students with learning disabilities. *The Journal of Special Education, 26,* 1 –19.

Cassel, J., & Reid, R. (1996). Use of a self-regulated strategy intervention to improve word problem-solving skills of students with mild disabilities. *Journal of Behavioral Education, 6,* 153–172.

Cates, G. L., Skinner, C. H., Watson, T. S., Meadows, T. J., Weaver, A., & Jackson, B. (2003). Instructional effectiveness and instructional efficiency as considerations for data-based decision making: An evaluation of interspersing procedures. *School Psychology Review, 32,* 601–616.

Chafouleas, S. M., Briesch, A. M., Riley-Tillman, T. C., & McCoach, D. B. (2009). Moving beyond assessment of treatment acceptability: An examination of the factor structure of the Usage Rating Profile–Intervention (URP-I). *School Psychology Quarterly, 24,* 36–47.

Chafouleas, S. M., Christ, T., Riley-Tillman, T. C., Briesch, A. M., & Chanese, J. (2007). Generalizability and dependability of direct behavior ratings to measure social behavior of preschoolers. *School Psychology Review, 36,* 63–79.

Chafouleas, S. M., Kilgus, S. P., & Hernandez, P. (2009). Using direct behavior rating (DBR) to screen for school social risk: A preliminary comparison of methods in a kindergarten sample. *Assessment for Effective Intervention, 34,* 224–230.

Chafouleas, S. M., Kilgus, S. P., Riley-Tillman, T. C., Jaffery, R., & Welsh, M. (2011). *Diagnostic accuracy of direct behavior rating as a behavior screener for elementary and middle school students.* Manuscript submitted for publication.

Chafouleas, S. M., McDougal, J. L., Riley-Tillman, T. C., Panahon, C. J., & Hilt, A. M. (2005). What do daily behavior report cards (DBRCs) measure? An initial comparison of DBRCs with direct observation for off-task behavior. *Psychology in the Schools, 42,* 669–676.

Chafouleas, S. M., Riley-Tillman, T. C., & Christ, T. J. (2009). Direct behavior rating (DBR): An emerging method for assessing social behavior within a tiered intervention system.

Assessment for Effective Intervention, 34, 195–200.

Chafouleas, S. M., Riley-Tillman, T. C., Christ, T. J., Kilgus, S. P., & Jaffery, R. (2011). *A multisite study of the use of direct behavior ratings single item scales for screening purposes.* Manuscript submitted for publication.

Chafouleas, S. M., Riley-Tillman, T. C., & McDougal, J. L. (2002). Good, bad, or in-between: How does the daily behavior report card rate? *Psychology in the Schools, 39,* 157–169.

Chafouleas, S. M., Riley-Tillman, T. C., & Sassu, K. A. (2006). Acceptability and reported use of daily behavior report cards among teachers. *Journal of Positive Behavior Interventions, 8,* 174–182.

Chafouleas, S. M., Riley-Tillman, T. C., & Sugai, G. (2007). *School-based behavioral assessment: Informing intervention and instruction.* New York: Guilford Press.

Christ, T. J. (2006). Short-term estimates of growth using curriculum-based measurement of oral reading fluency: Estimating standard error of the slope to construct confidence intervals. *School Psychology Review, 35,* 128–133.

Christ, T. J., & Boice, C. (2009). Rating scale items: A brief review of nomenclature, components, and formatting to inform the development of direct behavior rating (DBR). *Assessment for Effective Intervention, 34,* 242–250.

Christ, T. J., Riley-Tillman, T. C., Chafouleas, S. M., & Boice, C. H. (2010). Direct behavior ratings (DBR): Generalizability and dependability across raters and observations. *Educational and Psychological Measurement, 70,* 825–842.

Codding, R. S., Archer, J., & Connell, J. (2010). A systematic replication and extension of using incremental rehearsal to improve multiplication skills: An investigation of generalization. *Journal of Behavioral Education, 19,* 93–105.

Codding, R. S., Chan-Iannetta, L., Palmer, M., & Lukito, G. (2009). Examining a classwide application of cover–copy–compare with and without goal setting to enhance mathematics fluency. *School Psychology Quarterly, 24,* 173–185.

Codding, R. S., Archer, J., & Connell, J. (2010). A systematic replication and extension of using incremental rehearsal to improve multiplication skills: An investigation of generalization. *Journal of Behavioral Education, 19,* 93–105.

Codding, R. S., Burns, M. K., Lukito, G. (2011). Meta-analysis of mathematic basic-fact fluency interventions: A component analysis. *Learning Disabilities Research & Practice, 26*, 36–47.

Cohen, J. (1988). *Statistical power analysis for the behavioral sciences* (2nd ed.). Hillsdale, NJ: Erlbaum.

Colvin, G., Kame'enui, E. J., & Sugai, G. (1993). School-wide and classroom management: Reconceptualizing the integration and management of students with behavior problems in general education. *Education and Treatment of Children, 16*, 361–381.

Common Core Standards Initiative. (2010). Retrieved January 4, 2011, from *www.corestandards.org*.

Conderman, G., & Hedin, L. (2011). Cue cards: A self-regulatory strategy for students with learning disabilities. *Intervention in School and Clinic, 46*, 165–173.

Cook, B. G., Tankersley, M., & Landrum, T. J. (2009). Determining evidence-based practices in special education. *Exceptional Children, 75*, 365–383.

Cooper, J. O., Heron, T. E., & Heward, W. L. (2007). *Applied behavior analysis*, (2nd ed.). Columbus, OH: Prentice Hall.

Cowan, R., Dowker, A., Christakis, A., & Bailey, S. (1996). Even more precisely assessing children's understanding of the order-irrelevance principle. *Journal of Experimental Child Psychology, 62*, 84–101.

Cromley, J., & Azevedo, R. (2007). Testing and refining the direct and inferential mediation model of reading comprehension. *Journal of Educational Psychology, 99*, 311–325.

D'Agostino, J. V., & Murphy, J. A. (2004). A meta-analysis of reading recovery in United States schools. *Educational Evaluation and Policy Analysis, 26*, 23–38.

Daly, E. J., III, Martens, B. K., Hamler, K. R., Dool, E. J., & Eckert, T. L. (1999). A brief experimental analysis for identifying instructional components needed to improve oral reading fluency. *Journal of Applied Behavior Analysis, 32*, 83–94.

Daly, E. J., III, Martens, B. K., Kilmer, A., & Massie, D. (1996). The effects of instructional match and content overlap on generalized reading performance. *Journal of Applied Behavioral Analysis, 29*, 507–518.

Daly, E. J., III, Witt, J. C., Martens, B. K., & Dool, E. J. (1997). A model for conducting a functional analysis of academic performance problems. *School Psychology Review, 26*, 554–574.

De Civita, M., & Dobkin P. L. (2005). Pediatric adherence as a multidimensional and dynamic construct, involving a triadic partnership. *Journal of Pediatric Psychology, 29*, 157–169.

Dehaene, S., & Akhavein, R. (1995). Attention, automaticity, and levels of representation in number processing. *Journal of Experimental Psychology: Learning, Memory, and Cognition, 21*, 314–326.

Deno, S. L. (1985). Curriculum-based measurement: The emerging alternative. *Exceptional Children, 52*, 219–232.

Deno, S. L., & Mirkin, P. K. (1977). *Data-based program modification: A manual*. Reston, VA: Council for Exceptional Children.

Donovan, M. S., & Cross, C. T. (2002). *Minority students in special and gifted education*. Washington, DC: National Academy Press.

Driskell, J. E., Willis, R. P., & Copper, C. (1992). Effect of overlearning on retention. *Journal of Applied Psychology, 77*, 615–622.

Drummond, T. (1993). *The student risk screening scale (SRSS)*. Grants Pass, OR: Josephine County Mental Health Program.

DuPaul, G. J., Power, T. J., Anastopoulos, A. D., & Reid, R. (1998). *ADHD Rating Scale–IV: Checklists, norms, and clinical interpretation*. New York: Guilford Press.

Eckert, T. L. & Hintze, J. M. (2000). Behavioral conceptions and applications of acceptability: Issues related to service delivery and research methodology. *School Psychology Quarterly, 15*, 123–148.

Elbaum, B., Vaughn, S., Tejero, H. M., & Watson, M. S. (2000). How effective are one-to-one tutoring programs in reading for elementary students at risk for reading failure? A meta-analysis of the intervention research. *Journal of Educational Psychology, 92*, 605–619.

Fantuzzo, J. W., Rohrbeck, C. A., Hightower, A. D., & Work, W. C. (1991). Teachers' use of rewards in elementary school. *Psychology in the Schools, 28*, 175–181.

Feuer, M. J., Towne, L., & Shavelson, R. J. (2002). Scientific culture and educational research. *Educational Researcher, 31*, 4–14.

Fisher, W. W., Piazza, C. C., Bowman, L. G., &

Amari, A. (1996). Integrating caregiver report with a systematic choice assessment to enhance reinforce identification. *American Journal on Mental Retardation, 101*, 15–25.

Foegen, A., Jiban, C., & Deno, S. (2007). Progress monitoring in mathematics: A review of the literature. *Journal of Special Education, 41*, 121–139.

Gansle, K. A., & McMahon, C. M. (1997). Component integrity of teacher intervention management behavior using a student self-monitoring treatment: An experimental analysis. *Journal of Behavioral Education, 7*, 405–419.

Gardner, R., III, Heward, W. L., & Grossi, T. A. (1994). Effects of response cards on student participation and academic achievement: A systematic replication with inner-city students during whole-class science instruction. *Journal of Applied Behavior Analysis, 27*, 63–71.

Geary, D. C., Hoard, M. K., Byrd-Craven, J., Nugent, L., & Numtee, C. (2007). Cognitive mechanisms underlying achievement deficits in children with mathematical learning disability. *Child Development, 78*, 1343–1359.

Gersten, R., Beckmann, S., Clarke, B., Foegen, A., Marsh, L., Star, J. R., et al. (2009). *Assisting students struggling with mathematics: Response to intervention (RtI) for elementary and middle schools* (NCEE 2009-4060). Washington, DC: National Center for Education Evaluation and Regional Assistance, Institute of Education Sciences, U.S. Department of Education. Retrieved from *ies.ed.gov/ncee/wwc/publications/practiceguides*.

Gersten, R., Compton, D., Connor, C. M., Dimino, J., Santoro, L., Linan-Thompson, S., et al. (2008). *Assisting students struggling with reading: Response to intervention and multi-tier intervention for reading in the primary grades. A practice guide* (NCEE 2009-4045). Washington, DC: National Center for Education Evaluation and Regional Assistance, Institute of Education Sciences, U.S. Department of Education. Retrieved from *ies.ed.gov/ncee/wwc/publications/practiceguides*.

Gickling, E., & Thompson, V. (1985). A personal view of curriculum-based assessment. *Exceptional Children, 52*, 205–218.

Gickling, E. E., & Armstrong, D. L. (1978). Levels of instructional difficulty as related to on-task behavior, task completion, and comprehen-sion. *Journal of Learning Disabilities, 11*, 559–566.

Glenberg, A. M., Brown, M., & Levin, J. R. (2007). Enhancing comprehension in small reading groups using a manipulation strategy. *Contemporary Educational Psychology, 32*, 389–399.

Good, R. H., III, Simmons, D. C., & Kame'enui, E. J. (2001). The importance of decision-making utility of a continuum of fluency-based indicators of foundational reading skills for third-grade high-stakes outcomes. *Scientific Studies of Reading, 5*, 257–288.

Graham, S., Harris, K. R., & MacArthur, C. (2004). Writing instruction. In B. Y. Wong (Ed.), *Learning about learning disabilities* (pp. 281–313). San Diego, CA: Elsevier.

Graves, M. F. (2006). *The vocabulary book: Learning and instruction.* New York: Teachers College Press.

Graves, M. F., Cooke, C. L., & LaBerge, M. J. (1983). Effects of previewing difficult short stories on low ability junior high school students' comprehension, recall, and attitudes. *Reading Research Quarterly, 18*, 262–276.

Greenwood, C. R. (1996). The case for performance-based instructional models. *School Psychology Quarterly, 11*, 283–296.

Greenwood, C. R., Delquadri, J., & Hall, R. V. (1984). Opportunity to respond and student academic performance. In W. Heward, T. Heron, D. Hill, & J. Trap-Porter (Eds.), *Focus on behavior analysis in education* (pp. 58–88). Columbus, OH: Merrill.

Gresham, F.M. (2008). Best practices in diagnosis in a multi-tier problem solving approach. In A. Thomas & J. Grimes (Eds.), *Best practices in school psychology* (5th ed., pp. 281–294). Bethesda, MD: National Association of School Psychologists.

Guevremont, D. C., Onses, P. G., & Stokes, T. F. (1986). Programming maintenance after correspondence training interventions with children. *Journal of Applied Behavior Analysis, 21*, 45–55.

Hagermoser Sanetti, L. M., & Kratochwill, T. R. (2009). Toward developing a science of treatment integrity: Introduction to the special series. *School Psychology Review, 38*, 445–459.

Hanich, L. B., Jordan, N. C., Kaplan, D., & Dick, J. (2001). Performance across different areas of mathematical cognition in children with learning difficulties. *Journal of Educational Psychology, 93,* 615–626.

Happe, D. (1983). Behavioral intervention: It doesn't do any good in your briefcase. In J. Grimes (Ed.), *Psychological consultation* (pp. 15–41). Des Moines: Iowa State Department of Education.

Haring, N. G., & Eaton, M. D. (1978). Systematic instructional technology: An instructional hierarchy. In N. G. Haring, T. C. Lovitt, M. D. Eaton, & C. L. Hansen (Eds.), *The fourth R: Research in the classroom* (pp. 23–40). Columbus, OH: Merrill.

Harris, K. R., Graham, S., & Mason, L. H. (2003). Self-regulated strategy development in the classroom: Part of a balanced approach to writing instruction for students with disabilities. *Focus on Exceptional Children, 35*(7), 1–16.

Harris, K. R., Graham, S., Mason, L. H., & Friedlander, B. (2008). *POWERFUL Writing strategies for all students.* Baltimore, MD: Brookes.

Hartman, W. T., & Fay, T. A. (1996). Cost-effectiveness of instructional support teams in Pennsylvania. *Journal of Education Finance, 21,* 555–580.

Hasbrouck, J., & Tindal, G. (2005). *Oral reading fluency: 90 years of measurement* (Tech. Rep. No. 33). Eugene: University of Oregon, College of Education, Behavioral Research and Teaching.

Hattie, J. (2009). *Visible learning: A synthesis of over 800 meta-analyses relating to achievement.* New York: Routledge.

Haughton, E. C. (1980). Practicing practices. *Journal of Precision Teaching, 1,* 3–20.

Hawkins, J., Skinner, C. H., & Oliver, R. (2005). The effects of task demands and additive interspersal ratios on fifth-grade students' mathematics accuracy. *School Psychology Review, 34,* 543–555.

Hayes, S. C., Nelson, R. O., & Jarrett, R. B. (1987). The treatment utility of assessment: A functional approach to evaluating assessment quality. *American Psychologist, 42,* 963–974.

Hiebert, J., & Lefevre, P. (1986). Conceptual and procedural knowledge in mathematics: An introductory analysis. In J. Hiebert (Ed.), *Conceptual and procedural knowledge: The case of mathematics* (pp. 1–27). Hillsdale, NJ: Erlbaum.

Hintze, J. M., Volpe, R. J., & Shapiro, E. S. (2002). Best practices in the systematic direct observation of student behavior. In A. Thomas & J. Grimes (Eds.), *Best practices in school psychology IV* (pp. 993–1006). Bethesda, MD: National Association of School Psychologists.

Horner, R. H., & Sugai, G. (2001). "Data" need not be a four-letter word: Using data to improve schoolwide discipline. *Beyond Behavior, 11,* 20–22.

Houchins, D. E., Shippen, M. E., & Flores, M. M. (2004). Math assessment and instruction for students at-risk. In R. Colarusso & C. O'Rourke (Eds.), *Special education for all teachers* (3rd ed.) Dubuque, IA: Kendall/Hunt.

Hyman, I. A., & Perone, D. C. (1998). The other side of school violence: Educator policies and practices that may contribute to student misbehavior. *Journal of School Psychology, 36,* 7–27.

Individuals with Disabilities Education Improvement Act of 2004, Public Law 108-446, 108th Cong., 118 Stat. 2647.

Irvin, L. K., Horner, R. H., Ingram, K., Todd, A. W., Sugai, G., Sampson, N. K., et al. (2006). Using discipline referral data for decision making about student behavior in elementary and middle schools: An empirical evaluation of validity. *Journal of Positive Behavior Interventions, 8,* 10–23.

Irvin, L. K., Tobin, T. J., Sprague, J. R., Sugai, G., & Vincent, C. G. (2004). Validity of discipline referral measures as indices of school-wide behavioral status and effects of school-wide behavioral interventions. *Journal of Positive Behavior Interventions, 6,* 3–12.

ISTEP (2011). *ISTEP data management system for universal screening, progress monitoring and reporting.* Miami: ISTEP.

Iwata, B. A., Dorsey, M. F., Slifer, K. J., Bauman K. E., & Richman G. S. (1982). Toward a functional analysis of self-injury. *Analysis and Intervention in Developmental Disabilities, 2,* 3–20.

Jenson, W. R., Rhode, G., & Reavis, H. K. (1994). *The tough kid tool box.* Longmont, CO: Sopris West.

Jitendra, A. K. (2007). *Solving math word problems: Teaching students with learning disabilities using schema-based instruction.* Austin, TX: Pro-Ed.

Johnson, K. R., & Layng, T. V. J. (1992). Breaking the structuralist barrier: Literacy and numeracy with fluency. *American Psychologist, 47,* 1475–1490.

Johnson, T. C., Stoner, G., & Green, S. K. (1996). Demonstrating the experimenting society model with classwide behavior management interventions. *School Psychology Review, 25,* 199–214.

Jones, K. M., & Wickstrom, K. F. (2002). Done in sixty seconds: Further analysis of the brief assessment model for academic problems. *School Psychology Review, 31,* 554–568.

Joseph, L. M. (2000). Developing first graders' phonemic awareness, word identification, and spelling: A comparison of two contemporary phonic instructional approaches. *Reading Research and Instruction, 39,* 160–169.

Joseph, L. M. (2002). Helping children link sound to print: Phonics procedures for small-group or whole-class settings. *Intervention in School and Clinic, 37,* 217–221.

Kamphaus, R. W., & Reynolds, C. R. (2007). *Behavior assessment system for children (2nd ed.): Behavioral and emotional screening system (BESS).* Bloomington, MN: Pearson.

Kavale, K. A., & Forness, S. R. (2000). Policy decisions in special education: The role of meta-analysis. In R. Gersten, E. P. Schiller, & S. Vaughn (Eds.), *Contemporary special education research: Syntheses of knowledge base on critical instructional issues* (pp. 281–326). Mahwah, NJ: Erlbaum.

Kazdin, A. E. (1980). Acceptability of alternative treatments for deviant child behavior. *Journal of Applied Behavior Analysis, 13,* 259–273.

Kazdin, A. E. (2000). Perceived barriers to treatment participation and treatment acceptability among antisocial children and their families. *Journal of Child and Family Studies, 9,* 157–164.

Kelleher, C., Riley-Tillman, T. C., & Power, T. J. (2008). An initial comparison of collaborative and expert-driven consultation on treatment integrity. *Journal of Educational and Psychological Consultation, 18,* 294–324.

Kelshaw-Levering, K., Sterling-Turner, H. E., Henry, J. R., & Skinner, C. H. (2000). Randomized interdependent group contingencies: Group reinforcement with a twist. *Psychology in the Schools, 37,* 523–533.

Kern, L., & Clemens, N. H. (2007). Antecedent strategies to promote appropriate classroom behavior. *Psychology in the Schools, 44,* 65–75.

Kilpatrick, J., Swafford, J., & Finell, B. (Eds.). (2001). *Adding it up: Helping children learn mathematics.* Washington, DC: National Academy Press.

Klubnik, C., & Ardoin, S. P. (2010). Examining immediate and maintenance effects of a reading intervention package on generalization materials: Individual versus group implementation. *Journal of Behavioral Education, 19,* 7–29.

Konrad, M., Joseph, L. M., & Eveleigh, E. (2009). A meta-analytic review of guided notes. *Education and Treatment of Children, 32,* 421–444.

Kratochwill, T. R., Elliott, S. N., & Rotto, P. (1995). Best practices in school-based behavioral consultation. In A. Thomas & J. Grimes (Eds.), *Best practices in school psychology–III* (pp. 519–537). Washington, DC: National Association for School Psychologists.

Kratochwill, T. R., Sheridan, S. M., Carlson, J., & Lasecki, K. L. (1999). Advances in behavioral assessment. In C. R. Reynolds & T. R. Gutkin (Eds.), *The handbook of school psychology* (3rd ed., pp. 350–382). New York: Wiley.

LeFevre, J. A., Smith-Chant, B. L., Fast, L., Skwarchuk, S. L., Sargla, E., Arnup, J. S., et al. (2006). What counts as knowing? The development of conceptual and procedural knowledge of counting from kindergarten through grade 2. *Journal of Experimental Child Psychology, 93,* 285–303.

Lentz, F. E., & Daly, E. J. (1996). Is the behavior of academic change agents controlled metaphysically? An analysis of the behavior of those who change behavior. *School Psychology Quarterly, 11,* 337–352.

Lentz, F. E., & Shapiro, E. S. (1986). Functional assessment of the academic environment. *School Psychology Review, 15,* 346–357.

Lewis, T. J., & Sugai, G. (1999). Effective behavior support: A systems approach to proactive school-wide management. *Focus on Exceptional Children, 31,* 1–24.

Lienemann, T. O., Graham, S., Leader-Janssen, B., & Reid, R. (2006). Improving the writing performance of struggling writers in second grade. *The Journal of Special Education, 40,* 66–78.

Logan, G. D., Taylor, S. E., & Etherton, J. L. (1996). Attention in the acquisition and expression of automaticity. *Journal of Experimental Psychology: Learning, Memory, and Cognition, 22,* 620–638.

Mace, F. C., Yankanich, M. A., & West, B. J. (1988). Toward a methodology of experimental analysis and treatment of aberrant classroom behaviors. *Special Services in the Schools, 4,* 71–88.

MacQuarrie-Klender, L. L., Tucker, J. A., Burns, M. K., & Hartman, B. (2002). Comparison of retention rates using traditional, drill sandwich, and incremental rehearsal flashcard methods. *School Psychology Review, 31,* 584–595.

Madaus, M. M. R., Kehle, T. J., Madaus, J., & Bray, M. A. (2003). Mystery motivator as an intervention to promote homework completion and accuracy. *School Psychology International, 24,* 369–377.

Malone, L. D., & Mastropieri, M. A. (1992). Reading comprehension instruction: Summarization and self-monitoring training for students with learning disabilities. *Exceptional Children, 58,* 270–279.

Martens, B. K., Peterson, R. L., Witt, J. C., & Cirone, S. (1986). Teachers' perceptions of school-based interventions. *Exceptional Children, 53,* 213–223.

McCandliss, B., Beck, I.L., Sandak R., & Perfetti, C. (2003). Focusing attention on decoding skills for children with poor reading skills: Design and preliminary tests of the word building intervention. *Scientific Studies of Reading, 7,* 75–104.

McComas, J. J., Hoch, H., & Mace, F. C. (2000). Functional analysis. In E. S. Shapiro & T. R. Kratochwill (Eds.), *Conducting school-based assessments of child and adolescent behavior* (pp. 78–120). New York: Guilford Press.

McComas, J. J., & Mace, F. C. (2000). Theory and practice in conducting functional analysis. In E. S. Shapiro & T. R. Kratochwill (Eds.), *Behavioral assessment in schools: Theory, research, and clinical foundations* (2nd ed., pp. 78–103). New York: Guilford Press.

McGuinness, C., McGuinness, D., & McGuinness, G. (1996). Phono-graphix: A new method for remediation reading difficulties. *Annals of Dyslexia, 46,* 73–96.

McMaster, K. L., Fuchs, D., Fuchs, L. S., & Compton, D. L. (2005). Responding to nonresponders: An experimental field trial of identification and intervention methods. *Council for Exceptional Children, 71,* 445–463.

Messick, S. (1995). Validity of psychological assessment: Validation of inferences from persons' responses and performances as scientific inquiry into score meaning. *American Psychologist, 50,* 741–749.

Modi, A. C., & Quittner, A. L. (2006). Barriers to treatment adherence for children with cystic fibrosis and asthma: What gets in the way? *Journal of Pediatric Psychology, 31,* 846–858.

Montague, M. (2008). Self-regulation strategies to improve mathematical problem-solving for students with learning disabilities. *Learning Disability Quarterly, 31,* 37–44.

Montague, M., & Bos, C. S. (1986). The effect of cognitive strategy training on verbal math problem solving performance of learning disabled adolescents. *Journal of Learning Disabilities, 19,* 26–33.

Montarello, S. & Martens, B. K. (2005). Effects of interspersed brief problems on students' endurance at completing math work. *Journal of Behavioral Education, 14,* 249–266.

Moore, L. A., Waguespack, A. M., Wickstrom, K. F., Witt, J. C., & Gaydos G. R. (1994). Mystery motivator: An effective and time-efficient intervention. *School Psychology Review, 23,* 106–118.

Mortenson B. P., & Witt J. C. (1998). The use of weekly performance feedback to increase teacher implementation of a prereferral academic intervention. *School Psychology Review, 27,* 613–627.

National Council of Teachers of Mathematics. (2000). *Principles and standards for school mathematics.* Reston, VA: Author.

National Mathematics Advisory Panel. (2008). *Foundations for success: The final report of the National Mathematics Advisory Panel.* Washington, DC: U.S. Department of Education.

National Reading Panel. (2000). *Report of the national reading panel. Teaching children to read: An evidence-based assessment of the scientific research literature on reading and its implications for reading instruction* (NIH Publication No. 00-4769). Washington, DC: U.S. Government Printing Office.

National Research Council and Institute of Medicine. (2009). *Adolescent health services: Missing opportunities*. Washington, DC: National Academies.

Nist, L., & Joseph, L. M. (2008). Effectiveness and efficiency of flashcard drill instructional methods on urban first-graders' word recognition, acquisition, maintenance, and generalization. *School Psychology Review, 37*, 294–308.

No Child Left Behind Act of 2001, Public Law 107–110, 107th Cong., 115 Stat. 1425.

Noell G. H., Duhon G. J., Gatti S. L., & Connell J. E. (2002). Consultation, follow-up, and implementation of behavior management interventions in general education. *School Psychology Review, 31*, 217–234.

Noell, G. H., & Gansle, K. A. (2006). Assuring the form has substance: Treatment plan implementation as the foundation of assessing response to intervention. *Assessment for Effective Intervention, 32*, 32–39.

Noell, G. H., & Witt, J. C. (1996). A critical reevaluation of five fundamental assumptions underlying behavioral consultation. *School Psychology Quarterly, 11*, 3, 189–203.

Northrup, J., George, T., Jones, K., Broussard, C., & Vollmer, T. R. (1996). A comparison of reinforcer assessment methods: The utility of verbal and pictorial choice procedures. *Journal of Applied Behavior Analysis, 29*, 201–212.

O'Connor, R. E., Fulmer, D., Harty, K. R., & Bell, K. M. (2005). Layers of reading intervention in kindergarten through third grade: Changes in teaching and student outcomes. *Journal of Learning Disabilities, 38*, 440–455.

Pace, G. M., Ivancic, M. T., Edwards, G. L., Iwata, B. A., & Page, T. J. (1985). Assessment of stimulus preference and reinforcement value with profoundly retarded individuals. *Journal of Applied Behavior Analysis, 18*, 249–255.

Palinscar, A. S. & Brown, A. L. (1984). Reciprocal teaching of comprehension-fostering and comprehension-monitoring activities. *Cognition and Instruction, 1*, 117–175.

Paniagua, F. A., & Baer, D. M. (1982). The analysis of correspondence training as a chain reinforceable at any point. *Child Development, 53*, 786–798.

Pearson. (2008). *Aimsweb: Progress monitoring and RTI system*. Bloomington, MN: Author.

Petersen-Brown, S., & Burns, M. K. (2011). Adding a vocabulary component to incremental rehearsal to enhance maintenance and generalization. *School Psychology Quarterly, 26*, 245–255.

Piaget, J. (1971). Biology and knowledge: An essay on the relations between organic regulations and cognitive processes. Chicago: University of Chicago Press.

Plienis, A. J., Hansen, D. J., Ford, F., Smith, S., Stark, L. J., & Kelly, J. A. (1987). Behavioral small group training to improve the social skills of emotionally-disordered adolescents. *Behavior Therapy, 18*, 17–32.

Poncy, B., Skinner, C.H., & Jaspers, K.E. (2007). Evaluating and comparing interventions designed to enhance math fact accuracy and fluency: Cover, copy, and compare versus taped problems. *Journal of Behavioral Education, 16*, 27–37.

Porterfield, J. K., Herbert-Jackson, E., & Risley, T. R. (1976). Contingent observation: An effective and acceptable procedure for reducing disruptive behavior of young children in a group setting. *Journal of Applied Behavior Analysis, 9*, 55–64.

Power, T. J., Blom-Hoffman, J., Clark, A. T., Riley-Tillman, T. C., Kelleher, C., & Manz, P. H. (2005). Reconceptualizing treatment integrity: A partnership-based framework for linking research with practice. *Psychology in the Schools, 42*, 495–507.

Proctor, M. A., & Morgan, D. (1991). Effectiveness of a response cost raffle procedure on the disruptive classroom behavior of adolescents with behavior problems. *School Psychology Review, 20*, 97–109.

Public Agenda (2004). *Teaching interrupted: Do discipline policies in today's public schools foster the common good?* New York: Author.

Rasinski, T. V. (2003). The fluent reader: *Oral reading strategies for building word recognition, fluency, and comprehension*. New York: Scholastic.

Rathvon, N. (2008). *Effective school interventions: Evidence-based strategies for improving student outcomes* (pp. 81–83). New York: Guilford Press.

Read Naturally. (2004). *Read naturally*. St. Paul, MN: Author.

Reimers, T. M., Wacker, D. P., & Koeppl, G. (1987). Acceptability of behavioral treatments: A review of the literature. *School Psychology Review, 16*, 212–227.

Reinke, W. M., & Herman, K. C. (2002). Creating school environments that deter antisocial behaviors in youth. *Psychology in the Schools, 39*, 549–559.

Renaissance Learning. (2003). *Math facts in a flash*. Wisconsin Rapids, WI: Author.

Riley-Tillman, T. C., & Burns, M. K. (2009). *Evaluating educational interventions: Single-case design for measuring response to intervention*. New York: Guilford Press.

Riley-Tillman, T. C., Chafouleas, S. M., & Briesch, A. M. (2007). A school practitioner's guide to using daily behavior report cards to monitor interventions. *Psychology in the Schools, 44*, 77–89.

Riley-Tillman, T. C., Chafouleas, S. M., Christ, T., Briesch, A. M., & LeBel, T. J. (2009). Impact of wording and behavioral specificity on the accuracy of direct behavior rating scales (DBRs). *School Psychology Quarterly, 24*, 1–12.

Riley-Tillman, T. C., Chafouleas, S. M., & Eckert, T. (2008). Daily behavior report cards and systematic direct observation: An investigation of the acceptability, reported training and use, and decision reliability among school psychologists. *Journal of Behavioral Education, 17*, 313–327.

Riley-Tillman, T. C., Chafouleas, S. M., Sassu, K. A., Chanese, J. A. M., & Glazer, A. D. (2008). Examining the agreement of direct behavior ratings and systematic direct observation for on-task and disruptive behavior. *Journal of Positive Behavior Interventions, 10*, 136–143.

Riley-Tillman, T. C., Christ, T. J., Chafouleas, S. M., Boice, C. H., & Briesch, A. M. (2010). The impact of observation duration on the generalizability and dependability of direct behavior ratings (DBR). *Journal of Positive Behavior Interventions, 13*, 119–128.

Riley-Tillman, T. C., & Eckert, T. (2001). Generalization programming and school based consultation: An examination of consultees' generalization of consultation-related skills. *Journal of Educational and Psychological Consultation, 12*, 217–241.

Riley-Tillman, T. C., Methe, S. A., & Weegar, K. (2009). Examining the use of direct behavior rating methodology on classwide formative assessment: A case study. *Assessment for Effective Intervention, 34*, 224–230.

Risley, T. R., & Hart, B. (1986). Developing correspondence between the non-verbal and verbal behavior of preschooler children. *Journal of Applied Behavior Analysis, 1*, 267–281.

Rittle-Johnson, B., & Siegler, R. S. (1998). The relation between conceptual and procedural knowledge in learning mathematics: A review. In C. Donlan (Ed.), *The development of mathematical skill* (pp. 75–110). Hove, UK: Psychology Press.

Rittle-Johnson, B., Siegler, R. S., & Wagner, M. A. (2001) Developing conceptual understanding and procedural skill in mathematics: An iterative process. *Journal of Educational Psychology, 93*, 346–362.

Rivera, D. M., & Bryant, B. R. (1992). Mathematics instruction for students with special needs. *Intervention in School and Clinic, 28*, 71–86.

Robbins, K. P., Hosp, J. L., Hosp, M. K., & Flynn, L. J. (2010). Assessing specific graphic–phonemic skills in elementary students. *Assessment for Effective Intervention, 36*, 21–34.

Robinson, S. L., & Skinner, C. H. (2002). Interspersing additional easier items to enhance mathematics performance on subtests requiring different task demands. *School Psychology Quarterly, 17*, 191–205.

Rogevich, M. E., & Perin, D. (2008). Effects on science summarization of a reading comprehension intervention. *Exceptional Children, 74*, 135–154.

Rose, L. C., & Gallup, A. M. (2005). The 37th annual Phi Delta Kappa/Gallup poll of the public's attitudes toward the public schools. *Phi Delta Kappan, 87*, 41–57.

Rosenfield, S. A. (2002). Best practices in instructional consultation. In A. Thomas & J. Grimes (Eds.), *Best practices in school psychology* (4th ed., pp. 609–624). Bethesda, MD: National Association of School Psychologists.

Rosenshine, B. V., & Stevens, R. (1986). Teaching functions. In M. C. Wittrock (Ed.), *Handbook of research on training* (3rd ed., pp. 376–391). New York: Macmillam.

Rosenshine, B. V. (1986). Synthesis of research on explicit teaching. *Educational Leadership, 43*, 60–69.

Sackett, D. L., Rosenberg, W. M. C., Gray, J. A. M., Haynes, R. B., & Richardson, W. S. (1996). Editorial: Evidence based medicine: What it is and what it isn't. *British Medical Journal, 312*, 71–72.

Salvia, J., & Ysseldyke, J. E. (2004). *Assessment* (9th ed.). Princeton, NJ: Houghton Mifflin.

Samuels, S. J. (1979). The method of repeated readings. *The Reading Teacher, 32,* 403–408.

Severtson, J. M., Carr, J. E., & Lepper, T. L. (2008). Noncontingent reinforcement is an empirically supported treatment for problem behavior exhibited by individuals with developmental disabilities. *Research in Developmental Disabilities, 30,* 44–57.

Shanahan, T. (2006). *The national reading panel report: Practical advice for teachers.* Naperville, IL: Learning Point Associates.

Sheridan, S. M., Welch, M., & Orme, S. F. (1996). Is consultation effective: A review of outcome research. *Remedial and Special Education, 17,* 341–354.

Simonsen, B., Sugai, G., & Negron, M. (2008). Schoolwide positive behavior supports: Primary systems and practices. *Teaching Exceptional Children, 40,* 32–40.

Singer-Dudek, J., & Greer, R. D. (2005). A long-term analysis of the relationship between fluency and the training and maintenance of complex math skills. *Psychological Record, 55,* 361–376.

Skinner, B. F. (1983). *A matter of consequences: Part three of an autobiography.* New York: Knopf.

Skinner, C. H., Belfiore, P. J., Mace, H. W., Williams-Wilson, S., & Johns, G. A. (1997). Altering response topography to increase response efficiency and learning rates. *School Psychology Quarterly, 12,* 54–64.

Skinner, C. H., Hall-Johnson, K., Skinner, A. L., Cates, G. L., Weber, J., & & Johns, G. A. (1999). Enhancing perceptions of mathematics assignments by increasing relative problem completion rates through the interspersal technique. *The Journal of Experimental Education, 68,* 43–59.

Skinner, C. H., McLaughlin, T. F., & Logan, P. (1997). Cover, copy, and compare: A self-managed academic intervention across skills, students, and settings. *Journal of Behavioral Education, 7,* 295–306.

Skinner, C. H., Turco, T. L., Beatty, K.L., & Rasavage, C. (1989). Cover, copy, and compare: A method for increasing multiplication performance. *School Psychology Review, 18,* 412–420.

Sornson, R., Frost, F., & Burns, M. (2005). Instructional support teams in Michigan: Data from Northville Public Schools. *Communiquè, 33*(5), 28–29.

Sporer, N., Brunstein, J. C., & Kieschke, U. (2009). Improving students' reading comprehension skills: Effects of strategy instruction and reciprocal teaching. *Learning and Instruction, 19,* 272–286.

Sprague, J. R., Sugai, G., Horner, R. H., & Walker, H. M. (1999). Using discipline referral data to evaluate school-wide discipline and violence prevention interventions. *Oregon School Studies Council Bulletin, 42,* 1–17.

Stokes, T. F., & Baer, D. M. (1977). An implicit technology of generalization. *Journal of Applied Behavior Analysis, 10,* 349–367.

Stokes, T. F., Fowler, S. A., & Baer D. M. (1978). Training preschool children to recruit natural communities of reinforcement. *Journal of Applied Behavior Analysis, 11,* 285–303.

Stokes, T. F., & Osnes, P. G. (1989). An operant pursuit of generalization. *Behavior Therapy, 20,* 337–355.

Stone, S., McLaughlin, T. F., & Weber, K. P. (2002). The use and evaluation of copy, cover, and compare with rewards and a flash cards procedure with rewards on division math facts mastery with a fourth grade girl in a home setting. *International Journal of Special Education, 17,* 82–91.

Sugai, G., & Horner, R.H. (2002). The evolution of discipline practices: School-wide positive behavior supports. *Child and Family Behavior Therapy, 24,* 23–50.

Sugai, G., Horner, R., & Lewis, T. (2009). *OSEP technical assistance center on effective schoolwide interventions: Positive behavioral interventions & supports.* Eugene, OR: U.S. Department of Education, Office of Special Education Programs. Retrieved November 3, 2009, from *www.pbis.org.*

Sugai, G., Sprague, J. R., Horner, R. H., & Walker, H. M. (2000). Preventing school violence: The use of discipline referrals to assess and monitor school-wide discipline interventions. *Journal of Emotional and Behavioral Disorders, 8,* 94–101.

Swanson, H. L. (1999). Reading research for students with LD: A meta-analysis in intervention outcomes. *Journal of Learning Disabilities, 32,* 504–532.

Swanson, H. L. (2003). Age-related differences in learning disabled and skilled readers' working memory. *Journal of Experimental Child Psychology, 85,* 1–31.

Swanson, H. L., & Jerman, O. (2007). The influence of working memory on reading growth in subgroups of children with reading disabilities. *Journal of Experimental Child Psychology, 96,* 249–283.

Swanson, H. L., & Sachse-Lee, C. (2000). A meta-analysis of single-subject design intervention research for students with LD. *Journal of Learning Disabilities, 33,* 114–136.

Szadokierski, I., & Burns, M. K. (2008). Analogue evaluation of the effects of opportunities to respond and ratios of known items within drill rehearsal of Esperanto words. *Journal of School Psychology, 46,* 593–609.

Taylor, B. A., & Harris, S. L. (1995). Teaching children with autism to seek information: Acquisition of novel information and generalization of responding. *Journal of Applied Behavior Analysis, 28,* 3–14.

Tilly, D. W., III., & Flugum, K. (1995). Best practices in ensuring quality interventions. In A. Thomas & J. Grimes (Eds.), *Best practices in school psychology* (3rd ed., pp. 485–500). Washington, DC: National Association of School Psychologists.

Tobin, T., Sugai, G., & Colvin, G. (1996). Patterns in middle school discipline records. *Journal of Emotional and Behavioral Disorders, 4,* 82–94.

Treptow, M. A., Burns, M. K., & McComas, J. J. (2007). Reading at the frustration, instructional, and independent levels: Effects on student time on task and comprehension. *School Psychology Review, 36,* 159–166.

Tucker, J. A. (1989). *Basic flashcard technique when vocabulary is the goal.* Unpublished teaching materials, School of Education, University of Chattanooga. Chattanooga, TN: Author.

U.S. Department of Health and Human Services: (1999). *Mental health: A report of the surgeon general.* Rockville, MD: U.S. Department of Health and Human Services, Substance Abuse and Mental Health Services Administration, Center for Mental Health Services, National Institutes of Health, National Institute of Mental Health.

van den Broek, P., Lynch, J. S., Naslund, J., Ievers-Landis, C. E., &Verduin, K. (2003). The development of comprehension of main ideas in narratives: Evidence from the selection of titles. *Journal of Educational Psychology, 95,* 707–718.

VanDerHeyden, A. M., & Burns, M. K. (2005). Using curriculum-based assessment and curriculum-based measurement to guide elementary mathematics instruction: Effect on individual and group accountability scores. *Assessment for Effective Intervention 30 (3),* 15–29.

VanDerHeyden, A. M., & Burns, M. K. (2009). Performance indicators in math: Implications for brief experimental analysis of academic performance. *Journal of Behavioral Education, 18,* 71–91.

VanDerHeyden, A. M., & Witt, J. C. (2005). Quantifying the context of assessment: Capturing the effect of base rates on teacher referral and a problem-solving model of identification. *School Psychology Review, 34,* 161–183.

VanDeWalle, J. A., Karp, K. S., & Bay-Williams, J. M. (2010). *Elementary and middle school mathematics: Teaching developmentally* (7th edition). Boston: Allyn & Bacon.

Vaughn, S., Gersten, R., & Chard, D. J. (2000). The underlying message in LD intervention research: Findings from research syntheses. *Exceptional Children, 67,* 99–114.

Vaughn, S., Wanzek, J., Linan-Thompson, S., & Murray, C. S. (2007). Monitoring response to intervention for students at-risk for reading difficulties: High and low responders. In S. R. Jimerson, M. K. Burns, & A. M. VanDerHeyden (Eds.), *The handbook of response to intervention: The science and practice of assessment and intervention* (pp. 234–243). New York: Springer.

Vollmer, T. R., Iwata, B. A., Zarcone, J. R., Smith, R. G., & Mazaleki, J. L. (1993). The role of attention in the treatment of attention-maintained self-injurious behavior: Noncontigent reinforcement and differential reinforcement of other behavior. *Journal of Applied Behavior Analysis, 26,* 9–21.

Vollmer, T. R., Roane, H. S., Ringdahl, J. E., & Marcus, B. A. (1999). Evaluating treatment challenges with differential reinforcement of alternative behavior. *Journal of Applied Behavior Analysis, 32,* 9–23.

Vygotsky, L. S. (1986). *Thought and language* (A. Kozulin, Trans.). Cambridge, MA: MIT Press. (Original work published 1934)

White, A. G., & Bailey, J. S. (1990). Reducing disruptive behaviors of elementary physical education students with sit and watch. *Journal of Applied Behavior Analysis, 23,* 353–359.

White, R., Algozzine, B., Audette, R., Marr, M. B., & Ellis, E. D., Jr. (2001). Unified discipline: A school-wide approach for managing problem behavior. *Intervention in School and Clinic, 37*, 3–8.

Wildmon, M. E., Skinner, C. H., Watson, T. S., & Garrett, L. S. (2004). Enhancing assignment perceptions in students with mathematics learning disabilities by including more work: An extension of interspersal research. *School Psychology Quarterly, 19*, 106–120.

Witt, J. C. (1986). Teachers' resistance to the use of school-based interventions. *Journal of School Psychology, 24*, 37–44.

Witt, J. C., Cavell, T. A., Heffer, R. W., Carey, M. P., & Martens, B. K. (1988). Child self-reports: Interviewing techniques and rating scales. In E. S. Shapiro & T. R. Kratochwill (Eds.), *Behavioral assessment in schools* (pp. 384–454). New York: Guilford Press.

Witt, J. C., & Elliott, S. N. (1982). The response cost lottery: A time efficient and effective classroom intervention. *Journal of School Psychology, 20*(2), 155–161.

Witt, J. C., & Elliott, S. N. (1985). Acceptability of classroom intervention strategies. In T. R. Kratochwill (Ed.), *Advances in school psychology* (pp. 251–288). Hillsdale, NJ: Erlbaum.

Witt, J. C., VanDerHeyden, A. M., & Gilbertson, D. (2004). Troubleshooting behavioral interventions: A systematic process for finding and eliminating problems. *School Psychology Review, 33*, 363–381.

Wolfgang, C.H., & Wolfgang, M.E. (1995). *The three faces of discipline for early childhood: Empowering teachers and students* (pp. 223–225). Boston, MA: Allyn & Bacon.

Wright, J. A., & Dusek, J. B. (1998). Compiling school base rates for disruptive behaviors from student disciplinary referral data. *School Psychology Review, 27*, 138–147.

Ysseldyke, J., Thrill, T., Pohl, J., & Bolt, D. (2005). Using math facts in a flash to enhance computational fluency. *Journal of Evidence-Based Practices for Schools, 6*, 59–89.

Index

Page numbers in italics indicate figures or tables.